EVALUATION FOR WORKPLACE DISCRIMINATION AND HARASSMENT

BEST PRACTICES IN FORENSIC MENTAL HEALTH ASSESSMENT

Series Editors

Thomas Grisso, Alan M. Goldstein, and Kirk Heilbrun

Series Advisory Board

Paul Appelbaum, Richard Bonnie, and John Monahan

Titles in the Series

Foundations of Forensic Mental Health Assessment, Kirk Heilbrun, Thomas Grisso, and Alan M. Goldstein

Criminal Titles

Evaluation of Competence to Stand Trial, Patricia A. Zapf and Ronald Roesch

Evaluation of Criminal Responsibility, Ira K. Packer

Evaluating Capacity to Waive Miranda Rights, Alan M. Goldstein and Naomi E. Sevin Goldstein

Evaluation of Sexually Violent Predators, Philip H. Witt and Mary Alice Conroy

Evaluation for Risk of Violence in Adults, Kirk Heilbrun

Jury Selection, Margaret Bull Kovera and Brian L. Cutler

Evaluation for Capital Sentencing, Mark D. Cunningham

Eyewitness Identification, Brian L. Cutler and Margaret Bull Kovera

Civil Titles

Evaluation of Capacity to Consent to Treatment and Research, Scott Y. H. Kim

Evaluation for Guardianship, Eric Y. Drogin and Curtis L. Barrett

Evaluation for Personal Injury Claims, Andrew W. Kane and Joel Dvoskin

Evaluation for Civil Commitment, Debra Pinals and Douglas Mossman

Evaluation for Workplace Discrimination and Harassment, Jane Goodman-Delahunty and William E. Foote

Evaluation of Workplace Disability, Lisa D. Piechowski

Juvenile and Family Titles

Evaluation for Child Custody, Geri S.W. Fuhrmann and Robert A. Zibbell

Evaluation of Juveniles' Competence to Stand Trial, Ivan Kruh and Thomas Grisso

Evaluation for Risk of Violence in Juveniles, Robert Hoge and D. A. Andrews

Evaluation for Child Protection, Karen S. Budd, Jennifer Clark, and Mary A. Connell

Evaluation for Disposition and Transfer of Juvenile Offenders, Randall T. Salekin

EVALUATION FOR WORKPLACE DISCRIMINATION AND HARASSMENT

JANE GOODMAN-DELAHUNTY

WILLIAM E. FOOTE

OXFORD
UNIVERSITY PRESS

2011

OXFORD
UNIVERSITY PRESS

Oxford University Press

Oxford University Press, Inc., publishes works that further
Oxford University's objective of excellence
in research, scholarship, and education.

Oxford New York
Auckland Cape Town Dar es Salaam Hong Kong Karachi
Kuala Lumpur Madrid Melbourne Mexico City Nairobi
New Delhi Shanghai Taipei Toronto

With offices in
Argentina Austria Brazil Chile Czech Republic France Greece
Guatemala Hungary Italy Japan Poland Portugal Singapore
South Korea Switzerland Thailand Turkey Ukraine Vietnam

Published by Oxford University Press, Inc.
198 Madison Avenue, New York, New York 10016
www.oup.com

Library of Congress Cataloging-in-Publication Data

Foote, William E.
Evaluation for workplace discrimination and harassment / William Foote and
Jane Goodman-Delahunty.
p. cm. — (Best practices in forensic mental health assessment)
ISBN 978-0-19-537101-7 1. Discrimination in employment—Law and
legislation—United States. 2. Forensic psychology—United States. I.
Goodman-Delahunty, Jane. II. Title.
KF3464.F66 2011
344.7301'133—dc22
2010020179

9 8 7 6 5 4 3 2 1

Printed in the United States of America
on acid-free paper

About Best Practices in Forensic Mental Health Assessment

The recent growth of the fields of forensic psychology and forensic psychiatry has created a need for this book series describing best practices in forensic mental health assessment (FMHA). Currently, forensic evaluations are conducted by mental health professionals for a variety of criminal, civil, and juvenile legal questions. The research foundation supporting these assessments has become broader and deeper in recent decades. Consensus has become clearer on the recognition of essential requirements for ethical and professional conduct. In the larger context of the current emphasis on "empirically supported" assessment and intervention in psychiatry and psychology, the specialization of FMHA has advanced sufficiently to justify a series devoted to best practices. Although this series focuses mainly on evaluations conducted by psychologists and psychiatrists, the fundamentals and principles offered also apply to evaluations conducted by clinical social workers, psychiatric nurses, and other mental health professionals.

This series describes "best practice" as empirically supported (when the relevant research is available), legally relevant, and consistent with applicable ethical and professional standards. Authors of the books in this series identify the approaches that seem best, while incorporating what is practical and acknowledging that best practice represents a goal the forensic clinician should aspire to, rather than a standard that can always be met. The American Academy of Forensic Psychology assisted the editors in enlisting the consultation of board-certified forensic psychologists specialized in each topic area. Board-certified forensic psychiatrists were also consultants on many of the volumes. Their comments on the manuscripts helped ensure that the methods described in these volumes represent a generally accepted view of best practice.

The series' authors were selected for their specific expertise in a particular area. At the broadest level, however, certain general principles apply to all types of forensic evaluations. Rather than repeat those fundamental principles in every volume, the series offers them in the first volume, *Foundations of Forensic Mental Health Assessment*. Reading the first book, followed by a specific topical book, will provide the reader both the general principles that the specific topic shares with all forensic evaluations and those that are particular to the specific assessment question.

The specific topics of the 19 books were selected by the series editors as the most important and oft-considered areas of forensic assessment conducted by mental health professionals and behavioral scientists. Each of the 19 books is organized according to a common template. The authors address the applicable legal context, forensic mental health concepts, and empirical foundations and limits in the "Foundation" part of the book. They then describe preparation for the evaluation, data collection, data interpretation, and report-writing and testimony in the "Application" part of the book. This creates a fairly uniform approach to considering these areas across different topics. All authors in this series have attempted to be as concise as possible in addressing best practice in their area. In addition, topical volumes feature elements to make them user-friendly in actual practice. These elements include boxes that highlight especially important information, relevant case law, best-practice guidelines, and cautions against common pitfalls. A glossary of key terms is also provided in each volume.

We hope the series will be useful for different groups of individuals. Practicing forensic clinicians will find succinct, current information relevant to their practice. Those who are in training to specialize in forensic mental health assessment (whether in formal training or in the process of respecialization) should find helpful the combination of broadly applicable considerations presented in the first volume with the more specific aspects of other volumes in the series. Those who teach and supervise trainees can offer these volumes as a guide for practices to which the trainee can aspire. Researchers and scholars interested in FMHA best practice may find researchable ideas, particularly on topics that have received insufficient research attention to date. Judges and attorneys with questions about FMHA best practice will find these books relevant and concise. Clinical and forensic administrators who run agencies, court clinics, and hospitals in which litigants are assessed may also use some of the books in this series to establish expectations for evaluations performed by professionals in their agencies.

We also anticipate that the 19 specific books in this series will serve as reference works that will help courts and attorneys evaluate the quality of forensic mental health professionals' evaluations. A word of caution is in order, however. These volumes focus on best practice, not what is minimally acceptable legally or ethically. Courts involved in malpractice litigation, or ethics committees or licensure boards considering complaints, should not expect that materials describing best practice easily or necessarily translate into the minimally acceptable professional conduct that is typically at issue in such proceedings.

This book focuses on information critical to the forensic mental health professionals who are asked to evaluate issues related to claims of workplace discrimination. Bill Foote and Jane Goodman-Delahunty trace the history of laws that are designed to promote equality in the workplace. They review landmark federal and state statues and legal cases related to workplace discrimination. Specific ethical issues that may arise when conducting these assessments are discussed, along with suggestions to address and resolve them. Empirical research related to the frequency and types of workplace discrimination and its potential effects on employees is reviewed. Methodology that experts should consider when evaluating such cases is described, including the role of tests and structured interviews; and ways of addressing the possibility that a plaintiff is exaggerating or malingering is discussed. How the expert interprets numerous sources of data to form an opinion and present the findings in a focused, coherent report and in testimony is considered.

Alan M. Goldstein
Kirk Heilbrun
Thomas Grisso

Acknowledgments

We thank our reviewers, Alan Goldstein, Tom Grisso, Kirk Heilbrun, and David Vore, for their helpful guidance. The contribution from our research assistants, Kate O'Brien, and Mira Taitz, Hielkje Verbrugge, in compiling tables, references, and key words was invaluable.
In the 15 years that Bill and I have collaborated on projects, he has proven to be a stellar colleague and a formidable forensic scientist-practitioner. His enthusiasm and professionalism made this work a pleasure.

JGD

I want to thank my coauthor, Jane, for her hard work on this project. She is a wonderful editor and a great collaborator, even though she lives on the other side of the planet. I have appreciated the advice and kind words of Dr. Debra Saslawsky, who has always provided a sounding board for ideas. I could not have done this work without the constant support and care from my dear wife, Cheryl.

WF

Contents

FOUNDATION

The Legal Context

1

Perhaps the most prominent and central relationships in contemporary society are employment relationships. They affect the careers, livelihood, and well-being of individuals as profoundly and perhaps more extensively than family relationships. Work is how most people structure their time, focus their energies, and anchor their identities.

The goals of contemporary workplace discrimination legislation are to promote equality in the workplace and to make victims of discriminatory practices whole. The right to protection from and compensation for losses and injuries caused by discrimination has evolved slowly, over many hundreds of years.

In the feudal era and the Middle Ages, birth status defined people's social and workplace relationships. Following the Industrial Revolution, which started in Europe in the 1750s and culminated in the United States of America a century later, birthright was replaced by social Darwinism, and the economic philosophy and legal doctrine of "laissez-faire" prevailed. The unrestricted liberty and freedom of individuals and corporations to enter into contracts was paramount. From the 1850s, workers' rights were defined by the principle of employment-at-will, which gave an employer the right to discharge a worker for any reason at any time, with or without notice (*Hathaway v. Bennett*, 1854). This doctrine favored corporations, managers and employers.

Traditional craft guilds and apprenticeships were replaced by factories where wages and conditions of work were unregulated. Employees, including many children, worked long hours in appalling conditions, enriching a few enterprising industrialists and business magnates, some of whom were called "robber barons."

CASE LAW

Hathaway v. Bennett, 1854

- A New York court rejected the Statute of Laborers enacted by the British Parliament in the 14th century and returned to an "at-will" standard of employment, meaning an employee could be fired for any reason or no reason at all.

Workers who tried to rely on the common law to obtain redress from termination of their employment faced unsympathetic courts. Early in the twentieth century, the first legislation to enhance working conditions was enacted by the U.S. Congress, establishing minimum wage laws. Subsequently, in 1935, with the passage of the National Labor Relations Act, the first statutory exception to the doctrine of employment-at-will emerged, prohibiting employers from firing workers without just cause, and allowing workers to form unions.

The first antidiscrimination legislation was passed in the Civil Rights Acts of 1866, which outlawed discrimination based on color or race, and the Civil Rights Act of 1871 (prohibiting state agencies from using the law to discriminate against black Americans on the basis of race or color). Traditionally, *color* was applied to address discrimination against African Americans, whereas *race* referred more to ethnicity (e.g., Arabs, Jews), and *national origin* to one's place of birth (Germany, Mexico, Sweden). These laws reflected growing interest in social equality and the ideals of liberty, equality, and fraternity popularized by the French Revolution.

Civil rights have a basis both in philosophy and in religion, and often embody three principles. The principle of *equality of opportunity*, nowadays applied in the workplace, requires that decisions be neutral, not based upon categories or classifications such as race, color, or sex. The categories protected by antidiscrimination laws are often immutable. This principle seeks evenhanded, "colorblind" laws and decisions. A second relevant principle, the *anti-oppression principle*, is manifest in the 14th Amendment to the U.S. Constitution, and prohibits decisions designed to oppress or impose disadvantages on members of an identifiable or cognizable group or class. This principle also seeks to reverse laws and rules that maintain historic oppression of individuals, particularly those based on classifications such as race or sex. Third, the *antisubordination principle* prohibits decisions that subordinate or continue the subordination of a social group, and prohibits all actions that undermine the social or political standing of minority groups. This principle is applied to place persons with physical or psychological impairments or disabilities on an equal footing with non-disabled workers, and to ensure that workers with religious beliefs and practices are not subordinated because of their religion.

The first congressional bill to prohibit discrimination in employment was introduced in 1942, but did not pass. Only in the 1960s was the Civil Rights Act adopted, prohibiting workplace discrimination on the basis of race, color, national origin, gender, and religion. This Act, known as Title VII, applied the principle of antidiscrimination, as did other workplace discrimination legislation of that decade: the Equal Pay Act of 1963, and the Age Discrimination in Employment Act of 1967. Approximately 30 years later, the Americans with Disabilities Act of 1990 was enacted, extending workplace protection to persons with physical or psychological disabilities. The most recent antidiscrimination legislation was the Civil Rights Act of 1991, which amended and amplified the 1964 Act and expanded the right to compensation and the right to a jury trial, and the Administrative Dispute Resolution Act of 1995. The Americans with Disabilities Amendment Act of 2008 restored some antidiscrimination components of the ADA that had been eliminated by a series of U.S. Supreme Court decisions.

Thus, gradually, principles of equality and fairness in employment replaced the markers of birth or social status. These antidiscrimination laws address values of fairness and prejudice, the latter referring to unequal or differential treatment based on immutable human characteristics such as color, race, ethnicity, gender, age, disability, and national origin.

INFO

The following are three principles of civil rights:

1. Equality of opportunity
2. Anti-oppression
3. Anti-subordination

INFO
The Civil Rights Act of 1964, known as Title VII, prohibits workplace discrimination on the basis of race, color, national origin, gender, and religion.

Freedom to practice one's faith without persecution was a significant feature in the U.S. Constitution, as its European founders had fled from religious oppression by state-affiliated Christian churches.

Common-law doctrines evolved simultaneously. These doctrines ultimately were applied to abridge contract law of employment-at-will, and tort law claims developed. The first tort claim was brought in California in 1959, but it was not until the 1980s that the *tort of retaliatory discharge* was used to protect an employee from termination if he or she was fired in violation of a clear public policy. The difficulty was to identify a clear public policy that was breached. Other tort theories—such as intentional and negligent infliction of emotional distress, or the tort of outrage—were used. A statutory claim of discrimination may be accompanied by a related tort claim for intentional or negligent infliction of emotional distress, false imprisonment, invasion of the right to privacy, fraudulent misrepresentation, assault, battery, defamation, fraud, and/or whistle-blowing, depending on the case facts (Restatement of Law of Torts, Second, 1979).

Initially, workplace legislation focused on protecting employees from unfair or unjust termination of their employment. However, today all aspects of the working relationship are governed by a vast array of common-law doctrines, statutes, and state and federal administrative regulations. The impact of workplace antidiscrimination laws on corporate life has been significant. Despite some resistance and considerable skepticism over the operation of the antidiscrimination laws, they are fixtures in most countries. In the United States, most of the federal antidiscrimination statutes have state counterparts that may be more expansive, prohibiting marital discrimination as well as decisions based on sexual orientation and preference. The federal laws and cases are important because state courts often look to federal law for guidance in interpreting state and common law claims.

In sum, multiple sources of antidiscrimination law exist that can undergird a claim for psychological injury caused by workplace discrimination. The major federal laws are Title VII, the Age Discrimination in Employment Act of 1967, and the Americans with Disabilities Act of 1990. The filing of common-law claims alongside federal or state statutory claims is widespread.

Once the defendant employer's liability for an injury is established, evidence of the plaintiff's losses and injuries is assessed to determine the scope of monetary compensation recoverable. The goal of compensatory damage awards derives from the equitable principle *restitutio in integrum*—to arrive at a suitable financial sum in compensation to make the claimant "whole" by seeking to restore the plaintiff to the status enjoyed prior to the injury for which the defendant is liable. The traditional legal method to determine compensatory damages is based on *diminution in value* assessed by a comparison of the plaintiff's position before and after the unlawful conduct. Awards in compensation are most typically made in a lump sum. The amount of compensation, also known as the *damage award*, is computed with respect to two time frames: (i) past losses incurred from the time of injury to time of trial or assessment (settlement), and (ii) future losses in cases where the injuries are more enduring and will occur with certainty after the date of trial or assessment, and possibly for much of the remainder of the plaintiff's life. Most claims for psychological distress and injury are temporary losses or impairments, so typically the focus is on past losses incurred.

Initially, recoverable damages under Title VII excluded mental and emotional injuries, and were restricted to pecuniary losses and other tangible "make-whole" relief such as job reinstatement, lost wages and fringe benefits, and possibly some attorney fees. Compensation for psychological injuries was infeasible until the 1970s, unless it was accompanied by a physical injury (Young, Kane & Nicholson, 2007). Thus, only relatively recently have mental health issues in the workplace gained

INFO

Damages are usually awarded as a single lump sum and are calculated based on past and future losses.

CASE LAW
Harris v. Forklift Systems, Inc. (1993)

- The U.S. Supreme Court held that a person need not be damaged psychologically to demonstrate the presence of sexual harassment and a hostile work environment.
- The Court also held that it was not necessary for a plaintiff to show that her job performance had suffered as a result of the harassment.

credence and attention. For example, state workers' compensation systems now allow claims for psychological injuries for cumulative stress. In 1993, the U.S. Supreme Court acknowledged that fact finders could consider evidence of a diagnosable psychological injury to a sexually harassed complainant in determining whether her employer was liable (*Harris v. Forklift Systems, Inc.*, 1993).

Despite the fact that psychological injuries predominate in employment discrimination claims, and some changes have been made to the law, currently, damages for pain and suffering and for mental distress are still not available under the federal Age Discrimination in Employment Act. They are recoverable for age discrimination under some state laws. The Civil Rights Act of 1992, which allowed compensation for mental and emotional injuries and punitive damages to be awarded to prevailing plaintiffs in federal court, included a schedule that limited the recoverable amount based on the size of the employer, capping the damages at $300,000. Certain state antidiscrimination laws also "cap" or limit the maximum amounts recoverable in compensatory damages, and others do not. By comparison, most tort theories entitle a plaintiff to recover emotional distress damages, but the threshold for proof for some torts, such as intentional infliction of emotional distress, is more exacting than that under the antidiscrimination statutes. Legal scholars agree that the availability of non-pecuniary compensatory damages serves to discourage employers from continuing to discriminate in the future (Sanders, 2006; Sebok, 2007), although the statutory caps that limit the amounts recoverable for psychological injuries tend to undercut this goal.

Some commentators believe that the classifications inherent in antidiscrimination law serve to institutionalize and perpetuate in-group biases and prejudice (Chang, 1996). The effectiveness of antidiscrimination legislation in establishing social reform has been questioned, as least as far as race discrimination is concerned (Bell, 2004). Other scholars remain cynical about the effects of the legislation; while some claim that Equal Employment Opportunity (EEO) laws have had a modest effect, others believe they have had virtually none (Burstein, 1992). At a minimum, they appear to have a symbolic value.

Before discussing the mental and emotional injuries that can be caused by workplace discrimination, it is helpful to have an overview of the scope of workplace discrimination.

Scope of the Problem

Four broad types of employment actions can become the focus of a discrimination complaint. First, there are decisions affecting the terms and conditions of employment, such as decisions to hire, pay, train, promote, award benefits, discharge employees, and provide references to future employers. Second, employees cannot be segregated or classified based on their membership in protected cognizable groups (e.g., groups that have a common trait or characteristic, and are distinguished by statute) or categories. So, it is illegal to allocate only nondisabled or young workers to customer service positions, or to house Hispanic agricultural workers separately from non-Hispanic workers. Third, special consideration must be provided based on a worker's religion or disability, to accommodate those concerns. Finally, all employees who participate in procedures associated with the equal employment laws, such as by filing a complaint, or questioning or opposing particular employment practices or policies, are protected from reprisal or retaliation for this conduct, whether they are current or former employees. In all, the range of potential conduct that comes within the scope of the antidiscrimination laws is extremely broad, and new case facts are constantly emerging. New technologies lead to new offenses. For example, the advent of email and text messaging spawned a series of claims of discrimination committed via these technologies. Employment litigation has been marked as the fastest growing area of civil ligation in the United States.

Despite this variability in the kinds of cases that can be brought, most claims lodged with the U.S. Equal Employment Opportunity Commission (U.S. EEOC), the federal agency responsible for enforcing federal antidiscrimination legislation, are cases of unlawful discharge or termination of employment, after employees are fired or laid off from work. Approximately five million Americans are terminated from their employment each year, and this figure tends to escalate in times of economic adversity. However, claims of discriminatory working conditions or a hostile workplace environment have steadily increased. In a 2008 survey of business litigation, 29% of American companies reported involvement in discrimination cases, a slight increase over the previous year (Fulbright & Jaworski LLP, 2008). As was reflected in similar surveys over the past five years, the most common lawsuits facing American companies were labor-employment lawsuits and general discrimination suits (e.g., race, gender, national origin, retaliation). Disability and age-discrimination claims were also reported to have increased.

Importantly, a consideration for these companies is not only the litigation costs to defend against these claims, but the potential amount in compensatory damages in cases in which the plaintiff prevails. Although multi-million-dollar awards are rare (Nielsen, Nelson, & Lancaster, 2008), and more likely in a class action than an individual case, they can be substantial. For example, a judge reduced a $2.5 million award by a jury to $600,000 in a disability discrimination case in federal court in which an experienced pharmacist's assistant with cerebral palsy was assigned on his second day of work to collect shopping carts and pick up trash (*Brady v. Wal-Mart Stores, Inc.*, 2006). The sum of $40 million was allocated to compensate eligible Asian, Latino, and African American victims of systemic racial discrimination in proportion to their damages following settlement of a nationwide class

INFO
Most discrimination claims filed are cases of unlawful discharge or termination.

action opposing a "whites only" hiring policy by retailer Abercrombie and Fitch (*Gonzalez v. Abercrombie & Fitch*, 2005). In 2007, a $54.9 million settlement was reached in a race discrimination class action by African American and Latino employees challenging the performance evaluation and promotion system at FedEx Express (*Satchell et al. v. Fedex Express,* 2007). These figures demonstrate that employers are likely to contest claims for compensatory damages to minimize their litigation costs. When asked about the ten major types of employment litigation cases that involved the largest damages awards, U.S. companies pointed to race discrimination cases as creating the highest financial exposure, followed by claims stemming from sexual discrimination; wage-and-hour violations; ageism; harassment; retaliation; disability; noncompete disputes; and violations of the Family Medical Leave Act (Fulbright & Jaworski LLP, 2008).

Obtaining precise estimates of the prevalence of workplace discrimination is difficult because not all discrimination is reported. By all accounts, many employees prefer to resort to self help or avoidance rather than pursue a claim against a discriminatory employer. Thus, data based on official, formal complaints are underestimates of the prevalence. While not all discrimination claims proceed via the U.S. EEOC or parallel local state EEO agencies, the data maintained by the EEOC provide some reliable indicators of the trends. Statistics compiled by the EEOC in 2009 indicated that in excess of 93,000 charges were filed nationally (U.S. Equal Employment Opportunity Commission, 2010). About one-third of the claims filed include more than one basis of discrimination (Nielsen et al., 2008), e.g., race plus gender, disability plus retaliation. While charges of age discrimination and retaliation showed the greatest increase in the past year, charges alleging race discrimination (36%), retaliation (36%), and sex discrimination (30%) are the most frequent types of charges filed with the EEOC. In fact, EEOC charge filings alleging race/color discrimination have more than tripled since 1992. All antidiscrimination laws prohibit employers from taking adverse action against an employee for opposing what appear to be discriminatory violations of the law, or for participating in EEO processes, either as a claimant or

CASE LAW

Crawford v. Metropolitan Government of Nashville and Davidson County, Tennessee (2009)

- The U.S. Supreme Court held that an employee is protected against retaliation for answering questions during an employer's internal investigation.

a witness on someone else's behalf, or for speaking out about discrimination during an employer's investigation into another employee's internal complaint of discrimination (*Crawford v. Metropolitan Government of Nashville and Davidson County*, Tennessee, 2009).

Victimization claims based on reprisal or retaliation are among the most prevalent type of claim. Close behind in prevalence are sex discrimination claims, which also comprise a high proportion of the total number of charges, approximately two-thirds of which are for sexual harassment. The number of harassment charges filed with the EEOC and state fair employment practices agencies has risen significantly, from 10,532 in fiscal year 1992, to approximately 16,000 charges per year since 1997. These figures indicate either an increase in the experience of sexual harassment or an increase in willingness to report it (U.S. Equal Employment Opportunity Commission, 2007; 2010). Sexual harassment is particularly prevalent in male-dominated workplace settings, such as the military, police, and firefighting departments. More than 50% of women at four military service academies reported experiencing some form of sexual harassment, and more than 10% of women at these service academies had experienced some form of sexual assault (Cook et al., 2005).

In 2010, the EEOC reported an increase in charge filings in 2009 for certain types of discrimination, such as disability, religion, and national origin discrimination. The number of claims filed

INFO

According to the U.S. Equal Employment Opportunity Commission, more than 80,000 workers file discrimination claims against their employers each year. The bulk of these claims are charges of racial discrimination and unlawful retaliation.

Table 1.1 US Equal Employment Opportunity Commission Charge Statistics FY 1997- FY 2009

Basis of discrimination		Year 1997	2000	2003	2006	2009
Total Charges	N	80,680	79,896	81,293	75,768	93,277
Race	N	29,199	28,945	28,526	27,238	33,579
	%	36.2	36.2	35.1	35.9	36.0
Retaliation - all statutes	N	18,198	21,613	22,690	22,555	33,613
	%	22.6	27.1	27.9	29.8	36.0
Sex	N	24,728	25,194	24,362	23,247	28,028
	%	30.7	31.5	30.0	30.7	30.0
Age	N	15,785	16,008	19,124	16,548	22,778
	%	19.6	20.0	23.5	21.8	24.4
Disability	N	18,108	15,864	15,377	15,575	21,451
	%	22.4	19.9	18.9	20.6	23.0
National origin	N	6,712	7,792	8,450	8,327	11,134
	%	8.3	9.8	10.4	11.0	11.9
Religion	N	1,709	1,939	2,532	2,541	3,386
	%	2.1	2.4	3.1	3.4	3.6

Table 1.1 US Equal Employment Opportunity Commission Charge Statistics FY 1997- FY 2009 (*Continued*)

Basis of discrimination		Year				
		1997	2000	2003	2006	2009
Equal pay	N	1,134	1,270	1,167	861	942
	%	1.4	1.6	1.4	1.1	1.0

Source: Adapted from U.S. Equal Employment Opportunity Commission (2010). Note: "Total charges" reflects the number of individual charge filings. As some individuals claim multiple types of discrimination, the number of total charges for any given fiscal year is less than the total of the eight bases of discrimination listed.

based on age and disability is approximately even. Fewer claims are based on national origin and religion, and the Equal Pay Act is relatively underused. A 2009 congressional amendment to the Civil Rights Act of 1964, the Age Discrimination in Employment Act, the Americans with Disabilities Act, and the Rehabilitation Act of 1973 stated that the 180-day statute of limitations for filing an equal-pay lawsuit regarding pay discrimination resets with the issuance of each new discriminatory paycheck (The Lily Ledbetter Fair Pay Act of 2009, with a retroactive effective date of May 28, 2007). Whether this amendment will increase the number of unequal pay charges remains unknown.

Of course, the filing of the charge is just the beginning of the formal process. Most discrimination cases are settled before they get to trial. A comprehensive study that tracked claims of employment discrimination determined that as few as 5% of the cases proceed to trial (Nielsen et al., 2008). A substantial number, 13.5% of the claimants who settle with their employers prior to litigation obtain no monetary compensation (U.S. Equal Employment Opportunity Commission, 2009b). Figures on outcomes for discrimination claimants show that few prevail, despite extensive media coverage of large compensatory damage awards. One recent study tracking the disposition of EEOC claims revealed that only one in five of the claims is resolved in the plaintiff's favor (Hirsch, 2008). An early study of factors predicting outcomes in sexual harassment cases revealed that cases were more likely to be resolved in favor of the complainant when (a) the harassment behaviors were serious, or (b) the complainant had witnesses to support the charges, or (c) had given notice to management prior to filing formal charges (Terpstra & Baker, 1992). Whether the same factors predict outcomes in other types of discrimination cases is unknown. In cases that proceed to trial, some differences in outcome are attributable to the fact finder: juries find for the plaintiff over 30% of the time, whereas judges decide in favor of plaintiffs less than 7% of the time (Nielsen & Nelson, 2005).

The fact that employment discrimination plaintiffs litigating in federal court fare more poorly than other plaintiffs in the same venue has been formally acknowledged (Mehri, 2008):

> When employers win at trial, they are reversed by the U.S. Courts of Appeals 9% of the time. When employees win at trial, they are reversed 41% of the time. Juries in federal courts rule in favor of plaintiffs in workplace cases 38% of the time versus 44% in non-job cases. District court judges, however, rule in favor of jobs plaintiffs only 20%, while ruling in favor of non-jobs plaintiffs 46% of the time. (Clermont & Schwab, 2009, p. 110)

These trends in federal courts have been observed by plaintiffs' lawyers, many of whom advise their clients to lodge claims in state court, where the outcomes may be more favorable to plaintiffs. Unfortunately, data on outcomes of discrimination claims in state courts are less readily available. There is some indication that more lawyers have been opting to bring wage and hours claims under the Fair Labor Standards Act rather than file discrimination claims under Title VII. In any event, over a nine-year period from 1999 to 2007,

INFO

Employment discrimination cases rarely go to trial. When they do, they usually go to state court where the plaintiff is likely to fare better than in federal court. Still, employers are more likely to come out on top.

there was an absolute drop of 37% in employment discrimination cases filed in federal court of (Clermont & Schwab, 2009). This dramatic drop in federal civil litigation may be partially attributable to the fact that this period coincided with a growing practice among many employers of requiring employees to take any workplace disputes to binding arbitration as a condition of employment (Colvin, 2007). In employment arbitration, employee win rates and damage awards are significantly lower than in litigation.

The process for resolving employment discrimination disputes rarely results in a jury trial. These trials are increasingly staged in state as opposed to federal court because many states have passed statutes and have settled case law that provides a more hospitable climate for plaintiffs' cases. A review of cases that do go to trial indicates that plaintiffs are at a significant disadvantage relative to employers and are more likely to lose a case than win it before a federal judge (Clermont & Schwab, 2009).

Legal Concepts

In practice, a gap exists between laws that inhibit discrimination and the establishment of fair or equitable practices in the workplace. Even where employers fully comply with the antidiscrimination laws in the policies and workplace practices, this provides no absolute guarantee of fair and equal treatment. For example, there is no right to merit-based decision-making in the workplace (Goodman-Delahunty, 1999). Many unpleasant workplace actions and interactions, such as those based on favoritism or nepotism, as well as incivility and inconsideration, do not amount to unlawful discrimination. The significance of this fact for forensic psychologists is that employees may suffer psychological workplace injuries but may lack any legal recourse if the conduct at issue does not come within the legal definition of discrimination. These unpleasant, but non-compensable, wrongs may occur in the same time frame as events that constitute discrimination. For instance, the U.S. Supreme Court noted that EEO laws are not general civility codes, and that conduct that is merely offensive does not constitute discrimination (*Harris v. Forklift,* 1993). Only detrimental actions undertaken because of a worker's identity based on race, color, sex, pregnancy, national origin, disability, religion, age, or in reprisal are actionable, and may lead to employer liability.

Legally, it is important to realize that these classifications prohibit decisions that exclude *or* include members of these groups. In other words, it is illegal to select people based on their membership in a protected class just as much as it is to deselect them. Reverse-discrimination claims are fully within the law. In other words, legitimate claims can be brought by nondisabled workers, males, and non-minorities who allege that favored treatment was afforded to the disabled, to women, or to minorities. Second, not all discrimination that arises in the workplace is unlawful. First, there are some exceptions to the reach of the law. For example, small companies that employ few workers (fewer than 15 under federal law, and fewer under state laws) for 20 or more weeks in a year may be exempt. However, most private, local, state, and federal employers are covered.

INFO

Most claims of workplace discrimination can be categorized as one or more of the following:

- Disparate treatment—intentionally treating some people more favorably than others
- Adverse impact—using a facially neutral employment practice that has an adverse impact on members of a protected class
- Hostile work environment—offensive conduct in the workplace in the form of abusive harassment of one or more employees
- Refusal to accommodate—failure to provide reasonable accommodation to qualified individuals with disabilities or employees with sincere religious beliefs
- Retaliation and victimization—reprisal against an employee for opposing perceived or actual workplace discrimination

In addition, not all discriminatory actions in the workplace are sufficient to state a cause of action or support a viable claim. For example, unless certain challenged conduct is sufficiently severe and pervasive to rise to the level where a reasonable employee would regard it as hostile and abusive, the conduct may be dismissed as unpleasant but not discriminatory. Forensic mental health experts should consult local counsel to familiarize themselves with applicable standards of proof and rules of evidence in a particular jurisdiction to discern what the elements of proof for the offense are, and any relevant threshold of proof.

Next, we review the five key types of cases or legal theories that underlie most claims of workplace discrimination; namely: (1) disparate treatment; (2) adverse impact; (3) hostile or abusive work environment; (4) lack of reasonable accommodation; and (5) retaliation and victimization. Although the focus in this book is on assessment of consequences of discrimination rather than assessments of liability, it is helpful to have some understanding of the underlying theories of liability.

Disparate Treatment

To establish a claim of disparate treatment, the complainant must show that the employer treated some people more favorably than others because of race, color, religion, national origin, sex, age, or disability. This differential treatment must be intentional. The discriminatory intent can be established by direct, indirect, or circumstantial evidence, or by a combination of statistical and anecdotal evidence. Direct evidence of an improper motive can include comments revealing bias or prejudice. The evidence must be sufficient to raise an inference that the conduct was discriminatory and that discriminatory intent motivated the adverse employment decision, such as non-hire, a negative performance review, or exclusion from a workplace benefit such as training.

For example, an African American man was employed by a state highway department and was working in a rural setting where few people of color lived or worked. He was routinely given the hardest and most dangerous assignments, such as placing hazard signs to block lanes of a freeway before a crew began working.

Non-black workers were not routinely asked to do this work. When a vacancy opened for team foreman, he applied for the position, along with similarly qualified Hispanic or white applicants. He was never promoted, and the last time he applied for a position, another non–African American worker who was less qualified was given the position. At trial, he was able to prove that his status as an African American was the basis for his unfavorable treatment.

Adverse Impact

An adverse impact claim is one involving a facially neutral policy (i.e., a policy that "on its face" appears neutral) or practice that has a less favorable impact on members of one group than another. The policy may be an employment screening test or a recruitment strategy, etc. The plaintiff must show that the practice at issue resulted in an adverse impact on members of a protected group, by producing statistical evidence of this disparity. The employer may rebut the claim by showing that the practice was a business necessity.

For example, a truck parts depot had a warehouse in which the parts were sorted and stored. "Parts chasers" were employed to find the parts and take them to a central place where customers were served. In the warehouse, shelves were arrayed from floor level to about 7½ feet above the floor. Because of the difficulty shorter workers had in reaching the higher shelves, the employer instituted a rule that only employees 5'9" or taller could be employed as parts chasers. Female employees filed a complaint for disparate impact, noting that women (median height about 5'4") are generally shorter than men (median height about 5'8"), and that this policy, although appearing on its face to be gender-neutral, actually eliminated most women from consideration for this position.

Harassment

To establish a case of harassment based on race, color, sex, national origin, age, disability, or retaliation, an employee must prove that (a) he or she belongs to one of the protected groups; (b) he or she was subjected to unwelcome or offensive comments jokes, acts, or other verbal or physical conduct in the workplace; (c) the conduct substantially interfered with his or her ability to perform work, creating an intimidating, hostile or offensive workplace; and (d) the employer knew, or should have known of this conduct, and failed to take prompt corrective action. The conduct complained of must be offensive or abusive in the eyes of a reasonable person in the position of the plaintiff. The conduct must be frequent or severe enough to create a hostile work environment or result in a "tangible employment action." A tangible employment action is "a significant change in employment status, such as hiring, firing, failing to promote, reassignment with significantly different responsibilities, or a decision causing a significant change in benefits" (*Burlington Industries v. Ellerth,* 1998, p. 761). The EEOC's Enforcement Guidance on Vicarious Liability provides additional direction (U.S. EEOC, 1999).

Although the Civil Rights Act of 1964 did not encompass protection against a hostile workplace environment or harassment per se, the courts extended protection against discrimination to encompass harassing and abusive behavior that is motivated by considerations of race, age, disability, gender, and the like. The first legal case in which a hostile workplace environment was acknowledged to violate the law was a national origin claim brought by a Hispanic optometrist's assistant who was prohibited from working on Anglo-Saxon patients and was abused by her white coworkers. The court held that:

> An employee's psychological as well as economic fringes are statutorily entitled to protection from employer abuse.... [T]he phrase "terms, conditions, or privileges of employment" in Section 703 is an expansive concept that sweeps within its protective ambit the practice of creating a working environment heavily charged with ethnic or racial discrimination.... One can readily envision working environments so heavily polluted with discrimination to destroy completely the emotional and psychological stability of minority group workers...." (*Rogers v. Equal Employment Opportunity Commission,* 1972, pp. 237–238)

CASE LAW

Meritor Savings Bank FSB v. Vinson, 1986

- The U.S. Supreme Court held that sexual harassment by members of the opposite sex is a violation of the Civil Rights Act of 1964, Title VII.
- This was later extended to include same-sex harassment in the case of *Oncale v. Sundowner Offshore Services, Inc.*, 1998.

Similarly, legal protection against pregnancy discrimination and sexual harassment is not explicit in Title VII, but evolved from cases brought on the basis of gender-based discrimination. Initially, protection against harassment by members of the opposite sex was afforded (*Meritor Savings Bank FSB v. Vinson,* 1986); and some years later, same-sex harassment was included (*Oncale v. Sundowner Offshore Services, Inc.*, 1998; see Foote & Goodman-Delahunty, 1999). Whether discrimination on the basis of sexual orientation will be penalized under federal law varies from one jurisdiction to another. Two types of sexual-harassment cases exist. First, there are those that involve tangible employment actions by a supervisor. To establish a case on this basis, an employee must show that a tangible employment action occurred as a consequence of his or her acceptance or rejection of the supervisor's sexual advances. Second, when a claim does not involve a tangible employment action, the hostile workplace environment analysis applies.

For example, a woman was hired to work as a hostess in a sports bar. Although this setting is one where rough language was almost the norm, it was not the speech of the customers that bothered the claimant. It was her supervisor, an older male, who frequently came behind her in her station near the door of the bar, and pushed himself against her in a sexual way. He would often mutter in her ear, "Don't you know you want it, baby." In spite of her frequent rebuffs and complaints to the bar owner, this behavior continued until the woman decided that quitting was her only recourse.

Reasonable Accommodation

Employees who seek consideration from their employers so that they can observe religious holidays, or who seek accommodation for a physical or mental impairment that will enable them to perform their job duties, are entitled to special or preferential treatment under the law. Employers must accommodate reasonable requests based on sincere religious belief or from qualified disabled workers, unless this imposes an undue hardship or burden on the employer's business. Providing reasonable accommodation can include restructuring or modifying work schedules, providing special equipment to disabled workers, and making facilities accessible for them.

For example, a worker for a large computer parts manufacturer developed a severe depressive disorder, and became so disabled that he was no longer able to continue working. He took three months of medical leave, during which he began antidepressant medication and cognitive psychotherapy. These treatments are generally successful, and his doctor determined that he was ready to return to work but needed to continue his psychotherapy regime in order to maintain the gains made in his treatment and to be able to function in the workplace. Upon returning to the workplace, the worker asked his employer to change his schedule to give him time off each week to see his therapist. His employer refused to provide this accommodation, and the worker filed suit under the Americans with Disabilities Act.

Reprisal and Retaliation

Reprisal and retaliation claims can be brought on a "disparate treatment" or "hostile workplace environment" theory. The employee must show that he or she engaged in protected opposition to perceived discrimination, or participated in a discrimination proceeding, even as a witness interviewed in the course of an internal employer investigation, and as a consequence, was adversely treated or victimized. A review by the U.S. Supreme Court of prohibited retaliatory actions in 2009 clarified that it is not only formal or ultimate employment decisions (such as non-promotion or demotion, a negative performance appraisal, or denial of other employment benefits) that can constitute unlawful reprisal: less obvious adverse actions such as threats, reprimands, negative references, and workplace harassment may be actionable (*Crawford v. Metro. Gov't of Nashville and Davidson County*, 2009). The standard is whether the alleged retaliatory acts produced a material injury or harm to the affected employee, not whether the conduct occurred at the workplace or was instigated by management (*Burlington Northern & Santa Fe Railway Co. v. Sheila White*, 2006). A materially adverse or injurious act is defined as one that might deter or dissuade a reasonable worker from making or supporting a charge of discrimination. Commentators have noted that under this standard, social exclusion, hostility towards, and ostracism of a complainant by coworkers may be a prohibited form of retaliation in the workplace (Owens, Gomes, & Morgan, 2008).

For example, a Hispanic man was working for a sports franchise as the team's publicity director. In spite of his successful campaigns to gain community support for the team, and to stage a series of high-profile events in which team stars were featured, he was subjected to racial slurs such as "wetback" and was treated rudely by the team owner. He filed a complaint with the state fair employment practices division in an attempt to stop these actions. Once the suit was filed, his employer fired him. When the worker submitted a claim for unemployment insurance, the employer claimed that the worker was "lazy, incompetent, and spoke with an accent." Because of his high-profile activities in the community, the worker was nevertheless hired by another sports team and went to work. This job was short-lived, because the worker's new employer was called by his former employer and told that the worker was "paranoid, hypersensitive and a trouble-maker."

Damages Recoverable

Compensatory Damages

The Civil Rights Act of 1991 authorizes compensatory damages in cases of intentional discrimination in violation of Title VII of the Civil Rights Act of 1964, the Rehabilitation Act of 1973, and the Title I of the Americans with Disabilities Act of 1990. Compensatory

> **INFO**
> There are two types of compensatory damages:
>
> - Economic or pecuniary losses ("special damages")
> - Non-economic or non-pecuniary losses ("general damages")

damages are not available in disparate impact cases, or in cases under the ADA in which an employer has made a good-faith effort to provide reasonable accommodation to an employee, nor in age-discrimination cases. Typically, compensatory damages consist of two major types: (a) economic or pecuniary losses, sometimes called "special damages"; and (b) non-economic or non-pecuniary losses, sometimes called "general damages" (Restatement of Law of Torts [Second], 1979). This book outlines issues in assessing compensation for non-economic compensatory damages; namely, psychological and psychiatric injuries.

Punitive Damages

The Civil Rights Act of 1991 authorizes *punitive damages* against a private employer who acts "with malice or with reckless indifference to the federally protected rights of an aggrieved person." This book does not address punitive damages, although there is some evidence of leakage of damage awards from one category to another by fact finders (Dawson, Anderson, & MacCoun, 1999; Sunstein, Hastie, Payne, Schkade, & Viscusi, 2002).

Non-economic Compensatory Damages

Under different laws, the terminology applied to non-economic losses or damages varies. Under Title VII, the phrase "compensatory damages" is used, but elsewhere, the language "general damages," "extra-contractual damages," "emotional distress damages," or "pain and suffering" may be used. These phrases encompass a wide range of psychological reactions and responses, including fright, shock, nervousness, anger, shame, wounded pride, hysteria, embarrassment, grief, worry, mortification, indignity, and physical pain.

The federal agency charged with interpreting Title VII and other federal antidiscrimination legislation, the United States Equal

Employment Opportunity Commission, identified seven classes of non-pecuniary damages that may result from discrimination:

1. Emotional pain and suffering
2. Mental anguish
3. Loss of enjoyment of life
4. Loss of health
5. Inconvenience
6. Injury to one's character
7. Injury to one's professional standing

In addition, the EEOC distinguished fifteen possible symptoms of the above classes of harm (not intended as an exhaustive list), eight of which (anxiety, stress, depression, humiliation, emotional distress, loss of self-esteem, marital strain, and nervous breakdown) may be included in measures of general psychological well-being (Hemingway, 1994).

As can be inferred from this list, the injuries claimed need not be diagnosable as a mental disorder in order to be compensable. Surprisingly, little guidance is provided in the law regarding the meaning of the term *compensatory damages.* No available definitions of "pain and suffering" exist, nor is there legal direction or guidance on how to weigh and assess these injuries and how to translate the findings into a monetary award (Greene & Bornstein, 2000). Different writers have given the words different emphasis. To some, "pain and suffering" implies social and psychological consequences (Wissler, Evans, Hart, Morry, & Saks, 1997), but other commentators contend that this phrase applies most readily to physical injuries, and that "loss of amenities" more aptly describes the detriment to the plaintiff's happiness or lifestyle (Tilbury, 1979). Recently, scholars have begun to scrutinize the law governing monetary compensation for psychological injuries (Abel, 2006; Allen, Brunet, & Roth, 2006; Avraham, 2006; Sanders, 2006; Sebok, 2007).

INFO

Damages claimed need not be diagnosable as a mental disorder in order to be compensable.

Legal Procedures for Forensic Assessment

Although it is not necessary that a plaintiff suffer any emotional distress or psychological injuries in order to bring a successful claim of employment discrimination (*Harris v. Forklift Systems, Inc.*, 1993), and there is no presumption once liability is found that emotional distress must have occurred, in many cases, claimants will file a claim alleging that they were harmed by the discriminatory conduct.

Only if the claimant prevails in proving that the defendant is liable for discrimination will the issue of assessing and awarding monetary compensation arise. In some cases, the legal proceedings are bifurcated, or split, and issues related to a determination of whether the conduct was discriminatory are heard first, and only if the plaintiff prevails is a second proceeding opened to take evidence of the nature and scope of the consequential harm. In some jurisdictions, where the witnesses to liability overlap with those who will provide evidence of injuries, the court or administrative body may prefer to take all evidence related to damages and harm in the same proceeding as the evidence on liability.

To support a claim for mental and emotional distress, the law does not require that an expert provide a report or testimony to corroborate the claim. However, in practice, this form of corroborative evidence of mental and emotional distress is often helpful because of the nature of the harm. A survey of federal court judges revealed that in 64%–68% of federal trials in which expert witnesses provided testimony, the topic about which they were permitted to testify was the nature and scope of a plaintiff's injury and the cause of the alleged injuries (Krafka, Dunn, Johnson, Cecil, & Miletich, 2002).

A number of issues favor this practice. First, the injuries are difficult to assess and measure objectively, because few discrimination cases involve tangible injuries such as those that would result from a

INFO

Although helpful during trial, an expert's testimony or report is not required to support a plaintiff's claim of mental and emotional distress.

physical assault. Most injuries are invisible and intangible, compared to other workplace physiological injuries, and the measurement of these injuries is an inexact science. Second, self-reports by the complainant feature strongly in the description of the nature and scope of the alleged injuries, and not all complainants are articulate about their experiences or have insight into the impact of the discrimination on their lives. Third, there are widely different reactions and individual differences in response to experiences of discrimination, so identifying norms and average reactions is difficult. Fourth, research on the psychological sequelae or consequences of discrimination is fairly recent and difficult to access. Fifth, determining the cause of any observed injuries is a task that has to be conducted retrospectively and is complex. For example, a plaintiff may have pre-existing problems that worsen as a consequence of discrimination, or the plaintiff's theories about how events affected her may be misguided. There may also be concurrent stressors that need to be separated from the consequences of discriminatory conduct. Claims of exacerbation of pre-existing conditions will almost always require expert testimony.

Administrative procedural hurdles in bringing a discrimination claim can be quite complex (Livingstone, Shanor, & Mirengoff, 2005). Often the complainant must first exhaust all administrative remedies by filing a complaint with the employer or the local EEO agency and allowing these parties time to investigate the claim by interviewing witnesses and reviewing documents. In many jurisdictions, effort will be made to resolve the claim informally by conciliation prior to litigation. Thus, a psychologist may be asked to provide some indications of the claim at a pretrial phase if documentation of the injuries is relevant during conciliation, or at a mediation, to effect a settlement. More typically, however the forensic psychologist will be consulted by a lawyer for the complainant or the defendant employer after the administrative prerequisites are complete and the case has proceeded to litigation or the initial complaint has been filed in state or federal court.

Once a plaintiff alleges a psychological injury, the defense has a right to inquire about the nature and scope of the claim. Some courts distinguish between ordinary anticipated consequences of workplace discrimination, resulting in what have been called "garden-variety" damages, and more severe consequences that rise to the level of a psychological or emotional injury (see discussion in Chapter 3). If the plaintiff does not intend to call an expert witness and claims only emotional distress and not mental injury, then the plaintiff may not be required to submit to a Rule 35 mental examination by the opposing party (Foote & Goodman-Delahunty, 2005; Kovera & Cass, 2002). In a compelled evaluation, the inquiry will focus on the psychological history and status of the plaintiff.

Considerable variability exists from one jurisdiction to the next regarding when and whether a plaintiff may state the precise amount of money that he or she regards as appropriate compensation proportionate to the harm sustained in psychological or non-pecuniary damages and injuries. In certain states, a specific *ad damnum* or sum must be included in the complaint in the petition or prayer for relief, placing the court and the defendant on notice of the remedies that the plaintiff is seeking. However, other states have legislated to eliminate all *ad damnum* clauses or to exclude this information from trial on grounds that it leads to inflated damage awards and time-consuming amendments of the complaint.

A lawyer may not ask jurors to put themselves in the shoes of the plaintiff in arriving at a suitable determination of monetary damages. In certain jurisdictions, legal counsel may apply a per diem method, in which the jury is asked to assign a dollar value for each day the plaintiff had to suffer from the consequences of an injury. To convey the daily impact of the injuries, some courts allow the plaintiff's counsel to present a "day in the life" videotape (Avraham, 2006). Although courts and legal and psychological scholars have been concerned about implementing methods to reduce the variability in the amounts of money awarded for psychological injuries (McCaffery, Kahneman, & Spitzer, 1995), jurors are not provided with information about comparable amounts awarded in other similar cases. The issue of treating similar injuries alike to achieve horizontal equity in the law remains controversial (Sanders, 2006).

Legal Guidance and Procedures Governing an Evaluation

In 1992, the EEOC issued some preliminary guidelines to be addressed in determining the injuries in a discrimination claim (U.S. Equal Employment Opportunity Commission, 1992). While the field has advanced in the intervening years, these basic considerations provide some parameters to acquaint forensic psychologists with the issues:

- Was the alleged conduct overt or covert?
- Was management aware of the discriminatory conduct?
- Did the plaintiff seek counseling or therapy?
- Did plaintiff have other difficulties at the time?
- Is there corroboration from family members, friends, coworkers, and professionals?
- What indicators are there of the severity of harm experienced?
- What was the duration of the harm, or how much longer is it expected to continue?
- How susceptible was the plaintiff to this type of harm or injury?
- Is there any evidence of provocation by the plaintiff that may serve to mitigate the damages?

In assessing mental and emotional injuries, if the plaintiff has multiple legal claims, such as a Title VII claim and a tort claim for intentional infliction of emotional distress, the evaluator must be aware that injuries that are covered and the standards of proof for the claims may vary. Under federal statutes, the standard is whether the discrimination contributed to mental or emotional distress or injuries that the plaintiff would not otherwise have suffered. Some courts require that the plaintiff sustain severe injuries to be eligible for tort damages, whereas no such standard applies under Title VII (*Harris v. Forklift Systems, Inc.*, 1993). Loss of consortium claims

INFO
It is important to know that injuries covered and standards of proof may vary depending on the type of claim filed (e.g., Title VII claim versus a tort claim). Be sure to familiarize yourself with these differences.

may be not viable under Title VII in some jurisdictions, although the EEOC has allowed them (Gilbert, 2007). These are claims filed by a spouse or other family member of the target of discrimination, to compensate the family member for loss of sexual relations, or, in the case of children or other blood kin, the plaintiff's impairments resulting in the loss of counseling and affection for their family members. Although the Civil Rights Act specifies that compensatory damages for loss of value of life are recoverable, courts have generally found that claims for hedonic damages or loss of enjoyment of life are too speculative and unscientifically founded to be sustained.

Generally, distress attributable to the litigation (Binder, 1992) initiated by the plaintiff is not compensable. However, litigation stress must be distinguished from distress caused by acts of reprisal, retaliation or victimization against an employee after he or she complains of discrimination, as that is compensable. Research conducted on litigation stress is summarized in Chapter 3.

The scope of the inquiry a psychologist can make in the course of a psychological evaluation is limited by a 1994 amendment to Rule 412 of the Federal Rules of Evidence, a shield law that limits inquiries into the plaintiff's sexual history. This limitation is mainly relevant to claims of sexual harassment (Schuller & Klippenstine, 2004).

BEWARE
The sexual behavior or sexual predisposition of an alleged victim is admissible if its probative value substantially outweighs the danger of harm to any victim and of unfair prejudice to any party. Evidence of an alleged victim's reputation is admissible only if it has been placed in controversy by the alleged victim.

Conclusions

The legislative underpinnings and history of workplace antidiscrimination laws show that claims can be brought under a variety of state and federal laws. Lawyers may file multiple causes of action regarding a single complainant, based on the claimant's membership in more than one protected group (e.g., age plus gender plus retaliation), and may file both statutory and tort claims. Only relatively recently, following passage of the Civil Rights Act of 1991, were plaintiffs in federal court able to seek compensation for injuries caused by the discriminatory conduct they experienced at work. Many principles from tort law have been incorporated in the resulting statutory cases on damages. While, on average, discrimination plaintiffs fare better in state than federal court, state courts rely on federal court guidance in interpreting the applicable legal principles and standards. The legal framework to guide practicing psychologists in evaluating consequences of workplace discrimination is outlined in the next chapter.

Forensic Mental Health Concepts

2

Introduction

The purpose of this chapter is to acquaint the evaluating psychologist with analytical or conceptual models developed by past evaluators to help them prepare for and organize the task of conducting a workplace discrimination evaluation. The chapter introduces key legal concepts that the evaluating psychologist will encounter, such as *a mental state in controversy, "garden variety" damages, compelled mental examinations, proximate cause, eggshell skulls, the duty to mitigate,* and *malingering*. These concepts form the backdrop for our five-stage model to assess the nature and scope of injuries and causes of those injuries. A clear understanding of the concepts and issues described in this chapter will help the psychologist incorporate these concepts into the five-stage model that is elaborated in Chapter 5.

This knowledge, combined with familiarity with the research literature on workplace discrimination, will permit the evaluating psychologist to develop theoretical hypotheses about the validity of the complainant's claims. By collecting wide-ranging qualitative and quantitative data from the complainant, the psychologist can develop and refine these theoretical hypotheses about the complainant's claims. Finally, a process of *abductive reasoning* is applied to determine the best fit between the hypotheses and the available information (Goodman-Delahunty & Foote, 2009). Abductive reasoning is experience-based reasoning (Peirce, 1955) or "a method of reasoning in which one chooses the hypothesis which, if true, best explains the relevant evidence" (Stiles, 2009).

No Presumption of Harm

There is no presumption of any distress, harm, or injury to the claimant following a finding that a defendant employer engaged in discriminatory conduct. Some psychologists have endorsed a policy that presumes some minimal level of harm once liability is determined (Fitzgerald, 2003). Antidiscrimination statutes in a few state jurisdictions such as Massachusetts permit an inference of emotional harm and distress on the basis of a finding that the defendant is liable for discrimination (*Labonte v. Hutchins & Wheeler,* 1997). Emotional distress "is inferred as a normal adjunct of the employer's actions, even in the absence of physical injury or psychiatric consultation," (Gilbert, 2007, p. 169). A fact finder may award "nominal" damages when an employer is liable for discrimination and the plaintiff fails to provide evidence sufficient to sustain an award of compensatory damages. An award of nominal damages in the amount of $1–$500 may be appropriate when the plaintiff's experiences are no different from everyday stress. "Hurt feelings, anger and frustration are part of life" and at some level warrant little or no damages (*Patterson v. P.H.P. Healthcare Corp.*, 1996, p. 940). In federal courts and most state jurisdictions, the view that an inference without additional evidence is sufficient to sustain an award of compensatory damages has not been adopted, and the burden remains on the plaintiff to prove actual harm. Thus, the focus of an assessment related to a workplace claim for compensatory damages is twofold. The first issue is the presence, nature, scope, and duration of any harm or injuries; the second issue is causation.

CASE LAW

Patterson v. P.H.P. Healthcare Corp. (1996)

- The Court held that evidence of mental distress that is no different from everyday stress is insufficient to support anything more than a nominal damage award.

Proving and Rebutting Compensatory Damage Claims

To recover a monetary award in compensatory damages for workplace discrimination,

> **INFO**
> A workplace discrimination evaluation assesses the presence, nature, scope, and duration of any harm or injuries sustained by the plaintiff, as well as the cause of the harm.

the plaintiff must testify or present witnesses, documents, or other evidence sufficient to establish that the plaintiff was actually harmed or injured, and must establish that those injuries were caused by the discriminatory conduct of the employer. Proof of causation of harm usually turns on circumstantial evidence and inference drawn from, among other things, a differential diagnosis and a patient's psychosocial history. The personal history of the complainant is relevant because of the role of past history, level of coping skills, ongoing psychopathology or stress reactions, and other individual characteristics in modifying the complainant's reaction to experiences of discrimination.

Thus, the most significant questions that the forensic mental health professional can address to assist the fact finder are ways to provide evidence of emotional harm sustained by the plaintiff, or lack of it, and evidence that the unlawful conduct of the defendant employer was or was not the cause of any observed harm. In addressing these issues, four critical questions arise for the evaluator:

1. How to measure or quantify the severity of the distress claimed by or exhibited by the plaintiff
2. How to determine whether the distress is caused by workplace discrimination versus emotional or psychological difficulties that preceded the alleged discriminatory events
3. How to measure the extent to which any distress arose as a consequence of retaliation or victimization of the plaintiff at work
4. How to assess distress attributable to the litigation itself

To assist the court or jury in determining the nature, scope, and causes of any psychological injuries sustained by the plaintiff, the consulting expert must apply a methodology that is reliable and generally accepted within his or her profession. In a practical sense, if the plaintiff has sustained a condition that conforms to a DSM-IV diagnosis, that leg of the admissibility test may be met. Although differential diagnosis is one permissible methodology for ascriptions of causation of harm, it is not mandatory so long as the evaluating psychologist uses psychological tests that are generally used in the field and have been subjected to review in published peer-reviewed journals, and a reliable opinion may therefore be reached (*Pittman v. ANR Freight Sys.*, 2002). However, the presence of a diagnosis is not as important as the changes in functions sustained by the plaintiff as a result of the alleged discrimination (see discussion in Chapter 3).

The goal of the expert should be to express an opinion, supported by evidence, of the existence of any injury and related changes in functioning. In cases of workplace discrimination, this evaluation involves a review of all relevant documents, a structured interview, and the administration of one or more objective tests. A step-by-step description of this approach is set forth in Chapter 5. By the time an evaluating psychologist is consulted, most or all of the relevant events in dispute in a workplace discrimination claim have already transpired. These assessments are primarily retrospective, because it is rare than any test or interview will have been conducted prior to the alleged injury.

CASE LAW
Pittman v. ANR Freight Systems (2002)

- The Court held that differential diagnosis is not required to prove causation of harm. A reliable opinion can be reached using other means, so long as the means are reliable and generally accepted within the expert's profession.

Conducting a Retrospective Analysis

Four types of retrospective analysis were distinguished by Rogers (2002):

1. Corroborative analysis: where independent sources are consulted to

gather evidence to support or rebut the allegations of the complainant and the theories of causation of harm

2. Analogue analysis: offers accounts of ways in which various factors influence the ability of people to recall and relate past clinical events
3. Time-lapse analysis: an attempt to reproduce a given set of events or conditions
4. Biological marker analysis: reports are confirmed by a biological marker

In many mental health assessments, a multifactorial, biopsychosocial approach is recommended to frame conclusions about causation of harm (Schultz & Stewart, 2008; Young, 2008). The model we recommend incorporates features of the corroborative analysis and the multifactorial elements of a biopsychosocial approach. A strength of our model is that it avoids exclusive reliance on the subjective perspective and statements of the claimant. Given the skepticism of courts and fact finders about the credibility of plaintiffs and their susceptibility to suggestion, the evaluating expert should take care to avoid reliance on any methods that could be criticized as suggestive. For example, if the evaluator assessing the presence of traumatic reactions asks the plaintiff if he has experienced nightmares, intrusive recollections, or traumatic avoidance, the plaintiff must only affirm the presence of the symptoms in order to meet the criteria for the diagnosis of post-traumatic stress disorder (PTSD) (Young, Kane, & Nicholson, 2006). The approach we recommend is also adapted to assist the evaluator in teasing apart issues that are informative in determining causation of harm.

We describe a five-stage model of analysis to assess causation of harm. This model is a distillation of best practices that have long been recognized in forensic psychology as applied to tort and civil rights cases (Goodman-Delahunty & Foote, 1996; Greenberg, 2003), and it applies those practices in a systematic fashion. The focus of this model is the determination of the

BEWARE
Be sure not to rely on suggestive methods to inform your opinion on the causation of harm.

courses of the injuries sustained by the plaintiff to assist the court or jury in determining whether the defendant is liable for compensatory damages, and, if causation is attributed to the defendant, the basis to assess the amount recoverable in compensatory damages. This model results in a description of functional impairment in the plaintiff.

The five-stage model relies on inductive, deductive, and abductive reasoning to determine causation of harm. It is a best-practice model to prepare ethically sound, reliable reports. It connects theory and research to clinical practice and the law. By applying the five-stage model, a full range of possible influences is considered, including preexisting and secondary or unrelated ones, not only those related to the alleged discriminatory events and subsequent outcomes. Issues of potential malingering are also addressed. In addition, the assessment may take into account the future mental health of the plaintiff.

In our model, the forensic mental health expert applies hypothesis testing to determine if the plaintiff's or the defendant's theories of causation are supported. In addition, the expert develops theories in light of his or her clinical experience and knowledge. The systematic approach we outline allows practitioners who have an understanding of the literature to integrate the theories and findings of the literature and the case facts to reach an informed and evidence-based opinion on causation of harm. The evaluating psychologist works from the premise that, unless contrary evidence is uncovered, the claimant has no psychological or psychiatric disorder, and, if there is one, it may be caused wholly by preexisting stressors, psychological vulnerabilities, personality disorder, psychopathology, and so forth. Finally, abductive reasoning processes are used by the psychologist to link or connect the information gathered in the course of the evaluation to support or rebut several competing theories about the causes of the plaintiff's injuries, and to determine which is the best fit for the available case facts.

The evaluator must consider the context in which the discrimination occurred in the workplace, along with potential extrinsic influences on the way the impact of an experience of discriminatory workplace conduct may be registered. We have identified four ways that nondiscriminatory events can influence determinations of the causation of any harm observed. First, there may be problems experienced by the plaintiff that were caused by events unrelated to the alleged discrimination. Second, the plaintiff may have an ongoing problem that preexisted the alleged discrimination and that serves as a vulnerability factor, a risk factor, or more harm. For instance, for a plaintiff who has a history of childhood sexual abuse, the impact of sexually harassing conduct may be more profound and severe. Third, the presence of an ongoing problem may be exacerbated by exposure to workplace discrimination. Fourth, the plaintiff's social support system may be eroded by the discrimination. The complexity of this list of issues to address in reaching an opinion on the nature and severity of the injury and causation of harm can be daunting. The five-stage model we outline to manage the data collection, analysis, and assessment in a systematic fashion facilitates the determination of a defensible expert opinion on causation of harm.

In almost every evaluation of damages in workplace discrimination cases, the psychologist must determine if the defendant's actions proximately caused the plaintiff's injuries. That is, understanding that plaintiffs have lives before, during, and after the alleged harassment, were there events or processes occurring in those time frames apart from the alleged harassment, which could reasonably account for the plaintiff's symptoms? The psychologist

INFO

There are four categories or types of nondiscriminatory events that can influence determinations of the causation of harm in workplace discrimination claims:

1. Plaintiff problems unrelated to the alleged discrimination
2. Plaintiff problems that are ongoing and preexisting and that serve as risk factors for harm
3. Plaintiff problems that are exacerbated by the discrimination
4. The erosion of the plaintiff's social support system due to the discrimination

BEST PRACTICE

A comprehensive workplace discrimination evaluation should address the following areas of the plaintiff's life:

- On-the-job activities
- Social activities
- Mental and physical health

must examine whether any symptoms or problems present in the plaintiff are related to the alleged discrimination, harassment, or hostile workplace environment.

Workplace discrimination has been shown to affect three major dimensions in a target's life:

- On-the-job activities such as career opportunities, job satisfaction, work behaviors, and workplace functioning
- Off-the-job social and relationship activities
- Personal psychological and physical health consequences

A comprehensive evaluation should aim to address all three areas of activity, including "the severity and long-term stability of the individual's problems" (Butcher & Miller, 1999, p. 110).

To ensure that the fact finder has legally relevant information on emotional harm, the expert should aim to include details that specify precisely the physical or behavioral manifestations of the distress, and the duration of these symptoms. In all cases, the expert should provide examples of the impact of the distress while the plaintiff is at work and while he or she is not at work. To better assist the court, it is helpful to discuss the physical, behavioral, and emotional state of the plaintiff in these arenas before, during, and after the discriminatory events.

Duty to Mitigate

Although the duty to minimize or contain one's losses applies in cases of employment discrimination, this legal doctrine is relevant more to pecuniary than to non-pecuniary damage claims. Notably, the EEOC has held that a plaintiff has no duty to mitigate his or her compensatory damages (Gilbert, 2007, p. 276). Despite this

BEST PRACTICE

The duty of the plaintiff to mitigate compensatory damages is dependent on whether the claim is filed under federal or state statutes or tort law. Be sure to check relevant doctrines with the retaining attorney.

legal ruling, the extent to which a claimant takes action to seek help or to otherwise minimize damage and harm is still a fertile ground for cross-examination. Examples of ways to minimize compensatory damages might include prompt notice to the employer of the discriminatory events, consultation with a counselor available through an employee assistance program (EAP), seeking treatment from a medical or mental health care provider, and following the advice of a health care or mental health practitioner. Where discrimination claims are brought under the aegis of tort law rather than federal or state antidiscrimination statutes, the duty of the plaintiff to mitigate his or her compensatory damages may still apply. Evaluating psychologists should check with legal counsel in a particular case to ascertain whether this doctrine is relevant.

Causation of Harm

To determine causation of harm, although evidence from a health care provider is a not a mandatory prerequisite for recovery of compensatory damages for emotional distress, an expert may be better able to provide this information than the plaintiff or other lay witnesses.

In circumstances where the injuries sustained are primarily or exclusively psychological or emotional, however, assignment of responsibility for the injury is a complex task. Similarly, a determination of the degree of impairment or disability that is the result of the exposure to discriminatory conduct is complex. To assist in the task of specifying the degree of causation of harm to a plaintiff and the nature and scope of any impairment or consequential disability, psychologists with forensic expertise have devised various approaches or models. The six distinct models applied in the assessment of impairment or disability were distinguished and

INFO
Determining causation of harm, as well as degree of harm, is a difficult and complex task. A variety of methods and approaches can be used.

evaluated by Schultz and Stewart (2008); namely, the biomedical, forensic, psychosocial, ecological, economic, and biopsychosocial models. Other psychologists have emphasized procedural models. For example, Cocchiarella and Andersson (2001) recommended a procedure that draws on and incorporates the AMA Guides to the Evaluation of Permanent Impairment (2007). Similarly, Wilson and Moran outlined a matrix model (2004); and Greenberg, Otto, and Long (2003) discussed psychological testing to assess emotional damages. Other scholars have outlined steps to observe in assessing and documenting psychological injuries (Greenberg, 2004; White, Day, & Hackett, 2007; Young, Kane, & Nicholson, 2007). However, no comprehensive model has yet emerged to guide evaluating psychologists in the determination of causation of harm. These models, and the five-stage model that we recommend (Foote, 2009), all aim to facilitate the integration of data from multiple sources to indicate whether the defendant's actions at issue in a discrimination case were causally related to the plaintiff's injury.

General and Specific Causation

Courts often distinguish between notions of *general causation of harm*, which apply to most individuals, and *specific causation*, applicable only to the plaintiff in a particular case. The psychologist should be prepared to address both topics. Familiarity with the literature on issues of general causation, such as common nomothetic or common coping behavioral patterns and responses in victims of workplace discrimination, will help the evaluating expert develop specific hypotheses about how a typical person in circumstances similar to those of the plaintiff can be expected to react. "Specific causation" is the assessment of the ideographic or particular response of the individual plaintiff in the current case.

INFO

Familiarize yourself with base rates and common symptoms of certain injuries. This information can be helpful when evaluating general causation of harm.

To assist the expert in addressing issues of general versus specific causation, some familiarity with base rates of injury and with common symptoms of certain injuries is helpful. These can be determined through a review of relevant psychological studies, even if the researchers did not test the specific questions and circumstances presented in the current case.

Proximate Cause

To recover damages, guidance issued by the EEOC (1992) advises that the complaining party must prove that the employer's discriminatory act or conduct was the cause of his loss. The critical question is whether the complaining party incurred the losses as a result of the employer's discriminatory action or conduct. In civil cases, where the applicable burden of proof is a preponderance of the evidence, to be sufficient, evidence of causation must demonstrate that it is more likely than not that the discrimination caused the harm at issue; i.e., "a probability and not [a] mere possibility that the alleged tortious conduct caused the alleged injury" (*Harrison v. Edison Bros. Apparel Stores, Inc.*, 1998). Put another way, the question is whether the defendant employer's discriminatory conduct was one of several proximate causes of

CASE LAW

Merriweather v. Family Dollar Stores of Indiana, Inc. (1996)

- The U.S. Court of Appeals ruled that the plaintiff's emotional distress resulted in part from her discharge, and therefore she was entitled to compensatory damages. However, because termination was not the sole cause of distress, the damages awarded were adjusted.

the harm. The discriminatory conduct need not be the sole cause of emotional distress for the plaintiff to recover non-pecuniary damages, although an award of damages should be adjusted when there are multiple causes of the injury (*Merriweather v. Family Dollar Stores of Indiana, Inc.*, 103 F.3d 576, 581 [7th Cir. 1996]).

Eggshell Skulls

Even unusually sensitive plaintiffs may recover damages if the injuries were caused by the discrimination. More specifically, in the United States' legal context, the "eggshell skull" rule holds a defendant liable for all consequences resulting from his or her activities leading to an injury to another person, even if the victim suffers an unusually high level of damage (e.g., due to a preexisting vulnerability or medical condition). The term implies that if a person had a skull as delicate as the shell of an egg, and a *tortfeasor* or assailant who did not know of that condition were to hit that person on the head, causing the skull unexpectedly to break, the responsible party would be held liable for all damages resulting from the wrongful contact, even though they were not foreseeable.

The way the eggshell skull doctrine can apply in workplace discrimination cases is illustrated by the case of a worker hired by the U.S. Social Security Administration to answer telephones and perform computer data entry. Ten years before she was hired, the worker commenced treatment for depressive and obsessive-compulsive disorders. These disorders qualified her as a disabled employee within the meaning of the Americans with Disabilities Act. The worker sought reasonable accommodation for her disability in the form of duty and hours adjustments. Her request was denied, and soon thereafter, she was constructively discharged and filed a claim of disability discrimination. At trial, the plaintiff testified that she experienced anger, shame, and rejection, and that her preexisting mental disorder was exacerbated by the discriminatory treatment. Her treating psychiatrist testified that the discharge caused a severe emotional injury in the form of feelings of worthlessness and low self-esteem which lasted for a period of five years.

INFO

The eggshell skull rule says that you take your victim as you find him. It holds a defendant liable for all consequences resulting from his or her activities leading to an injury to another person, even if the victim suffers an unusually high level of damage (e.g., due to a preexisting vulnerability or medical condition).

The emotional symptoms, supported by the medical evidence, were found to justify an award of $100,000 in compensatory damages for the additional harm to the plaintiff caused by the illegal discrimination (*Holland v. Barnhart*, 2003).

A common issue arising in the context of employment discrimination cases, especially discrimination on the basis of gender or sexual harassment, is the vulnerability of the plaintiff who has an "eggshell skull" to injuries because of the experience of past sexual abuse. Although a reasonable-person standard applies on issues of liability in a discrimination case, the eggshell skull doctrine applies to determinations of damages. In other words, a plaintiff who is unusually sensitive to workplace conduct that other reasonable workers did not regard as offensive may not prevail, even if the sensitivity is the consequence of a prior trauma, unless that individual qualifies as a disabled worker who requires reasonable accommodation. However, if that worker prevails on the issue of liability, and the discriminatory conduct aggravated a preexisting condition, the plaintiff can recover for the worsening of the symptoms. Thus, the evaluating expert must be able to determine, retrospectively, the existence of any prior pathology or underlying disorder.

Mental State "In Controversy"

Different legal procedures may be observed depending on the severity of the distress or injuries claimed by the plaintiff. The procedures that are most significantly impacted by this distinction are the involvement of expert witnesses by one or more parties, and

CASE LAW
Schlagenhauf v. Holder (1964)

- The U.S. Supreme Court held that the defense must show that the plaintiff's mental state is "in controversy" and that "good cause" exists for ordering mental or physical examinations of the plaintiff.

the opportunity for a formal mental-state examination or assessment by an evaluating psychologist. A prerequisite to the right of the defense's evaluating expert to examine the plaintiff is whether the mental state of the plaintiff is "in controversy" (*Schlagenhauf v. Holder*, 1964).

In some courts, when a plaintiff's alleged distress has ended, his or her mental state is no longer "in controversy." Thus, if the lapse of time between the discriminatory events and the trial is lengthy, as is typically the case, by the time a claim is prepared for trial, the plaintiff's suffering occasioned by the discrimination may be significantly reduced, leading courts to conclude that the benefit to be derived from any examination is too minimal to justify the intrusion into the plaintiff's life (*Hodges v. Keane*, 1993). Moreover, the decision by a plaintiff not to call an expert witness does not fully resolve the issue of whether the plaintiff's mental state is in controversy in the case, but tends to indicate that it is not. Other factors that establish a controversy and that may provide a basis for a compelled mental examination of the plaintiff, pursuant to Federal Rule of Civil Procedure 35 (2007), or state analogues, are claims of more severe outcomes, such as depressive disorders or clinical depression following workplace discrimination. Thus, in determining whether or not a controversy exists, some courts distinguish between the ordinary anticipated consequences of workplace discrimination, resulting in what have been called "garden variety" damages, and more severe consequences that rise to the level of a psychological or emotional injury.

"Garden Variety" Damages

In many discrimination cases, the psychological sequelae or consequences may be intense for a number of weeks and then dissipate. Garden-variety damages are more temporary and ordinary consequences of workplace discrimination. A majority of jurisdictions distinguish between claims of serious emotional distress and injury and claims of lower-level distress, humiliation, and embarrassment (Bresticker & Fitzgerald, 2005). General allegations of mental anguish and humiliation may support a modest compensatory damages award. Support for a claim of compensatory damage via the testimony of the plaintiff is legally acceptable in cases in which there is no substantial harm and the amounts claimed are not large. For example, where a plaintiff did not seek any medical treatment, and the complainant was the sole witness who testified about the mental-distress damages that she experienced, an award of $25,000 was reduced to $10,000, in part because her testimony on this topic was sparse (*Iroquois Nursing Home v. NYSDHR*, 2008).

Most commonly, parties claiming garden-variety damages will not introduce medical evidence or consult mental health professionals. In these cases, if the defendant employer wants to retain an expert, that expert may not be allowed to examine the plaintiff unless the court first determines that the plaintiff has placed his or her "mental state in controversy" in the case, and the defendant can show good cause why the plaintiff should submit to the examination. In other words, a claim limited to ordinary emotional harm, distress, and disruption (not psychological or psychiatric injury) may be inadequate to establish any controversy, and thus may foreclose the defendant's right to compel a Rule 35 mental examination of the plaintiff by the opposing party (Foote & Goodman-Delahunty, 2005; Kovera & Cass, 2002). Federal Rule of Civil Procedure 35 allows one party, usually the defendant, to compel a medical or psychological evaluation of a party once that party's mental condition has been placed "at issue."

INFO

Rule 35 of the Federal Rules of Civil Procedure states that the court may order a party whose mental or physical condition is in controversy to submit to a physical or mental examination by a suitably licensed or certified examiner.

Where no mental examination of the plaintiff is allowed, the defense expert will have access to the plaintiff's statements, deposition testimony, and other pleadings (e.g., complaint, interrogatory questions and answers, workplace records, and the like) to provide an opinion. An interview with the plaintiff may be granted, in the presence of legal counsel. These circumstances may preclude the evaluating psychologist from obtaining a full history from the plaintiff. The consulting expert will have to determine whether it is feasible ethically and practically to prepare an expert report in these circumstances. Because of this reduced database, the psychologist may determine that there are insufficient data upon which to base a reliable professional opinion. Even if there are sufficient data, the expert is required to describe any limitations to the conclusions drawn that may result from a reduced fund of information (see APA Ethical Standard 9.01b, American Psychological Association, 2002).

Compensatory Damages and the Privacy of the Complainant

The only way a plaintiff can avoid all inquiries into his or her private life is to forego any claim for compensatory damages. Some plaintiffs who do not wish to submit to a compelled mental examination and to disclose private information about their personal history may choose to forego compensation for any injury sustained as a consequence of the discrimination.

To support a claim for only garden-variety damages, some thresholds of privacy must be crossed—the plaintiff will have to articulate and describe the injuries suffered in some detail at deposition and before a judge and jury. The plaintiff may also have to identify witnesses such as family members, friends, coworkers, physicians, or therapists who can corroborate that he or she suffered the alleged harms. While the defendant employer is not permitted to contact these

INFO

If a claimant is seeking compensatory damages, he should expect that there will be inquiries into his private life. The only way to avoid this type of questioning is to claim "garden variety" damages.

individuals solely to harass or embarrass a plaintiff, the employer has the right to determine whether other factors in the plaintiff's life caused the alleged injuries. By seeking non-*pecuniary* or non-economic compensatory damages, the plaintiff, and his or her family, friends, coworkers, and physicians or therapists may be contacted and may be required to provide testimony concerning matters of a personal, private, or sensitive nature. The extent to which the plaintiff may have to disclose personal and private information is determined by the judge or by agreement of the parties.

The rape shield law, Federal Rule of Evidence 412, was extended in 1994 to apply to civil cases by amendments to Rule 412. This limitation is mainly relevant to claims of sexual harassment and may impose some limits on the evidence that a lawyer may introduce at trial. For example, in a sexual harassment case, the scope of the inquiry a lawyer may cover in the trial about the plaintiff's past sexual behavior is limited in terms of the plaintiff's sexual history regarding the (a) the plaintiff's sexual predisposition and (b) previous engagement by the plaintiff in any other sexual behavior. To overcome this limitation, permission must be obtained from the court showing a need for the evidence, and that the relevance outweighs the potential harm to the plaintiff and the risk of unfair prejudice. What is difficult is that this rule does not prohibit the lawyer or forensic mental health expert from making these inquiries in depositions, in writing, or in the course of an independent medical examination by an evaluating psychologist of the plaintiff. However, in light of this shield rule, pretrial queries to the plaintiff along these lines may raise objections to them as unnecessary violations of the plaintiff's privacy.

Compelled Mental Examinations

In certain circumstances, the parties may reach an agreement that the plaintiff will submit to an examination by a defense expert, or the parties may agree to rely on evidence from a single independent evaluating expert.

The case law makes it clear that even when more extensive, protracted, and severe psychological injuries from workplace discrimination are alleged, there is no requirement that the plaintiff call expert witnesses to give evidence on this topic, but that is the more likely procedure. A plaintiff who consults an expert at the request of his or her attorney will expect to submit to a mental examination.

However, if an evaluating expert is retained by defense counsel, as previously indicated, one cannot assume that the plaintiff will be available for an interview and the testing that the psychologist may wish to conduct to prepare a report. Where substantial injuries are claimed, the defendant may seek an order from the court requiring the plaintiff to submit to an examination by an independent physician and/or mental health professional designated by the defendant, as provided for in Rule 35 of the Federal Rules of Civil Procedure (2007) or similar state rules.

Psychological and Psychiatric Injuries

Evidence of psychological and psychiatric injuries may emerge in various ways. For example, they may be apparent in the form of physical or somatic symptoms, psychological symptoms, and workplace-related symptoms.

Symptoms of Employment Discrimination

Although some individuals are far more resilient than others, and research on consequences and sequelae of workplace discrimination is still relatively new (Goodman-Delahunty, 1999; Foote & Goodman-Delahunty, 2005), the body of relevant literature is growing dramatically. This body of literature has provided a range of symptoms and problems commonly seen in employment discrimination cases. Understanding this range of reactions allows the expert to focus evaluation procedures and to determine if the reactions reported by a particular plaintiff fall within predictable patterns.

Not all complainants who experience more enduring and severe injuries following workplace discrimination will consult a mental health professional. For example, a clinical pharmacist who was discriminated against on the basis of her race (Caucasian), religion (Jewish), and retaliation for filing a complaint of discrimination against her supervisors, relied primarily on medical evidence from her physician to support her claim for compensatory damages. Over a five-year period, she experienced an increase in the frequency and duration of migraine headaches and was diagnosed with intestinal distress consistent with irritable bowel syndrome. She also suffered from an irrational fibroma caused by persistent biting of her cheeks due to stress, and this had to be surgically removed (*Glockner v. Dept of Veterans Affairs,* 2004). On the basis of this evidence, she was awarded $200,000 in non-pecuniary compensatory damages.

Some of the more serious mental injuries associated with workplace discrimination are depression, agoraphobia, acute stress disorder, and PTSD. For example, profound and enduring suffering was experienced by a complainant who was harassed by a letter of reprimand, humiliated during a staff meeting, and criticized over her performance of a job task after she prevailed in a claim of unlawful retaliation for prior EEO activity. She was unable to sleep, experienced suicidal thoughts and anxiety, and was hospitalized in two occasions. She consulted a psychiatrist who diagnosed a severe major depression, and, for over a year she was prescribed antidepressants and psychotropic medications. This evidence supported an award of $100,000 in compensatory damages (*Leatherman v. England*, 2001).

Disorders versus Functional Impairments

A diagnosis will not assist the courts in determining why an individual reacted the way he or she did to certain events (Melton, Petrila, Poythress & Slobogin, 2007) such as workplace discrimination. Numerous commentators have noted that a diagnosis of a disorder may make little difference in the context of a "before-and-after" analysis to determine the extent of compensatory damages (Slovenko, 2002), as the focus in legal cases is more on

INFO

Damages caused by workplace discrimination can manifest in various ways, including physically and psychologically.

functional impairment than on any particular diagnosis. A plaintiff whose injuries do not satisfy the elements for diagnosis of any disorder can be impaired; a plaintiff who meets criteria for the diagnosis of a disorder may nonetheless function ably. For example, some experts have argued that disorders such as PTSD are overdiagnosed because researchers and clinical practitioners do not define functioning in context (Wakefield, 2003; Wakefield & First, 2003). To discern functional impairments, the evaluating psychologist must consider the plaintiff in context (Greenberg & Wheeler, 2004).

Consider the case of a corrections officer who prevailed in a claim of gender discrimination, hostile workplace environment because of her sexual orientation, and retaliation for filing an EEO complaint. She and her coworkers testified that she experienced increased stress, sleeping and eating difficulties, nosebleeds, and physical, mental, and emotional distress, and that the harasser made her fear for her life. She was diagnosed as suffering from an adjustment disorder with depressive features. However, she received only four counseling sessions, did not take any leave from work, and was not prescribed any medication. As a consequence, an award of $850,000 in compensatory damages was reduced to $200,000 on appeal on the grounds that the original award amount was excessive because the capacity of the plaintiff to continue working, and the short duration of the treatment indicated that the injuries sustained were not so severe or pervasive, notwithstanding the diagnosis of a psychological disorder (*New York State Dept of Correctional Services v. NYSDHR*, 2008). However, an employee who manages to function in the workplace without revealing her distress to others is nonetheless entitled to an award of compensatory damages.

INFO

The focus in legal cases is on functional impairment, not on the diagnosis of a disorder.

Of course, a diagnosis of a disorder can influence the prognosis for the plaintiff, as some symptoms tend to diminish over time, while others do not. This topic is discussed in more detail in Chapter 6.

Impairments and Disabilities

Any deficits experienced by the plaintiff as a consequence of workplace discrimination or other events must be expressed in terms of functional impairments in the workplace and in other life arenas (Bryant, 2005). Impairment is loss of, loss of the use of, or disturbance of a mental, psychological, or physiological function (Schultz & Brady, 2003). Thus, impairment is defined functionally, behaviorally, or by examples of dysfunctions in the workplace and in other contexts. A more thorough review of this topic is presented in Chapter 6. Thus, a diagnosis of psychopathology is distinct from an "impairment." A disability is "an alteration of an individual's capacity to meet personal, social, or occupational demands because of impairment" (Cocchiarella & Andersson, 2001, p. 8).

The evaluating expert should provide a longitudinal history of the impairment, its scope, its treatment, and efforts at rehabilitation (Melton et al., 2007). The American Medical Association (AMA) developed tables that assess eight classes of impairment: of intelligence, thinking, perception, judgment, affect, behavior, ability, and potential (AMA, 2007). For each class, a five-point rating scale is applied regarding the degree of impairment observed. These tables are familiar to many judges, and can be useful to an evaluating expert as dimensions to consider in determining whether the plaintiff has experienced any deficits, and how these deficits impact the person's work performance, physical activities, social activities, and personal and family activities. This approach is helpful in focusing the evaluating expert on functional dimensions that will be of interest to the court, but will be of limited utility in determining causation of harm, a critical issue for the finder of fact. Chapter 6 and the five-stage model we present will help the evaluating expert integrate these data in determining the causation of harm as well as the nature and scope of injuries and impairments.

Standard of Certainty for Expert Opinion in Civil Cases

In expressing a conclusion on any issue, experts are often asked whether they endorse the conclusion "to a reasonable degree of medical/psychological certainty." There has been some debate in the literature as to what the phrase implies and whether the threshold of expert certainty in a civil case differs from that applied in criminal cases, given that the burden of proof in civil cases, "a preponderance of the evidence," is less onerous than that applied in criminal cases, "beyond a reasonable doubt." Some commentators have noted that the goal is to allow the forensic expert to make a qualitative statement that he or she is "reasonably certain" that the conclusion is correct, while acknowledging that absolute certainty in many areas of testimony cannot be reached (Bradford, 2001; Poythress, 1982). The precise meaning of this phrase has remained elusive.

In actual practice, psychologists attempt to obtain information from multiple sources to provide a basis for an expert opinion. Rarely does all this information point to the same conclusion, and the expert is frequently required to reconcile contradictory information. However, after this process is complete, the evidence should weigh more heavily on one side of the scale than on the other. If the evidence is in virtual equipoise, the expert is required to say that no clear conclusion could be reached. In cases where the evidence supports one conclusion over the other, the expert must have a logical and defensible basis for choosing that alternative. The reader is directed to the first volume in this series on this topic—the reasonable degree of psychological certainty (Heilbrun, Grisso, & Goldstein).

Standards for the Admissibility of Expert Evidence

To be admissible in court, the opinions and conclusions reached by the evaluating expert must comply with the standards set forth in Federal Rule of Evidence 702 on the Testimony by Experts:

> If scientific, technical, or other specialized knowledge will assist the trier of fact to understand the evidence or to determine a fact in issue, a witness qualified as an expert by knowledge, skill, experience, training, or education, may testify thereto in the form of an opinion or otherwise, if (1) the testimony is based

upon sufficient facts or data, (2) the testimony is the product of reliable principles and methods, and (3) the witness has applied the principles and methods reliably to the facts of the case.

In a landmark civil case, *Daubert v. Merrell Dow Pharmaceuticals, Inc.* (1993), the U.S. Supreme Court specified the factors pertinent to a determination of whether opinions of a scientific expert are sufficiently reliable to be admitted into evidence (Nordberg, 2009):

- whether the theories and techniques employed by the scientific expert have been tested;
- whether they have been subjected to peer review and publication;
- whether the techniques employed by the expert have a known error rate;
- whether they are subject to standards governing their application; and
- whether the theories and techniques employed by the expert enjoy widespread acceptance.

Subsequently, in another case, *Kumho Tire Co. v. Carmichael* (1999), in which the expert relied on specialized but non-scientific knowledge, the U.S. Supreme Court held that the factors applied to screen the expert evidence for its reliability may vary depending on the field of expertise in issue. Whether the evidence proffered by an evaluating forensic psychologist fits entirely within the *Daubert* scientific-knowledge model or fits better within the *Kumho* specialized-knowledge model is a topic of ongoing debate. However, many courts apply the *Daubert* criteria to all forms of psychological expert evidence, so the evaluating expert is best advised to adhere to those standards.

CASE LAW

Daubert v. Merrell Dow Pharmaceuticals, Inc. (1993)

- The Court ruled that judges be given the role of "gatekeeper," using a number of criteria (testing, peer review, error rate, underlying science, and acceptance) to determine admissibility of expert testimony.

CASE LAW
Kumho Tire Co. v. Carmichael (1999)

- The U.S. Supreme Court held the *Daubert* factors may apply to the testimony of experts who are not scientists.

Forensic experts may wish to note that psycholegal scholars identified seven discrete actions by a clinical evaluating psychologist that may trigger a *Daubert* inquiry (Sales & Shuman, 2005, interpreting the court's opinion in *Antoine-Tubbs v. Local 513*, 1999) when the proffered expert is not a research psychologist and the basis of the testimony indirectly relies on research. These proposed actions are: personally conducting an assessment of the plaintiff; undertaking a thorough evaluation of the plaintiff's relevant history; using differential diagnosis and etiology; reviewing assessments conducted by other professionals; evaluating other facts or data that are "reasonably relied on" by other professionals in the field to draw inferences and develop an opinion; including references to appropriate professional literature; and using professional training and experience (Sales & Shuman, 2005, p. 8).

To the factors specified by the Supreme Court in *Daubert*, the Advisory Committee on the Federal Rules of Evidence (Mueller & Kirkpatrick, 2007) added five suggested areas of consideration based on court rulings that succeeded the 1993 *Daubert* opinion:

a. Whether experts are proposing to testify about matters growing naturally and directly out of research they have conducted independently of the litigation, or whether they have developed their opinions expressly for purposes of testifying;

b. Whether the expert has unjustifiably extrapolated from an accepted premise to an unfounded conclusion;

c. Whether the expert has adequately accounted for obvious alternative explanations;

BEWARE
Most courts apply *Daubert* as opposed to *Kumho* standards, so it is best to adhere to the model set by the former when providing expert testimony.

d. Whether the expert "is being as careful as he would be in his regular professional work outside his paid litigation consulting" (*Sheehan v. Daily Racing Form, Inc.*, 1997); and

e. Whether the field of expertise claimed by the expert is known to reach reliable results for the type of opinion the expert would give.

Only rarely has expert psychological testimony proffered in a workplace discrimination case been challenged on appeal (Nordberg, 2009), and only a handful of those challenges pertained to assessments of psychological injury and a determination of compensatory damages. It is instructive to look at cases where psychological expert testimony on mental injuries has been challenged, reflecting legal concerns with the reliability of the expert opinions proferred. For instance, in a case in which a victim of a stroke sued the employer for retaliatory discharge under the Americans with Disabilities Act, testimony on causation of harm by a physician and a treating psychologist was excluded from trial in part on grounds that the opinions were developed expressly for purposes of testifying (*Franklin v. Consolidated Edison Co. of New York*, 2002). The court questioned the basis for the expert's assertion that the discriminatory treatment caused the stroke in light of multiple sources of stress in the employee's life and the absence of any reliable information on which to base a retrospective pre-stroke evaluation.

A similar outcome occurred in a case of sexual harassment in which a psychologist's testimony was offered to establish that the harassment caused the plaintiff to suffer from Post-Traumatic Stress Disorder. The trial court found that the expert did not follow any established recognized methodology to reach this conclusion. Exclusion of the evidence on this basis was affirmed on appeal (*Siljak v. Ravenswood Disposal Serv.*, 2002). A psychological autopsy was proffered by an expert in another employment case. The court found that the expert had never before performed a psychological autopsy, did not review any medical records of the plaintiff, and relied entirely on anecdotal information to form her opinion. The expert evidence was excluded on the basis of a lack of expertise and a field of expertise not known to yield reliable conclusions (*Halvorsen v. Plato Learning, Inc.*, 2006).

Conclusions

This chapter has introduced a series of key concepts integral to questions at the core of psycholegal damages determination. Familiarity with these forensic mental health concepts will equip the evaluating psychologist to test relevant theories of causation of harm, and to better distinguish injuries caused by discriminatory and nondiscriminatory events. In the next chapter, we describe some of the ways the evaluating forensic mental health professional can bring to bear relevant knowledge from group research published in the peer-reviewed social scientific literature; forensic case studies in psychology, psychiatry, and legal literatures; and experience as an expert in forensic cases.

Empirical Findings: Foundations and Limits

3

Introduction

Past studies have shown that the majority of experts (40%) who appear in courts are mental health experts; as few as 3% are active research scientists (Krafka et al., 2002). This pattern is replicated in employment cases on the issue of non-pecuniary compensatory damages (Landy, 2005a). The focus of this expert evidence is the mental health consequences of discrimination and an analysis of risk factors and protective factors that may tend to increase or decrease the nature and the duration of these sequelae. In offering expertise on these topics, the experts may draw on a range of empirical studies on responses to workplace discrimination, occupational injuries, and psychological injuries.

First, we describe the types of empirical studies that have been conducted to acquaint readers with the range of topics and resources available for more in-depth study in the context of a specific case. Next, we review some of the major topics of research pertinent to an assessment of psychological injuries, and findings that have emerged in these studies. We conclude by presenting research related to the responses of judges and jurors to evidence on compensatory damages from complainants and experts.

Empirical Studies on Workplace Discrimination

The majority of the research literature on workplace discrimination, including a spate of recent books on the topic (Blanck, 2005; Borgida & Fiske, 2008; Colker, 2005; Crosby, Stockdale, & Ropp, 2007; Dipboye & Coalella, 2005; Landy, 2005b; Nielsen &

Nelson, 2005; Rudman & Glick, 2008; Stefan, 2002; Stockdale & Crosby, 2004; Wrench, 2007), has focused almost exclusively on issues pertaining to liability determinations (i.e., on circumstances that elicit or foster prejudice or biased perceptions [e.g., Wiener & Winter, 2007], and psychological mechanisms of discrimination, such as stereotyping based on age, race, gender and disability: Fiske & Borgida, 2009). These resources offer much useful information on the manifestation of unlawful employment discrimination. However, the reactions and responses of targets of bias or discrimination that are integral to the issue of compensatory damages have received comparatively little research attention. Newcomers to this literature should be aware that the research corpus is somewhat uneven, and on some topics remains underdeveloped.

The research review presented in this chapter does not address liability determinations in discrimination cases, but is confined to the consequences or outcomes of discrimination. The purpose of this chapter is to provide an overview of the content, nature, and types of empirical research relevant to the assessment of psychological injuries in employment discrimination cases.

Research on Psychological Injuries

A significant issue that underlies much of the research on psychological injuries is what some psychologists have referred to as "a double standard" in the treatment of physical versus psychological injuries (Bornstein, 2009; Bornstein & Schwartz, 2009). The law has resisted putting psychological injuries on a par with physical injuries (Perrin & Sales, 1993). For example, on a commonly used nine-point scale of injury severity (Sowka, 1980), the lowest level is reserved for emotional injuries where no physical injury occurred, below temporary insignificant physical injuries that include very superficial reactions, such as a rash, laceration, or minor scar, with no recovery delay. Recent studies of

BEWARE
There is relatively little research literature that focuses on the consequences and outcomes of workplace discrimination. Most research addresses issues of liability, which is not helpful for determining damages.

psychological injuries flowing from psychosocial events such as ostracism have demonstrated that psychological pain and suffering experienced in the absence of any physical injury may have consequences that are more profound and enduring than those generated by physical trauma and physical injuries (Chen et al., 2008). These findings are in line with those in retrospective and prospective studies consistently showing that individuals exposed to human-generated traumatic events or conflict situations carry a higher risk of developing Post-Traumatic Stress Disorder, PTSD (Charuvastra & Cloitre, 2008). Both risk and recovery are highly dependent on psychosocial phenomena, such as social support.

Workplace discrimination qualifies as a human-generated traumatic event. Extensive research on PTSD has enabled the early identification of the one in four individuals most likely to develop chronic PTSD after exposure to a trauma (Bryant & Guthrie, 2007). For example, a self-administered self-report scale, the acute stress disorder (ASD) scale, can predict those who will develop PTSD with 91% accuracy (Bryant, Moulds, & Guthrie, 2000). Therefore, an ASD diagnosis is predictive of PTSD (Bryant, 2005b). However, the absence of an ASD diagnosis may not necessarily indicate a good prognosis, as many of those who go on to develop PTSD have not met criteria for ASD (Creamer et al., 2004).

Much of the extant relevant research on psychological injuries has addressed civil claims and cases in other contexts distinct from workplace discrimination, such as personal injury tort claims for accidental, not intentional, injuries (Bornstein et al., 2008; Feigenson, 2001; Greenberg, 2003; Greene & Bornstein, 2003; Koch et al., 2006; Samra & Koch, 2002; Schultz & Brady, 2003; Simon & Shuman, 2002; Young, Kane, & Nicholson, 2007; 2006). For example, major advances in studies of PTSD have focused on claims of distress and impairment in claims for compensation lodged by war veterans (Blanck, 2008). To the extent that this line of research is informative about the nature, scope, and duration of psychological injuries and their assessment, these resources are useful to experts in workplace discrimination cases. For example, these studies have shown that individuals who, before exposure to the trauma occurs, have maladaptive self-appraisals such as beliefs that they are incompetent, are more likely to develop PTSD (Bryant & Guthrie, 2007). Other studies have indicated that cognitive behavior therapy (CBT) is the most effective treatment promoting recovery from acute stress disorder and PTSD (Riggs & Foa, 2009). Drawing on this research, an evaluating mental health professional in a discrimination case who is informed that a claimant with maladaptive self-appraisals who was harassed at work and then attended 12 months of counseling that did not involve CBT may reach a different conclusion about the prognosis for recovery than an evaluating expert who is informed only that a claimant attended 12 months of counseling therapy.

In general, the risk for developing PTSD following even a serious injury is low—about one in four survivors of a seriously traumatic event (Kessler et al., 1995; O'Donnell et al., 2006). Although this is a general finding, the rate of PTSD following some events, like rape or sexual assault, is much higher, with more than half the survivors developing the syndrome (Kessler et al., 1995). Findings on the cumulative nature of trauma experiences can also help evaluating experts assess the impact of workplace discrimination on an individual who has a history of exposure to other trauma. For instance, studies conducted with firefighters and police officers who were exposed to multiple traumatic events have demonstrated that multiple exposures to trauma increase the risk of developing PTSD (McNally, Bryant, & Ehlers, 2003; O'Donnell et al., 2009).

The relevance of PTSD research to employment discrimination cases may be limited by the very definition of the disorder. The DSM-IV requires that in order to diagnose the disorder, "1. the person experienced, witnessed, or was confronted with an event or events that involved actual or threatened death or serious injury, or a threat to the physical integrity of self or others; 2. the person's response involved intense fear, helplessness, or horror" (American Psychiatric Association, p. 467). As observed by Foote and Goodman-Delahunty (2005), adverse events in the workplace rarely meet this criterion. In most cases, "physical integrity" is not threatened, nor is life and limb. Nevertheless, the person may respond to the trauma with "fear, helplessness, or horror," especially in cases of sexual harassment involving physical contact.

Research on Workplace Psychological Injuries

Empirical research on general workplace injuries is pertinent, as injuries caused by workplace discrimination comprise a discrete subset of the occupational injuries studied. For example, many studies have addressed the topic of workplace strain by applying Agnew's "General Strain Theory" (Agnew, 2001; Clarke et al., 2007). This theory posits that when people experience too much strain, they may act out in some way. Others have explored the impact of general occupational stressors (Barling, Kelloway, & Frone, 2005; Underhill, 2008). In addition, a large body of research explores claims for occupational injuries in the context of workers' compensation (Lippel, 2007). In former years, workers' compensation research focused exclusively on physical injuries (Janutis, 2008), but the more recent trend has been to allow psychological injury claims, including claims for psychological injuries attributable to general workplace harassment. In response to this development, the past decade has seen an explosion in studies of workplace harassment, and the formation of the Global Occupational Health Network, which provides a forum for sharing information concerning occupational injuries across national borders.

Many of these findings are directly relevant to claims of workplace harassment motivated by a worker's membership in a category protected under the antidiscrimination legislation. For example, one robust outcome of the general workplace harassment studies is a gender difference in response to harassment, indicating that women and men perceive and interpret situations of harassment differently and have different claim and compensation patterns (Lippel, 1999; Salin, 2010). Findings show that in response to higher levels of perceived exclusion or ostracism, men indicated lower satisfaction and psychological health compared to women. In addition, several studies have shown that gender and racial or ethnic discrimination affect occupational health and access to compensation (Bond et al., 2004; Katzen, 2006; Lippel, 1999; 2003). Recent studies on psychological distress in Asian-Americans following racial discrimination showed that ethnic attachment was a protective factor for older individuals who were born in the United States, but not for individuals born outside the United States (Yip, Gee, & Takeuchi, 2008).

Theories and Models of Psychological Injuries Caused by Workplace Discrimination

As might be anticipated from the foregoing section, research on compensatory damages in discrimination cases has drawn extensively from occupational stress models (Rospenda & Richman, 2005). The most widely applied model is the interactional Person x Situation model that takes into account social interactions in the workplace. This model, developed from earlier work by Lazarus and Folkman (1984), is based on the transactional model of stress, the leading theoretical model of human responses to stressors for the past 25 years. A feature of this model is consideration of "the critical role of the individual's subjective experience in understanding his/her psychological and emotional responses" to a stressor (Keashley & Harvey, 2004, p. 211), in this case, workplace discrimination.

The transactional model of stress posits that the employee target first undertakes "primary" or "threat appraisal" to assess positive or negative attributes of an event such as being subjected to inappropriate workplace behavior. If the employee views the event or behavior as potentially stressful or harmful, the second stage, "secondary" or "coping appraisal," proceeds. At this stage, the target evaluates his or her resources. In the case of discrimination, this might include the ability to defend themselves against the perpetrator(s) and a determination as to whether they can cope with the threat. The process of appraising a stressor to decide if it is potentially harmful is influenced by individual characteristics of the worker, or "person-factors," as well as contextual elements or "situation-factors." For example, recent studies have shown that the nature of an employee's attributions about workplace stressors, such as ostracism, moderate the relationship between ostracism and consequential emotional distress (Robinson, 2009).

Thus, the Person x Situation model provides a theoretical frame of reference to explore salient factors that may influence an assessment of compensatory damages. Both individual factors related to the employee and contextual factors related to the workplace are examined, as are features of the unlawful discriminatory conduct at issue, such as its severity, pervasiveness, and duration.

> Some individual difference variables (e.g., pre-existing psychological distress, gender, risk-taking) will increase the risk of suffering a tortious injury, while some individual difference variables will mediate between the tortious injury and the severity of the loss (e.g., cognitive appraisal, coping styles, occupation-injury interaction). The model also suggests that some individual difference variables will directly influence litigation (e.g., trait anger, anti-defendant attitudes), and that litigation itself will have some effect on the individual (e.g., increasing psychological distress). Further, systemic variables (e.g., intra-organizational policies and resolution procedures) may lessen or increase the likelihood of a tortious event occurring, may mediate between the tortious injury and the severity of the ensuing losses, and may influence the likelihood of initiating formal litigation. . . ." (Samra & Koch, 2002, pp. 300–301)

Researchers have applied this model to examine the antecedents and consequences of a variety of workplace stressors, including workplace discrimination (e.g., Fitzgerald, Swan, & Fischer, 1995; Fitzgerald, Swan, & Magley, 1997; Langhout et al., 2005; Magley et al., 1999; Rospenda, 2002; Williams, Fitzgerald, & Drasgow 1999).

Research on Psychological Injuries Related to Workplace Discrimination

The majority of the research reviews that have emerged that are relevant to assessments of psychological injuries and compensatory damages in employment discrimination cases have focused on cases involving sexual harassment (Beiner, 2005; Foote & Goodman-Delahunty, 2005; Goodman-Delahunty & Foote, 2009; Gold, 2004; Lenhart, 2004; Rospenda & Richman, 2005). Research on consequences of workplace discrimination on topics other than sexual harassment relevant to compensatory damages has lagged. Newly emerging areas of research include the consequences of discrimination based on disability, same-sex harassment (Foote & Goodman-Delahunty, 1999), sexual orientation (Badgett & Frank, 2007), race (Deitch et al., 2003) and age (Mujtaba et al., 2006; Orpen,). Research findings pertinent to the consequences and damages experienced by targets of discriminatory retaliation are also located under other conceptual labels, such as "whistleblowing" (Brown, 2008; Miceli, Near, & Dworkin, 2008; Rehg et al., 2008), ostracism (Williams, 2007; Chen et al., 2008); stalking (Kamphuis & Emmelkamp, 2001; Wilczak, 2009); bullying or mobbing (Mayhew et al., 2004), workplace harassment (Einarson et al., 2003; Knox-Haly, 2008; Matthiesen & Einarsen, 2004; Tehrani, 2004), workplace victimization (Aquino & Thau, 2009), and workplace incivility (Cortina et al., 2001).

Disparities in the research coverage and the dearth of studies on certain topics compared to others raises questions about the applicability of some research findings, particularly those regarding victims of sexual harassment, to victims of other types of workplace discrimination, such as discrimination based on race, age, national origin, or disability. Clearly, the law makes no distinction between the methods to prove damages depending on whether a claim is framed legally on the grounds of race, sex, religion, disability, or retaliation. From a legal standpoint, scholars note that a common mistake in evaluating cases for damages is to look for cases involving similar kinds of discrimination as a point of reference—i.e., in a case of racial discrimination, to compare the complainant with another complainant who experienced racial discrimination (Hadley & Laws, 2008). The legal focus when determining damages is not on the type or basis of discrimination, but on the similarity in the harm experienced by the complainant and other cases involving that type of outcome or harm to the complainant: namely, the symptoms of harm experienced by the complainant, the severity of those symptoms, and the period for which they persisted or are expected to persist (Hadley & Laws, 2008).

Undoubtedly, some experts will espouse the view that responses to discrimination in the form of sexual harassment are fundamentally different from responses to disability discrimination, racial discrimination, or other types of discriminatory conduct. This argument may be premised on the notion that sexual harassment is similar to sexual assault, and that workplace harassment that threatens an employee's sexual identity has the potential to be more damaging because sexual identity is so integral to personal identity and interpersonal social relationships. Other researchers have theorized that psychological injuries stemming from racial discrimination are particularly profound because of the integral nature of race to individual identity (Carter, 2007). Research findings have shown that victim reactions to sexual harassment are comparable to those of victims of sexual assault (Kilpatrick, Dansky, & Saunders, 1994). However, findings from studies of the consequences of racial discrimination have also shown that the responses of these victims are similar to responses observed in sexual harassment victims (Buchanan & Fitzgerald, 2008; Corbie-Smith et al., 1999; Griffith, 2007). With respect to the experience of harm from the standpoint of a victim or target of discrimination, the existing studies provide little basis to sustain an argument that a worker's racial or ethnic identity is less integral to that worker's social identity than the worker's gender. Currently, there are no data to support a distinction between the nature, severity, and duration of a worker's response to harassment based on sex versus harassment based on race, age, disability, gender, national origin, religion, etc. What seems plausible is that general workplace harassment and harassment motivated by considerations of a worker's membership in a group protected by the civil rights legislation (age, disability, race, national origin, religion, gender, etc.) produce similar reactions. This conclusion is supported in part by research on the similarity of outcomes of exposure to different types of sexually harassing conduct.

Types of Empirical Research on Consequences of Workplace Discrimination

Much useful information on compensatory damages appears in expert reports and testimony offered at trial or in pretrial motions in courts of first impression (courts in which a legal issue is first presented), or trial courts where employment discrimination cases are heard. However, information presented in court and decisions of the trial court are difficult to access, as these data are not typically reported or publicly available unless a decision is appealed. Lawyers often gain access to trial court information by consulting jury verdict publications. For example, when a jury returns a decision at the conclusion of a trial, the verdict and a summary of the core facts are recorded by local or national verdict reporting services, many of whom belong to the National Association of State Jury Verdict Publishers. These databases are useful repositories of information about similar cases and can be searched by geographical location, by expert, by type of injury (e.g., depression, "emotional breakdown"), and type of discrimination (race, age, disability, etc.). In addition, many resources are compiled to aid lawyers in summarizing case facts and evidence presented on compensatory damages. Evidence presented by plaintiffs in federal workplace discrimination cases is reviewed by Gilbert (2007), who provides examples addressing causation of harm, the impact of preexisting injuries, and multiple causes of emotional harm, drawn from decisions on compensatory damages involving a diverse array of injuries ranging from reduced self-confidence to suicide attempts.

Research on compensatory damages within the discipline of psychology commenced with single, anecdotal case studies and has evolved to the point that there are now large scale meta-analyses collating responses from thousands of participants. The research corpus encompasses both qualitative and quantitative studies, some of which have examined the issues from the standpoint of victims or targets of discrimination, while others have examined the workplace organization, and still others have explored the perspectives of fact finders: judges and juries who render decisions in

INFO

The following types of available research on compensatory damages can be helpful to experts who perform workplace discrimination evaluations:

- Victim studies
- Case studies (first-person or third-party)
- Archival studies
- Simulation studies (role-play)
- Stakeholder surveys
- Employee surveys

employment discrimination cases about the awards of compensatory damages. Variations in the types of studies influence the weight that experts should accord to their findings and the extent to which the findings may be generalized to the case at hand.

Studies of Victims or Targets and Claimants

Studies of actual targets and victims who have experienced mental and physical pain and suffering and emotional distress as a consequence of employment discrimination are an important resource for evaluating experts to consult to gain insight into patterns of responses to unlawful workplace discrimination. Both qualitative and quantitative research involving actual victims and litigants has been published in scholarly journals.

Qualitative Case Studies on Individual Targets, Litigants, and Class Members

Case-study reports by third parties such as lawyers, treating therapists, and evaluating experts have documented symptoms reported by victims of different types of workplace discrimination, such as disability (Holzbauer & Berven, 1996), gender-based harassment (Antilla, 2002), sexual harassment (Foote & Goodman-Delahunty, 2005; Gold, 2004; Salisbury et al., 1986), or age (Gregory, 2001). These case studies demonstrate that targets of many different types of discrimination have similar experiences (Rospenda & Richman, 2005), both in terms of the basis (e.g., race, gender, etc.), and in terms of the nature of the unlawful conduct experienced (verbal, nonverbal, etc.).

Some firsthand qualitative accounts by plaintiffs have been published. An articulate report is a case study by Crangle (2007), a research scientist in the Medical School at Stanford University, who prevailed on a claim of unlawful reprisal, was awarded the maximum available amount under the statutory cap for compensatory damages, but sacrificed her academic career in the process. Other firsthand accounts include details of seven years of litigation endured by Ann Hopkins, the plaintiff in a landmark nonpromotion claim against Price-Waterhouse (*Price Waterhouse v. Hopkins,* 1989; Hopkins, 1996; 2007). The accounts of groups of individuals such as multiple class-action claimants who experienced similar forms of discrimination within the same workplace or organization provide further qualitative insights into the damaging consequences of protracted exposure to workplace harassment. For example, a group of female employees at the Eveleth Taconite Mines in Minnesota comprised the first-ever class of sexual harassment plaintiffs, in a case that took 14 years to resolve. The lead plaintiff, Lois Jenson, worked in an environment of harassment for 12 years until she was disabled by PTSD. Following a review of their evidence on compensatory damages, the Eighth Circuit Court of Appeals commented:

> It should be obvious that the callous pattern and practice of sexual harassment engaged in by Eveleth Mines inevitably destroyed the self-esteem of the working women exposed to it. The emotional harm, brought about by this record of human indecency, sought to destroy the human psyche as well as the human spirit of each plaintiff. The humiliation and degradation suffered by these women is irreparable. Although money damage cannot make these women whole or even begin to repair the injury done, it can serve to set a precedent that in the environment of the working place such hostility will not be tolerated. (*Jenson v. Eveleth Taconite Company,* 1997, p.33)

Soon after this opinion was issued, the 15 plaintiffs settled for $3.5 million. The experiences of the women were chronicled in a book, *Class Action* (Bingham & Gansler, 1999) and a fictionalized motion picture, *North Country*.

Responses to a written survey from a larger group of 915 women who comprised the nationwide class of plaintiffs in a gender-based case against their employer were quantitatively analyzed by the plaintiffs' expert, Professor Louise Fitzgerald. The survey results prompted a settlement (*Cremin et al. v. Merrill Lynch Pierce Fenner & Smith, Inc.*, 1997). Other aspects of the case formed the basis of subsequent empirical reports on common experiences of plaintiffs who litigate, such as demoralization, anxious arousal, fear, and self-blame (Wright & Fitzgerald, 2007), decisions to litigate were influenced more by workplace climate or context than by the severity of injuries to the plaintiff (Wright & Fitzgerald, 2008). Another account of a gender-based class action against a multistate corporation, drafted by the counsel for the plaintiffs (Ryu & Larkin, 2007), described how the case settlement, achieved on the eve of trial, included provisions for compensatory damages to be awarded to all eligible class members. To gather an estimate of those damages, 10 to 20 members of the plaintiff class were formally evaluated by a team of two psychologists. Results of these evaluations offered insight into common patterns of consequences and injuries experienced by the claimants. Those findings formed the basis for a settlement formula, although class members were also permitted to seek individualized relief (Ryu & Larkin, 2007).

Archival Studies of Claimants

Archival studies that aggregate the data of individual claimants in different cases have also shed light on the commonalities and differences in reactions to workplace discrimination. These studies are less susceptible to selection biases that may be characteristic of case studies (Brun & Kedl, 2006), particularly when the data are randomly selected. For example, a series of comprehensive studies conducted by the Discrimination Research Group at the American Bar Foundation used archival quantitative data obtained from the EEOC, court outcomes, and qualitative interviews with the parties and legal counsel to explore trends in damage awards in employment discrimination cases. Their findings are summarized in *The Handbook of Employment Discrimination Research: Rights and Realities* (Nielsen & Nelson, 2005). Subsequent reports described outcomes in 1,788 randomly selected employment discrimination cases tried in federal court in the period from 1987 to 2003 (Nielsen et al., 2008). This large-scale analysis discerned that most parties opt to settle their cases because of the uncertainty of outcomes in court. A further significant finding was that the current antidiscrimination laws provide either modest or no relief to most plaintiffs; only a select few plaintiffs secured substantial compensatory damage awards (Nielsen, Nelson, & Lancaster, 2008; Berrey, 2009).

Other quantitative studies using convenience samples of claimants and litigants are also instructive, although the findings must be interpreted in light of the fact that, when sampling procedures do not permit random selection, some biases may be present in the results. For example, a sample of 192 women and 14 men who initiated claims of workplace discrimination was referred to members of a team of researchers to assess the severity of their injuries. An analysis of the Minnesota Multiphasic Personality Inventory 2 (MMPI-2) scores achieved in the course of evaluations revealed that 28% of the female profiles fell within normal limits (Long et al., 2004), highlighting the variability of individual responses to workplace discrimination and the fact that some litigants who seek compensatory damages experience "garden-variety damages" and present no diagnosable psychological injury at the time of trial.

Experimental Simulations

Laboratory studies often require participants to role-play or to assess vignettes that are randomly assigned so the researchers can draw causal inferences from the outcomes. Although constraints are imposed by ethical limits as to what researchers can expose participants to, some powerful findings have emerged using this methodology, particularly regarding manipulations of social-psychological variables in simulated studies of the impact of ostracism in studies of cyber-bullying (Williams, 2007). Many employees experience ostracism as a form of workplace discrimination, or as a consequence of lodging a complaint about perceived discrimination in the workplace.

Other simulation studies have presented participants with workplace vignettes to determine their perceptions of conduct and injuries. This research provides insight into factors that may influence the responses of targets of discrimination, coworkers, managers, and fact finders who are involved in workplace discrimination cases. To examine factors that influence compensatory and punitive damages assessments, descriptions of injuries were rated for their severity (Bright & Goodman-Delahunty, 2010; Wissler et al., 1997; Wissler, Hart, & Saks, 1999; Vidmar, 1995). Other research has examined the influence of procedural variables on damage awards; for example, individual versus class complaints (Horowitz & Bordens, 1990); and bifurcated versus unitary trials (Kagehiro, 2004; Greene, 2000); or the influence of expert evidence on the magnitude of damages awarded (Raitz et al., 1990).

Surveys of Stakeholders

Researchers have conducted surveys with many stakeholder groups (those who are most affected by changes in legal standards or procedures) who have experience with workplace discrimination claims, including workers, managers, human resource professionals, mental health experts, judges, magistrates, and jurors or jury-eligible citizens.

Interviews with Federal Judges

A series of 14 interviews with federal judges who hear employment discrimination cases in federal district courts was conducted to canvas their views on and responses to expert evidence in these cases (Landy, 2005a). Results revealed that judges were more familiar with clinical than social or organizational psychologists, and were skeptical about expert evidence in discrimination cases.

Employee Surveys

A major source of information on the consequences of employment discrimination is the outcomes of surveys of workers canvassed in a variety of occupational settings. These surveys have explored both the antecedents and consequences of discrimination. Some datasets comprising large-scale studies were conducted by the Department of Defense and replicated over a number of years, examining race discrimination (Scarville et al., 1999) and sex discrimination (Bastian, Lancaster, & Reyst, 1996; Magley et al., 1999) at all levels of the organization. Other studies have focused on specific occupational segments of the workforce, such as white collar workers, pink collar workers, blue collar workers, or employees within specific occupations, such as police, or nurses.

One early criticism of using employee surveys to assess the prevalence of experiences of discriminatory conduct or harassment was that the participants were not always provided legal definitions of unlawful behavior. Even when these definitions were provided, the participants' subjective understanding of these definitions might not have been accurate. Regardless, the outcomes provide insight into problems experienced and perceived by employees in the workforce (Magley et al., 1999). A second criticism was the lack of a standardized instrument to measure the consequences. A third criticism was the extensive focus on sexual harassment. Since then, numerous studies applying a similar approach have examined other forms of discrimination, such as discrimination based on age and gender (Pavalko, Mossakowski, & Hamilton, 2003; Waldo, Berdahl, & Fitzgerald, 1998), race (Gee & Walsemann, 2009; Scarville et al.,1999; Schneider, Hitlan, & Radhakrishnan, 2000), sexual orientation (Badgett & Frank, 2007; Krieger & Sydney, 1997) and disability (Schur et al., 2009). These correlational and cross-sectional studies advanced our knowledge regarding the prevalence, nature, and duration of common reactions to discriminatory workplace conduct.

INFO

Data gathered through research studies address three broad types of outcomes of discrimination:

- Psychological consequences
- Physical or somatic consequences
- Workplace consequences

Numerous studies have suggested a link between perceived

discrimination and poor health, particularly depression and other mental health problems (Almeida et al., 2005; Clark et al., 1999; Finch, Kolody, & Vega, 2000; Kessler, Mickelson, &Williams, 1999; Krieger, 1990; 1999; 2003; Pavalko, Mossakowski, & Hamilton, 2003; Williams & Williams-Morris, 2000). Studies have shown that even low-level, repeated verbal comments have can be debilitating (Magley et al., 1999). This body of research has also demonstrated that victims experience more profound psychological, health, and job-related problems when the atmosphere in the workplace is seen as tolerant of discriminatory conduct (Wright & Fitzgerald, 2008). However, the likelihood that a victim of discrimination will seek appropriate medical or mental health care decreases in response to perceived discrimination. In the United States, workers drawn from a multi-ethnic sample who perceived that they were discriminated against underused medical and mental health care services (Burgess et al., 2008).

The major weakness identified in the past research was the difficulty of drawing causal inferences from the data, given their cross-sectional and correlational nature, because this research only demonstrated that these phenomena occurred at the same time, not that one caused the other. This concern has been addressed in a number of ways. First, where studies on antecedents and consequences of sexual harassment used similar variables, meta-analyses were feasible and several have been conducted (e.g., Ilies et al., 2003; Lapierre, Spector, & Leck, 2005; Rotundo, Nguyen, & Sackett, 2001; Willness, Steel, & Lee, 2007). In some meta-analyses, researchers have aggregated data from as many as 60 independent samples drawn from several countries, canvassing up to 106,948 participants (Topa et al., 2008). The results of the meta-analyses do not fully resolve the issues regarding causation, but have demonstrated the most robust evidence of outcomes of workplace discrimination.

In addition, a series of longitudinal studies has now been conducted (Glomb et al., 1999; Munson, Hulin, & Drasgow, 2000; Murrell, Olson, & Frieze, 1995; Pavalko, Mossakowski, & Hamilton, 2003; Richman et al., 2004), which has allowed the issue of cause-and-effect relationships to be scrutinized more directly.

For example, with respect to outcomes of racial discrimination, a subset of data from 1979 to 1983 of the U.S. National Longitudinal Study of Youth focused on consequences following exposure to racially based discrimination by comparing participants of Black (n = 1851), Hispanic (n = 1170), White (n = 3450) and Other (n = 1387) descent. The findings indicated that exposure to race discrimination in seeking employment predicted health-related work limitations (Gee & Walsemann, 2009). Perceived interpersonal racial discrimination has been associated in epidemiological studies with higher rates of common mental disorders; and more recently, with higher rates of psychosis. Initial cross-sectional work was supplemented by a longitudinal study, which demonstrated that victims of discrimination were at an increased risk of developing a psychosis (Mackenzie, 2006). Additionally, a team of researchers in Illinois commenced a series of longitudinal studies using random digit-dial phone survey samples at two points in time to examine whether exposure to workplace harassment or discrimination mediates the relationship between membership in a protected category (such as gender, race, ethnicity, age, etc.), and subsequent work-related illness or injury (Shannon et al., 2009). By controlling for the influence of individual demographic characteristics and job and life stressors, the researchers demonstrated that exposure to workplace discrimination explained additional variance in problem drinking and mental health challenges beyond life and job stressors, particularly for women.

An example of research that explored relationships between discrimination and workplace consequences is the meta-analysis of 41 studies and almost 70,000 respondents by Willness, Steel, and Lee (2007). Employees exposed to sexual harassment expressed greater dissatisfaction with the interpersonal aspects of their work (interactions with coworkers and supervisors) than with the work itself. Sexual harassment experiences were negatively correlated with organizational commitment (e.g., psychological attachment to the workplace organization) and work-group productivity, and were positively correlated with work withdrawal and job withdrawal. Sexual harassment targets were significantly more likely to "withdraw" from work (e.g., avoid or neglect tasks, miss work) than to quit. Sexual harassment had a negative impact on mental and physical health, and was moderately correlated with increased PTSD symptoms.

With respect to the relationship between absenteeism and psychological injury, a meta-analysis of 275 effects from 153 separate studies revealed positive but small significant associations between absenteeism and work strain, psychological illness, and physical illness (Darr & Johns, 2008).

Many workers who experience discrimination experience periods of unemployment, either because they are fired, constructively discharged, or simply quit their jobs to evade the source of stress. A series of meta-analyses across 237 cross-sectional and 87 longitudinal studies of the impact of unemployment on mental health showed more distress in unemployed than in employed persons, with significant differences on several indicator variables of mental health (mixed symptoms of distress, depression, anxiety, psychosomatic symptoms, subjective well-being, and self esteem). Findings from both longitudinal studies and natural experiments have endorsed the assumption that unemployment is not only correlated with distress, but also causes it (Paul & Moser, 2009).

Consequences of Workplace Discrimination

Consensus has emerged in the field that is it most helpful if consequences of discrimination are addressed at individual, group, and organizational levels (Goldman et al., 2008). Accordingly, research findings are often presented by reporting the findings in terms of their impact on the professional and personal consequences of discrimination and outcomes that affect the worker's physical and mental health and occupational opportunities; the effects of workplace discrimination within an organization; and the responses of fact finders to evidence on compensatory damages in employment discrimination cases. Most evaluating experts will focus their attention on the findings that center on the consequences of workplace discrimination for an individual worker.

Drawing primarily on the findings that have emerged in longitudinal studies and in meta-analyses of individual consequences of workplace discrimination, we have grouped the symptoms and outcomes into three broad categories, depending on whether they were indicators of (a) mental or psychological anguish, pain, and suffering; (b) physiological or somatic symptoms; or (c) work-related or vocational consequences. These findings are summarized in Table 3.1. The purpose of this analysis is to provide a readily accessible overview of the research findings produced when data were aggregated from many individuals. This summary does not imply that other symptoms or consequences that a claimant may report in a particular case are not feasible or sincere. As was noted above, particular care must be taken in assessing individuals from non-Western cultures where conventions for reporting pain and suffering may differ and an emphasis on physical symptoms may be more common. Within the interactional model of workplace discrimination, the extent to which any claimant manifests these symptoms will be moderated or mediated by a variety of factors that will influence the nature, scope, and duration of his or her reactions to workplace discrimination.

Individual Variability in Response to Discrimination

Research on exposure to traumatic events outside of the workplace has demonstrated variability in the ways that different individuals respond to the same stressor, and that most individuals (approximately 75%) will recover from a traumatic experience within three to six months (O'Donnell et al., 2006), particularly if they receive mental health care treatment that has proven effective in helping individuals recover from trauma, such as cognitive behavior therapy (Riggs & Foa, 2009). Generally, it is the duration of the harm and not the duration of the unlawful conduct that is most relevant to a determination of compensatory damages, although in some cases, the duration of the wrongful conduct may bear directly on the harm experienced by the plaintiff (Gilbert, 2007; Rospenda, 2002).

Table 3.1 Symptoms and Consequences of Workplace Discrimination

Psychological outcomes	Physiological or somatic outcomes	Work-related outcomes
Anxiety Richman et al. 1999[c] Topa Cantisano et al. 2008[a]	**Alcohol consumption increase** Richman et al. 1991[c] Rospenda et al. 2002, 2008[b]	**Decreased productivity** USMSPB 1995
Depression Kessler et al. 1999[c] Richman et al. 1999[c] Scarville et al. 1999[c] Street, Gradus, Stafford, & Kelly 2007[c]	**Binge-eating** Gutek & Koss 1993[c] Harned & Fitzgerald 2002[c]	**Lower job satisfaction** Longhout et al. 2005[c] Glomb et al. 1999[b] Willness, Steele, & Lee 2007[a] Chan et al. 2008[a] Topa Cantisano et al. 2008[a] Laprierre et al. 2005[a]
Distress Pavalko et al. 2003[b] Langhout et al. 2005[c] Waldo et al. 1998[c] Chan et al. 2008[a]	**Blood pressure change** Krieger 1990[c] James et al. 1994 Hill, Kobayashi, & Hughes 2007	**Organizational withdrawal** Fitzgerald et al. 1997[c] Miner- Rubino & Cortina 2007[c] Willness, Steele, & Lee 2007[a] Chan et al. 2008[a] Glomb et al. 1999[b]
Fear Scarville et al. 1999[c]	**Chronic fatigue syndrome** Antilla 2002	**Diminished job performance** Topa Cantisano et al. 2008
Hostility Richman et al. 1999[c]	**Crying spells** Gutek & Koss 1993[c]	**Quit job** USMSPB 1995 Gutek & Koss 1993[c] Sims, Drasgow, & Fitzgerald 2005[b]
Loss of control Hasswell & Perrewe 1993	**Gastrointestinal complaints** Gutek & Koss 1993[c]	**Decreased commitment to the organization** Willness, Steele, & Lee 2007[a] Topa Cantisano et al. 2008[a] Chan et al. 2008[a]
Life-satisfaction decrease Schneider et al. 2000[c] Willness, Steele, & Lee 2007[a]	**Headaches** Gutek & Koss 1993[c] Goldenhar et al. 1998[c]	**Decreased workgroup productivity** Willness, Steele, & Lee 2007[a]
Poor overall well-being Fitzgerald et al. 1997[c] Fitzgerald et al. 1999[c]	**Hypertension** Krieger 1990[c]	**Decreased satisfaction with supervisor and coworkers** Willness, Steele, & Lee 2007[a]

Table 3.1 | Symptoms and Consequences of Workplace Discrimination (*Cont.*)

Psychological outcomes	Physiological or somatic outcomes	Work-related outcomes
Glomb et al. 1997; 1999[b] Goldenhar et al. 1998[c] Gunnarsdottir et al. 2006[c] Magley et al. 1999[c] Miner-Rubino & Cortina 2007[c] Munson et al. 2000[b] Piotrkowski 1998[c] Street, Gradus, Stafford, & Kelly 2007[c] Topa Cantisano et al. 2008[a]		Topa Cantisano et al. 2008[a] Chan et al. 2008[a]
Post-Traumatic Stress Disorder		
Symptoms Re-experiencing, avoidance, numbing, hyperarousal Palmieri & Fitzgerald 2005[c] Dansky & Kilpatrick 1997 Street et al. 2007[c] Willness, Steel, & Lee 2007[a] Wolfe et al. 1998[c]	**Nausea** Goldenhar et al. 1998[c] Gutek & Koss 1993[c]	
Self-esteem loss Hasswell & Perrewe 1993	**Poor general health** Blindt 2005	
Suicidal thoughts Antilla 2002	**Somatization** Klonoff et al. 2000[c] Schneider et al. 2001[d]	
	Sleep disturbances Gutek & Koss 1993[c]	
	Teeth-grinding, jaw tightening Gutek & Koss 1993[c]	
	Weight loss/gain Gutek & Koss 1993[c]	

Note: Superscripts indicate source of documented injuries:

[a]Meta-analysis
[b]Longitudinal study
[c]Cross-sectional or other study
[d]Experimental study

Psychological injury is not a universal reaction to discrimination (Foote & Goodman-Delahunty, 2005), and there is no "one size fits all" response (Beiner, 2004, p. 82). Research on general workplace stress and on workplace discrimination has demonstrated that employees vary extensively in their responses to workplace stressors. Depending on an individual's history and his or her appraisal of the discriminatory conduct (whether it is perceived as threatening), employees who are discriminated against can display markedly different reactions, ranging from general annoyance and upset to the experience of symptoms associated with PTSD, including re-experiencing of the stressor through nightmares, avoidance of the perpetrator or the workplace, and hyperarousal or hypervigilance (Brodsky, 1976; Einarsen & Raknes, 1997; Leymann, 1990; Price-Spratlen, 1995). The fact that individuals who are discriminated against are differentially affected by discrimination has been attributed in part to their coping capability (Pavalko, Mossakowski, & Hamilton, 2003). Some individuals are more resilient than others and are able to adapt and cope successfully when faced with threatening or challenging situations (Agabi & Wilson, 2005).

Reactions to discriminatory conduct have been shown to vary systematically according to gender and minority status (e.g., regarding sexual harassment, see Magley et al., 1999). Reactions to workplace retaliation have varied according to the same factors (Aquino & Thau, 2009; Rehg et al., 2008).

Exposure to Multiple Types of Workplace Discrimination

As was noted in Chapter 1, many workers who bring claims of discrimination belong to more than one group that is protected by the civil rights antidiscrimination legislation; for example, age plus disability, gender plus race. These individuals may experience what has been termed "double discrimination"; that is, discrimination based on more than on type of prejudice or bias, such as gender discrimination plus disability discrimination (Reina, Adya & Blanck, 2007) or race plus sexual orientation (Krieger & Sidney, 1997).

A nationally representative random-digit-dial phone survey conducted in 2003–2004 with 2,151 participants showed that experiencing multiple types of workplace discrimination was common (Shannon et al., 2009).

In many situations, double discrimination cases arise because after the worker raises one allegation of discrimination (e.g., based on race or gender), the response of the employer is to treat that complainant less favorably than before, leading to a second complaint of retaliation. The number of retaliation claims filed with the U.S. Equal Employment Opportunity Commission has doubled since 1992 (Zimmerle, 2005). In instances in which a worker alleges double discrimination, he or she may not prevail on one claim, such as the underlying race or gender claim, but may prevail on the subsequent reprisal claim. Alternatively, complications for the evaluating expert in untangling the chain of causation can arise when double discrimination is alleged and one allegation allows a statutory claim of compensatory damages and the other does not. For example, no compensatory damages are available in federal court for age-based discrimination. A claimant who prevails on a claim of age and disability discrimination may be eligible for compensation only for harm caused by disability discrimination. Thus, in certain cases, the evaluating expert may be asked to address causation of harm attributable to just one set of unlawful behaviors, even if others were alleged and resulted in a finding of liability.

From the standpoint of causation, it is helpful to conduct research to examine outcomes in individuals who were targets of multiple types of discrimination, such as a combination of racial bias and gender discrimination (Mays, Coleman, & Jackson, 1996). The findings in these studies show that the risk of harm is increased when an employee is exposed to more than one type of discrimination (Bergman & Drasgow, 2003: Rospenda & Richman, 2005). Nonetheless, researchers have cautioned that the type of discrimination experienced (i.e., race versus disability versus gender) does not predict the severity of the harassment or the extent of the harm. With respect to sexual harassment, researchers have cautioned that it would be an error "to equate sexual harassment severity with sexual harassment type" (Langhout et al., 2005, p. 1000). Put another way, one can not presume that quid pro quo sexual harassment—whereby a tangible employment benefit is contingent upon sexual favors—is more severe than harassment in the form of hostile, verbal, gender-based comments or persistent, unwanted sexual and romantic overtures.

Exposure to Multiple Workplace Stressors

Six distinct categories of psychosocial risk factors for stress at work were identified by National Institute of Occupational Safety and Health (Sauter, Murphy, & Murrell, 1990): (a) workload and work pace, (b) job content, (c) work schedule, (d) role stressors, (e) work security and advancement, and (f) interpersonal relations. Even in the absence of discrimination, experience of these forms of workplace stress can precipitate changes in a worker's health (Goldenhar, Williams, & Swanson, 2003). Often, the presence of discrimination is experienced via the psychosocial factors. For example, a common interpersonal form of discrimination is social ostracism, although socially ostracizing behaviors may also be unrelated to unlawful discrimination. Research has shown that ostracizing behaviors can lead to the development of severe mental health problems, including depression, anxiety, difficulty concentrating, and bizarre thoughts (Matthiesen, 2004). Workers exposed to comments that they are incompetent because of their age or gender, or who are ridiculed, ignored, or treated with a hostile or dismissive attitude, or whose work style was insulted, were significantly more likely to manifest symptoms related to the occurrence of psychiatric distress and PTSD (Matthiesen & Einarson, 2004; Glasø et al., 2009).

When researchers compared consequences of nondiscriminatory occupational stress (caused by an intense or increased workload) with consequences of general workplace harassment and sexual harassment (e.g., Shannon et al., 2009), the nondiscriminatory conduct did not produce statistically significant consequences, but the discriminatory conduct did.

Cultural Differences in Workplace Discrimination Injuries

Because in many non-Western cultures it is more accepted to discuss and express anguish, pain, and suffering via physiological symptoms, criteria used to assess the extent of psychological injuries must reflect those conventions. Symptoms of extreme distress that may qualify as indicators of PTSD may differ in non-Western cultures from those applicable in Western cultures (Andary, Stolk, & Klimidis, 2003), and can include dizziness, nausea (but no vomiting), difficulty passing urine, persistent back pain, sleepiness or hallucinations (Bryant & Njenga, 2006).

Workplace discrimination precipitated elevated risk for women and racial and ethnic minority workers on the psychosocial risk factors identified by the National Institute of Occupational Safety and Health (Sagresanto, 2004). If racial and ethnic minority workers are more frequently the targets of discrimination than their white counterparts, consultation of professional help may vary along cultural lines (Burgess et al., 2008).

Cultural differences have been noted in responses to sexual harassment (Shupe et al., 2002; Wasti et al., 2000; Zimbroff, 2007). For example, cross-racial sexual harassment researchers found an indirect (but not direct) mediated effect on post-traumatic stress via participants' appraisals of their harassment. Specifically, the more negative appraisal in response to cross-racial sexual harassment was associated with increased post-traumatic stress symptoms (Woods, Buchanan, & Settles, 2009).

The Impact of Litigation

In reviewing whether litigation exacerbates psychological losses, Samra and Koch (2002) concluded that there was little support for the existence of the "litigation response syndrome" posited by some practitioners (Lees-Haley, 1988). The viability of the theory of "compensation neurosis" or a litigation response syndrome has been undercut by research findings that (a) individuals who litigate have often experienced more extreme and profound injuries than those who do not (Blanchard et al., 1998); (b) individuals who have received compensation continue to experience the negative impact of psychological injuries (i.e., the pain and suffering persists) after the litigation has been settled or the compensation has been awarded (Bryant & Harvey, 2003); and (c) ongoing injuries are observed in discrimination victims who never sought compensation, lasting as long as 11 years after the discriminatory events (Dansky & Kilpatrick, 1997). Moreover, symptoms of injuries such as chronic post-traumatic stress syndrome are difficult to simulate (Bryant & Harvey, 2003). Some studies revealed that both litigation and employment were significant factors influencing recovery from injuries (Suter, 2002), but litigation was not the most important variable in distinguishing between employed and unemployed chronic pain sufferers. Together, these results indicate that the suspicion and disbelief with which litigating parties are often treated is unfounded (Shuman, 2000; Tunks, 1992; Walfish, 2006).

Research on Responses of Fact Finders

Converging evidence from several sources points to the likelihood that victims of workplace discrimination will be undercompensated. Despite legal prohibitions against reprisal and retaliation against workers who file a claim of discrimination, anti-plaintiff biases exist in the workplace. Claimants are often regarded as unwanted whistleblowers. The public perception of litigating plaintiffs is skeptical, not sympathetic (Hans, 1996; 2000; Hans & Albertson, 2003). Trial consultants confirm that:

> One of the greatest obstacles plaintiffs' personal injury and employment attorneys face today is how to convince jurors that psychological injuries like emotional distress and pain and suffering are worthy of compensation. Emotional distress has become a buzzword for the anti-lawsuit crowd and is synonymous with frivolous lawsuits and out of control damage awards. (Bauss, 2009, p.9)

Psychological studies have examined situations that may lead fact finders to "blame the victim," the plaintiff (Walster, 1966).

Where claims for purely psychological and psychiatric injury are allowed, the claimant is often viewed very skeptically. This skepticism has been enhanced by studies which show that the nature of claims and the duration of alleged pain and suffering are often related to the types of causes of action available and the speed with which the case reaches trial (Binder & Rohling, 1996). Attorneys who advise their clients to delay litigation proceedings until their injuries have stabilized, so that greater certainty exists about the actual losses suffered, may contribute to the perception that plaintiffs experience "compensation neurosis." Experts retained to assess compensatory damages claims have described plaintiffs as persons seeking "a green [money] poultice."

The same hostility in attitudes of jurors towards plaintiffs has been observed by legal practitioners who represent plaintiffs in court. Clinical and legal practitioners have noted that women who bring sexual harassment claims are not taken seriously (Burns, 1995; Jensvold, 1993). These anecdotal reports have been confirmed by empirical studies. For example, in a carefully controlled study to assess the effects of labeling and reporting sexual harassment, women who used the term "sexual harassment" were attributed greater blame for the incident and were viewed as less trustworthy and less feminine (Marin & Guadagno, 1999). As a consequence, plaintiffs are often regarded with disdain, and their claims for compensation as bogus or trivial (Brown & Seymour, 1998), and undercompensation is likely.

Reports from experimental studies and legal practitioners have been confirmed by analyses of archival data. For example, an empirical study of outcomes in the first decade after the Americans with Disabilities Act was implemented in 1991 showed that trial courts and appellate courts were pro-defendant, and appellate courts were particularly hostile to ADA claims (Colker, 2005). The employment rate for disabled persons has declined since the ADA went into effect (Colker, 2005). ADA plaintiffs win approximately a third of the time if they appear before a judge or jury, but their cases are often dismissed before that (Colker, 2005).

Rates at which all employment-discrimination plaintiffs prevailed in federal court and the proportion of plaintiff verdicts that were reversed on appeal were analyzed in a large-scale study to investigate trends in workplace discrimination litigation. The results revealed that defendants fared far better at the trial and the appellate level in workplace cases than on other types of litigation, producing what the researchers identified as "plaintiphobia" or a clear and troublesome "anti-plaintiff effect." Plaintiff win rates in employment cases (15%) were much lower than in other litigation (51%). Certain circuit courts were more hostile to plaintiffs than others; namely courts in the Fourth, Fifth, Sixth, Eighth, and Eleventh Circuits, which encompass the American South and Midwest. Win rates in jury trials exceeded those in judge trials, but were still lower than win rates in jury trials in non-employment cases.

As a consequence of this treatment, the percentage of plaintiffs bringing claims in federal court has dropped dramatically, even though the rates at which complainants are filing EEOC charges have not dropped. Based on the inference that the judges were harsher on employment discrimination plaintiffs than were juries, plaintiffs' lawyers have been advising their clients to lodge their claims in another forum (Clermont & Schwab, 2009).

Perceived Consequences of Workplace Discrimination

Aside from the biases against all types of plaintiffs litigating in federal courts, gender biases have been observed in archival studies of workplace compensation. For example, male Canadian workers-compensation claimants who bring stress related cases receive two to three times as much in compensation as do similarly situated female claimants (Lippel, 1999). International data have revealed that in most countries, claims by male employees for industrial accidents are compensated more often than claims by female employees (Kjellberg, 1998). Judges and juries may rely on gender-based stereotypes in rendering verdicts (Curcio, 1988). Findings of this sort point to the need to explore ways in which the legal system can ensure that steps to assess psychological injuries are fair and unbiased.

Underestimation of Psychological Injuries Caused by Discrimination

Victims of employment discrimination rarely manifest physical injuries. Findings in studies of compensation in cases of physical injuries sustained in tort cases suggest that when the injuries are serious, jurors are motivated to alleviate the plaintiff's suffering and award higher damages (Bornstein, 1998). Whether these findings will generalize to cases of serious psychological injuries in workplace discrimination claims remains somewhat unknown. Judges and jurors have reported that awarding compensatory damages is the hardest part of their duties (Mott, Hans, & Simpson, 2000). The intangible nature of workplace discrimination injuries may lead fact finders to treat them with more skepticism and opprobrium than plaintiffs who sustain physical injuries. To some measure, this tendency may be attributable to their unfamiliarity with common sequelae of workplace discrimination.

In one demonstration of this, male and female non-victims were asked to gauge how distressing certain incidents of sexual harassment would be. They responded that these events were on a par with other mildly distressing life experiences, such as being stuck in traffic, failing a test in school, or having an argument with the boss (Lees-Haley et al., 1994). These findings tend to indicate that many coworkers and jurors will not anticipate that workplace discrimination can have more severe and enduring mental health consequences. Just as the law has privileged physical injuries over intangible psychological injuries, so do many fact finders.

An example of a workplace discrimination case tried before a jury in federal court in which this occurred comes from a qualitative case study of a sexual harassment case conducted by one of the authors based on observations of the trial; a review of exhibits entered into evidence; interviews conducted with the judge, lawyers for plaintiff, and defense; and interviews of real and shadow jurors (Report of the Special Committee ABA Section of Litigation, 1990; Greene & Goodman-Delahunty, 1995). The post-trial jury interviews and videotaped deliberations of a shadow jury decisions confirmed this skeptical response to the plaintiff's extensive psychological injuries.

The case involved a vulnerable female sheriff's deputy who alleged sexual harassment during her training on the job. Thereafter, she was threatened by coworkers and supervisors and received no support from her coworkers. She went through a divorce in the same period as the alleged discrimination. Later, she attempted suicide, was under psychiatric care, and was unable to work again in law enforcement. Most of the jury deliberation time was devoted to a discussion of the source or cause of the plaintiff's problems and whether she brought the problems on herself because of her difficult personality. The jurors lacked empathy for her predicament, some concluded she brought these events on herself, and agreed that she was an unbalanced person who had arrived in the department with a psychological problem. The jurors did not find the expert evidence helpful in resolving those issues. The plaintiff's treating psychiatrist was seen as too partisan, and the evaluating forensic psychiatrist was seen as a hired gun. Testimony of a vocational rehabilitation counselor was disregarded because she had never interviewed the plaintiff, so seemed to lack an adequate basis for her testimony. In considering compensation for injuries claimed by the plaintiff, the jurors espoused the view that compensation for psychological injuries was not warranted—that relative to physical impairments, such as losing one's sight or losing an arm, the injury seemed insubstantial. The jury awarded $50,000 in compensatory damages, only on the claim for discriminatory retaliation.

The tendency of workers and lay jurors to underestimate the impact of psychological injuries was confirmed in a series of experimental studies in which workers, jurors, and mental health experts read a brief description of a workplace accident caused by either physical negligence (falling off a ladder), a work stress injury (coworker leaves all the work to one employee), or a form of workplace discrimination (sexual harassment). They then indicated what the outcomes would be by rating the type, severity, and expected duration of any injuries. The consequences of the physical accident and of ordinary work stress were regarded as significantly more egregious and likely to produce more pain and suffering than the intangible injuries resulting from workplace sexual harassment (Goodman-Delahunty & O'Brien, 2009a).

Significantly less impact on the victim's life was perceived to result from exposure to sexual coercion or a hostile work environment than from work stress or a physical injury. Significantly more psychological distress was anticipated in response to unwanted sexual attention and workplace stress, and these were identified as issues for which a worker might seek professional help. Significantly more negative somatic symptoms were anticipated to follow from work stress than from a physical injury or workplace discrimination. Hostile work environments were perceived to have fewer work-related consequences than other forms of sexual harassment and workplace stress. Together, these findings indicated that an expert witness may be helpful in communicating clearly to the fact finder that invisible, intangible psychological injuries can be profound.

A follow-up experimental study using the same vignettes compared perceived harm and injuries regarding three types of sexual harassment by a group of 99 mental health experts in the United States and 237 venire persons on jury duty in Dade County, Florida. This study confirmed similar misperceptions by jurors and a substantial gap between perceived consequences of workplace discrimination anticipated by mental health experts versus lay jurors (Goodman-Delahunty & O'Brien, 2009b). The experts were significantly more likely than jurors to report that sexual harassment would negatively impact the target's daily life for a longer period and require professional counseling or therapy than were jurors. Interestingly, both experts and jurors anticipated that the impact on an employee of unwanted sexual attention was more severe than that of exposure to a hostile work environment or quid pro quo sexual harassment, and unwanted sexual attention was also expected to have significantly more severe psychological effects and work-related consequences than other forms of sexual harassment. In general jurors, did not anticipate somatic effects or work-related outcomes from sexual harassment—on these dimensions, expected injuries were seen as far less likely than what experts predicted. Other studies examining jury deliberation demonstrated that, when an expert testified on damages, even if no specific guidance was provided on how to assess compensatory damages, the presence of an expert increased the tendency for jurors to discuss and consider the plaintiff's pain and suffering during deliberation (Greene, Downey, & Goodman-Delahunty, 1999).

Conclusions

Empirical studies of the consequences of workplace discrimination apply a variety of methods and encompass topics beyond the consequences experienced by individual complainants in their personal lives and in their careers. This research has important implications for social justice, procedures to manage complaints and workplace conflict, the efficacy of the deterrent function of monetary legal sanctions, the capacity of organizations for positive change, and future compliance with the antidiscrimination laws. Many of those topics may bear on the outcomes in a particular discrimination case.

APPLICATION

Preparation for the Evaluation

4

From the beginning of her or his involvement in a civil rights case, the expert must view professional activities through a lens of fairness, balance, and honesty (Vasquez, Baker, & Shullman, 2003). The psychologist's ethical stance is derived from the American Psychological Association's (APA) "Ethical Principles of Psychologists' Code of Conduct" (APA, 2002) and the "Specialty Guidelines for Forensic Psychology" (Committee on Ethical Guidelines for Forensic Psychologists, 1991). In this context, the ethical principle that guides the psychologist's actions, Principle D (Justice), states:

> Psychologists recognize that fairness and justice entitle all persons to access to and benefit from the contributions of psychology and to equal quality in the processes, procedures, and services being conducted by psychologists. Psychologists exercise reasonable judgment and take precautions to ensure that their potential biases, the boundaries of their competence, and the limitations of their expertise do not lead to or condone unjust practices. (APA, 2002, p. 1062)

The ethical guidelines adopted by the American Academy of Psychiatry and the Law (American Academy of Psychiatry and Law, 2004) reflect a similar aspiration:

> IV. Honesty and Striving for Objectivity. When psychiatrists function as experts within the legal process, they should adhere to the principle of honesty and should strive for objectivity. Although they may be retained by one party to a civil or criminal matter, psychiatrists should adhere to these principles when conducting evaluations, applying clinical data to legal criteria, and expressing opinions.

Although the expert witness is sometimes appointed by the judge in a civil rights case, in most cases the expert is hired by counsel for the plaintiff or defendant. In all cases, the expert should view every retention as though it came directly from the judge. This perspective is appropriate in light of the stature of expert testimony in court proceedings, as defined by Federal Rule of Evidence 702. This rule states:

> If scientific, technical, or other specialized knowledge will assist the trier of fact to understand the evidence or to determine a fact in issue, a witness qualified as an expert by knowledge, skill, experience, training, or education, may testify thereto in the form of an opinion or otherwise, if (1) the testimony is based upon sufficient facts or data, (2) the testimony is the product of reliable principles and methods, and (3) the witness has applied the principles and methods reliably to the facts of the case. (Mueller & Kirkpatrick, 2007)

This rule defines the role of the expert as one who assists the trier of fact—the judge or jury—in understanding the other evidence in the case or in determining one or more essential facts of the case. This is a special role, because experts may provide an opinion, whereas percipient witnesses are precluded from doing so. Opinion testimony brings together disparate facts of the case in a comprehensible way so that the trier of fact may make connections between various aspects of the case.

For example, in many cases, the psychological expert provides opinions concerning the relationship between the alleged acts of the defendant and the emotional or other problems claimed by the plaintiff. This connection informs the fact finder about the extent to which the defendant is responsible for causing harm to the plaintiff and whether the defendant's conduct "proximately caused" any injuries. The legal concept of *proximate cause* (Hart & Honore, 1959) takes into consideration that the cause in question (such as the alleged sexual harassment) may be just one of many causes contributing to produce a specific outcome (such as a phobic reaction). However, in order for an event or series of events to be the proximate cause of damages, the damage must not have occurred "but for" the alleged workplace event. That is, the principle of proximate cause requires a direct causal relationship and a clear connection between the damages and the alleged workplace event(s), even if other contributors to the final result occur before, during, or after the alleged causative event.

INFO

Proximate cause requires a finding that an injury would not have occurred but for a defendant's act.

The evaluator can assist the trier of fact in making this connection by referring to scientific theories, research findings, and the case facts to draw a line between events that might not otherwise be seen as connected. The ability to provide opinions on these issues raises the ante. Those who serve as experts have responsibilities that extend beyond the relationship with the referral source to the justice system and the community.

From this perspective, the expert enters the case with a determination to resist pressures to become partisan. In most employment discrimination cases, lawyers working for the plaintiff or the defendant will contact the expert concerning an evaluation. This retention call is critical because it provides an opportunity for an exchange of information between the potential retaining counsel and the expert. These pressures arise first in the context of the retention process, and from that first contact, the expert should be sensitive to those who may push the expert "offsides," usually in a direction that aids the lawyer's case. Recognize, however, that when a lawyer is attempting to exert this influence, it is not an act of an unethical professional. To the contrary, lawyers are required by their professional code of ethics to zealously represent their clients, and zealous representation may, in the lawyers' eyes, begin by trying to convince the expert of the merits of the plaintiff's or defendant's perspective.

Consider, for example, how the beginning of the referral conversation in a sexual harassment case may differ, depending upon the source. The plaintiff's lawyer may begin by explaining how the claimant has been badly damaged by an employer who negligently allowed the workplace to become sexualized and failed to prevent a supervisor from repeatedly sexually harassing the plaintiff. In the same case, the defense lawyer may open the conversation with a discourse about how the plaintiff is a litigious, paranoid individual who misperceives much of what is going on and erroneously claimed that a supervisor was doing something that was not observed by anyone else, and moreover, that the acts alleged would have never been committed by the well-regarded supervisor, who is a leader in the community and committed family man. In both cases, the lawyers are certainly doing their job to provide zealous representation of their clients, and are likely to be reflecting their own perspective on the case.

Notwithstanding these caveats, this retention conversation is an important occasion for an exchange of information between the lawyer and the expert, because it will provide information that will help both determine if the expert is the appropriate professional to work on the case and will establish ground rules for a professional relationship that may endure for several years to come. We begin our discussion of this process by examining the information that must be gathered from the potential retaining lawyer, then examine considerations of the expert at this stage.

The Retention Conversation: Information from the Lawyer

The Nature of the Case

In the initial conversation with potential retaining counsel, the expert should ascertain the basic nature of the case. Will the case be governed by state or federal law? If it is a civil rights case, which body of civil rights law applies? For example, will it fall under Title VII of the Civil Rights Act of 1964? What is the essence of the plaintiff's claim? Is it a disparate treatment, hostile work environment, or retaliation claim? What are the main defenses put forward by the defendants in the matter? For example, in a sexual harassment case, counsel for the defense may ask an expert to determine whether the complainant "welcomed" the sexual conduct in issue and to determine whether any of the alleged injuries

BEST PRACTICE
It is important to explore alternative causes of emotional distress, regardless of who requests the evaluation (plaintiff or defendant). This allows you to produce a balanced and comprehensive assessment.

were caused by other factors in the complainant's life, such as distress over the breakup of the relationship with the alleged harasser and resentment at his new girlfriend. Even in cases in which the complainant's evaluation is requested by the complainant's counsel, exploration of alternative causes for evident emotional distress is necessary to produce a balanced and comprehensive evaluation (see Foote & Goodman-Delahunty, 2005; Gilbert, 2007).

In addition, it is good practice to ask the retaining counsel what general questions the evaluation should address (Heilbrun, 2001). Is it a damages case as opposed to a case in which liability issues are more important, or do the referral questions encompass both some liability issues as well as damages issues, such as in the preceding example of a sexual harassment case? This discussion is critical, because early in the case, the expert must determine whether those questions can be addressed using the techniques available to the expert. For example, the lawyer may ask the expert to determine whether the plaintiff or the defendant is lying about the alleged discrimination. Although experts are becoming more adept at determining who is lying and who is telling the truth (Ennis, Vrij, & Chance, 2008; Leal & Vrij, 2008; Vrij et al., 2008), lie detection is still not usually one of the skills of a forensic clinician. In such cases, the expert should decline the case.

BEWARE
Decline any referral in which the attorney asks you to determine whether the plaintiff or the defendant is lying about the alleged workplace discrimination. This is beyond the realm of your expertise.

The Retention Conversation: Tasks for the Expert

Clarifying the Professional Role

The first task for the expert is to clarify the expert's role. This task begins with an understanding that the forensic expert's client is the retaining lawyer, not the plaintiff or evaluee. In this situation, the plaintiff is the object of the evaluation, and will ultimately surrender their rights of privacy in order to complete the evaluation, but they are not the consumer of the expert's expertise. The relationship between the lawyer and expert is one of agency. That is, the expert is the agent of the lawyer, and works under the general direction of the lawyer, notwithstanding the expert's obligation to principles of fairness and balance.

In the context of defining one's role in a case, the ethical requirement to avoid multiple relationships may arise. The APA Ethics Code speaks of this issue:

> 3.05 Multiple Relationships (a) A multiple relationship occurs when a psychologist is in a professional role with a person and (1) at the same time is in another role with the same person, (2) at the same time is in a relationship with a person closely associated with or related to the person with whom the psychologist has the professional relationship, or (3) promises to enter into another relationship in the future with the person or a person closely associated with or related to the person.

A psychologist refrains from entering into a multiple relationship if the multiple relationship could reasonably be expected to impair the psychologist's objectivity, competence, or effectiveness in performing his or her functions as a psychologist, or otherwise risks exploitation or harm to the person with whom the professional relationship exists. (APA, 2002, p. 1065)

Ethical guidelines promulgated by the American Academy of Forensic Psychiatry express the same sentiment in the commentary related to the guideline for objectivity listed earlier:

> Psychiatrists who take on a forensic role for patients they are treating may adversely affect the therapeutic relationship with them. Forensic evaluations usually require interviewing corroborative sources, exposing information to public scrutiny, or subjecting evaluees and the treatment itself to potentially damaging cross-examination. The forensic evaluation and the credibility of the practitioner may also be undermined by conflicts inherent in the differing clinical and forensic roles. Treating psychiatrists

should therefore generally avoid acting as an expert witness for their patients or performing evaluations of their patients for legal purposes.

BEWARE It is unethical to enter into multiple relationships. Do not take on more than one role at a time.

To avoid dual relationships in forensic settings, the forensic evaluator should undertake only one role at a time. The guidelines deal specifically with simultaneous dual roles. In the context of working in forensic settings, concern has been expressed about both simultaneous and sequential dual roles (Greenberg & Shuman, 1997; Shuman et al., 1998). In civil rights cases, psychologists may assume four potential roles: fact (percipient) witness, consultant, examining expert, and scientific framework expert (O'Connor, 2007). Each role has both limitations and strengths.

Percipient Witness

The expert may enter the courtroom as a witness concerning events or facts learned through the expert's five senses, called a "percipient witness." In some cases, although the witness is a professional and may have sufficient experience, education, and training to testify as an expert, the lawyer who subpoenas the professional is adducing testimony about the professional's observations, rather than their opinions. Most often, this occurs when the expert has served as the therapist for the plaintiff either before or after the lawsuit was filed. Calling the therapist to provide testimony in deposition or court is often necessary for both the defense and plaintiff's lawyers because that testimony may be relevant to the plaintiff's damages by providing information concerning, for example, the nature of the plaintiff's problems, how the plaintiff described the origin of the problems, the treatment provided, and the timing of the reported symptoms or problems.

Current ethical practice indicates that the roles of percipient and expert witness should not be mixed (Greenberg & Shuman, 1997). Most academics agree (Shuman et al, 1998; Bush, Connell, & Denney, 2006) that the plaintiff's therapist should avoid testifying about some legal issues, such as proximate cause. This recommendation is

BEWARE If you are the plaintiff's therapist, you should avoid testifying about the legal issues of the case. You may, however, provide testimony regarding the plaintiff's working diagnosis, observations of the plaintiff's behavior in treatment, their progress in treatment, and their prognosis.

based in part upon limitations of the therapist's sources, most often reliant upon information provided solely by the plaintiff. It is also based on the bias that the therapist may necessarily have for the plaintiff, because of the supportive role. An attempt to shift roles may distract the therapist from the primary role of change agent for the patient. Nonetheless, the therapist can provide valuable testimony about the plaintiff based upon behavioral observations and conversations, including a provisional diagnosis, the effectiveness of interventions, and prognosis.

Consultant Role

The consultant is hired by defense or plaintiff counsel to assist in preparation and execution of the case. This role is one in which the expert is distinctly partisan: the work is to help one side prevail. The consultant may review the reports of the opposing side's expert to assist in preparation of deposition questions or cross-examination. This role may include assisting counsel in developing case strategy, including development of theories and themes of the case and sequencing witnesses. The consulting expert may assist the lawyers in preparing witnesses for deposition or court testimony. Although in some jurisdictions, federal rules of evidence and relevant case law have established that the consulting expert may be called to testify by the opposing counsel (e.g., *Baki v. B.F. Diamond Construction Co.*, 1976), in most cases, the existence of a consulting expert may not be disclosed by retaining counsel because of the potential to disclose attorney work product (Sales & Shuman, 2005).

INFO The existence of a consulting expert need not be disclosed by the retaining attorney.

Examining Expert

A more familiar role is that of the examining expert. In civil rights cases, the examining expert will generally conduct a psychological evaluation of the plaintiff. This is the role this book is primarily focused on, as it requires integrating multiple sources of information to support an expert opinion. In Chapter 2 we discuss how the Federal Rules of Civil Procedure (2007) define this role. However, in most cases, the examining expert is asked by the plaintiff or defense counsel to evaluate the plaintiff. The evaluation must embody the values of balance and fairness previously discussed. This does not mean that the expert does not advocate a position in a deposition or in-court testimony. In every case, the examining expert conducts the evaluation with the plaintiff and weighs the evidence from multiple sources and uses that evidence to arrive at conclusions concerning the plaintiff. Those conclusions are defended in sworn testimony, because these are the vehicles for bringing the expert's scientific knowledge as applied to the particular facts of the case to the trier of fact.

INFO

The role of the examining expert is to evaluate the plaintiff and use the data obtained to form a reliable opinion.

The Social Framework Expert

Another testifying expert role is one in which the expert has some case-relevant knowledge concerning the scientific research or clinical practice on a particular topic (Goodman-Delahunty & Croyle, 1989; Monahan, Walker, & Mitchell, 2008). The court may benefit from general information by a mental health professional regarding generic aspects of a particular consequence of workplace discrimination. For example, a plaintiff is diagnosed as suffering from PTSD and alleges that the disorder was caused by the employer's unlawful conduct in failing to promote her. Without conducting any evaluation of the plaintiff, a social framework expert may present evidence on whether non-promotion is consistent with the kind of traumatic event normally associated with PTSD, and whether this conduct could cause the disorder (Gilbert, 2007, p. 213).

In this role, the expert usually does not conduct an evaluation of the plaintiff. Rather, this expert role is one in which the expert serves as teacher to the jury or judge to provide a better understanding of the events that transpired (Borgida & Fiske, 2008). Of course, the scientific findings they describe must still be relevant to the issue before the court (Federal Rule of Evidence 402) and must be more probative than prejudicial (Federal Rule of Evidence 403). This is a role that social psychologists, industrial-organizational psychologists, cognitive psychologists, and health psychologists who do not necessarily have clinical expertise may fulfill to assist the court. For example, in an ADA case, a rehabilitation expert may testify about the research on the cost and complications involved in providing reasonable accommodations to workers with psychiatric disabilities. Other examples of evidence relevant to damages that a social or industrial/organizational expert may offer include a review of the impact of preventive measures undertaken by the employer to control discrimination and its aftermath, or a summary of findings based on studies of past cases of workplace discrimination (O'Connor, 2007). Evidence about the workplace atmosphere or organizational climate can be helpful in regard to the claimed severity of the consequences, as injuries are typically more profound when the organization is perceived to tolerate discrimination (Fitzgerald & Collinsworth, 2007). In other words, evidence about a lack of effective policies, training, and procedures to prevent or control discrimination has a bearing on the extent to which victims are injured.

One difficulty faced by non-clinicians is the lack of familiarity of many judges with psychological fields other than clinical and counseling psychology, and with social framework evidence. A recent survey of 150 federal judges revealed that as few as 8% had heard of industrial/organizational psychology (Wingate & Thornton, 2004). Judicial confusion between the disciplines of psychiatry and psychology is not uncommon (White, Day, & Hackett, 2008).

INFO

A social framework or state of the science expert does not evaluate the plaintiff, but instead presents general scientific findings that may help the court better understand the issues at hand.

Determining if the Psychologist Is Qualified to Do the Job

Ethical standards require that psychologists agree to engage in work that they are qualified to perform. Ethical Standard 2.01 states: "Boundaries of Competence (a) Psychologists provide services, teach, and conduct research with populations and in areas only within the boundaries of their competence, based on their education, training, supervised experience, consultation, study, or professional experience" (APA, 2002, p. 1064). The expert considering a referral in a civil rights case should determine if he or she has sufficient practical expertise to perform the expert's duties. The ethical standard defines the parameters of this expertise and helps the expert frame questions for considerations. The first question is whether the psychologist's education encompasses the skills and knowledge required by the case. For example, if the expert was trained to work only with adults, a case involving an alleged civil rights violation for a nine-year-old child may well be outside the parameters of the psychologist's knowledge. Similarly, a clinical therapist who has worked with few or no patients diagnosed with PTSD may lack the requisite expertise to address damages in the case of an employee who has had a previous diagnosis of PTSD if the referral question centers on the extent to which the preexisting injury was exacerbated by exposure to discriminatory conduct in the workplace. As years pass following the psychologist's formal graduate education, continuing education plays a central role, and a series of workshops in a particular area may provide sufficient information for the expert to take on a case in a new area.

The second question is whether the psychologist's training, supervision, and consultation are sufficient for this task. In this regard, not only practicum training in graduate school is considered, but also consultation and supervision by other professionals. This ad hoc training can be quite beneficial. Whether this training is sufficient is an ethical question itself, but in many cases, the consulting or supervising expert may advise one if the training is sufficient for the task. Remember, if the expert is under supervision for forensic work, the supervising expert is legally responsible for the work and may be called to testify in the case. For this reason, supervision of forensic work is best conducted in institutional settings rather than in private practice, and any advice gained from other professionals should be in the context of peer consultation.

The third question is whether study or professional experience have adequately prepared the expert for the case. One of the true joys of forensic psychology is the necessity to keep up to date on the research and current professional standards in the area in which one practices. In some cases, if one's training and education are sufficient, extending expertise through reading books and professional articles can appropriately prepare the expert to work on the case. Some forensic cases are quite specific and require searches of the literature in particular areas. For example, suppose an expert has had experience working on cases of sexual harassment, but receives a referral for a case in which the plaintiff was employed as a police officer at the time of the alleged harassment. This case may require reading the particular research on sexual harassment in police departments and other quasi-military occupational settings, which the expert may supplement with consultation with an expert who has had experience in police sexual harassment cases. One way for an expert to test whether he or she possesses sufficient training and background to conduct an evaluation of a particular plaintiff is to imagine being on the witness stand and being grilled by the opposing lawyer, answering questions about training and education. If one can honestly claim an appropriate background to support the work on the case, then further reading and consultation can make up for lack of specific experience with that particular type of case.

The fourth question is whether the expert has enough familiarity with the law in the area of concern to qualify to work on that case. APA ethical standards indicate that psychologists should know enough about the law applicable to the case to be able to properly frame their evaluation or consultation. Standard 2.01 (f) states: "When assuming forensic roles, psychologists are or become reasonably familiar with the judicial or administrative rules governing their roles" (APA, 2002, p. 1064) In the context of civil rights cases, knowledge of Title VII, the Americans with Disabilities Act, and the Civil Rights Act of 1991 is critical. Also important is a grasp of the principles inherent in the cases discussed in Chapter 2.

> **INFO**
>
> When qualifying the expert, the court considers the expert's
>
> - education
> - training
> - professional experience
> - familiarity with the law

Although this general background is essential, a grasp of the law in the particular case is also necessary. For example, the case may be brought under your state's civil rights act or as a tort case, and may be governed by a body of law totally separate from the federal civil rights acts listed above. Also, there may be case law in the jurisdiction in which your case is being tried which modifies the general tenets of the major civil rights acts. In the course of early conversations with retaining counsel, you as the expert should enquire about such specific legal constraint or demand.

Evaluating Potential Conflicts

Prior Professional Relationships

In addition to concerns about within case conflicts, psychologists must avoid between-case conflicts. APA Ethical Standard 305 just discussed also applies to this situation. Particularly in forensic cases, the expert must determine if prior professional relationships with the principals in a case may prohibit his or her retention in the current matter.

This discussion begins by developing a list of *dramatis personae in* the case: What is the plaintiff's name? Who are the opposing counsel? Who are the experts disclosed by opposing counsel? If the expert has had any professional or personal experience with the plaintiff or any member of the plaintiff's family, it is probably best to steer clear of work on the current case. In many cases, the prior contact with the plaintiff or a member of her family may be a matter covered by a professional confidentiality, and even disclosing that the expert has worked with that person before may constitute a violation of her rights to privacy. These situations are best handled by the expert's waiting until identities of all the people involved are known before simply stating, "I'm sorry, but I have a conflict here."

The expert has similar concerns about patient-therapist confidentiality in cases in which the expert has had therapeutic or other forensic contact with the counsel in the case. For example, the expert may have evaluated the opposing counsel when that person was involved in a divorce. As noted before, this professional relationship may be confidential, and may require that the expert recuse himself or herself from the case.

In most cases, having worked for either the plaintiff's or defense's counsel in prior cases does not constitute a conflict and requires no specific action on the psychologist's part. In fact, if the expert has worked with opposing counsel in prior cases, this fact may go some distance to dispel doubt about the psychologist's bias in the case.

Concerns about Known Biases

Although psychologists strive to prevent personal biases from entering into their professional functioning (APA Ethical Standard 2.06), avoiding all biases is often impossible. Still, the requirement to prevent such biases from adversely affecting one's professional work compels the expert to consider whether personal biases may prevent their effective professional work in a particular case. For example, because of religious beliefs, they may harbor a negative view of gay, lesbian, or bisexual individuals. In such cases, the expert should not work on cases involving these issues. Another expert may have strong feelings about the participation of large corporations in ongoing wars. Being aware of this bias and acting to preclude work on cases in which the bias would interfere with fair and balanced views on the case will not only avoid conflicts in the case but will assure more comfortable professional work.

BEWARE
Do not accept a referral for a case in which you have had prior therapeutic contact with the plaintiff, the plaintiff's family, or either of the counsel in the case.

BEWARE
Take heed of any personal bias or preconceived notions that may interfere with your objectivity in a particular case.

The worst-case scenario is an expert who takes a case in which they have a clear bias, their final professional opinion is congruent with the bias, and this alignment is revealed in discovery or on the witness stand.

Organizational Matters

Deadlines

A concern that is sometimes overlooked by a harried expert is a realistic appraisal of whether he or she has sufficient time to devote adequate attention to the case. Remember to account, not just for the time set aside to meet with the plaintiff, but also the time necessary to review documents, conduct collateral interviews, and prepare the report or prepare for depositions and testimony. Discovery deadlines in federal civil rights cases are often quite short, and care should be taken in the referral conversation to ensure that there is no need to rush one's professional work or cut corners.

Fees

An essential part of the retention conversation concerns fee arrangements. Psychologists are ethically bound to have clear financial arrangements before the case begins (APA Ethics Code, Standard 6.04a). In general, the psychologist's fees should provide fair compensation for the anticipated work. Setting the level of fees is a matter of several factors, including the prevailing fees for such services in the community and the demand for the psychologist's expertise. Some psychologists who conduct therapy charge a higher rate for forensic services, believing that the stress, the time taken from practice, and inconvenience involved

BEST PRACTICE
Before accepting a referral, make sure there is enough time before the hearing to thoroughly prepare. It is important to provide the attorney with a realistic estimate of the time it will take to conduct interviews and obtain records. If time is an issue, it is best to decline the referral.

merits more pay. Also, if the expert possesses particular expertise that is not otherwise available in the region, higher fees may be justified. Although some will disagree (Connell, 2007; Heilbrun, 2001) and express concern that differential fees may raise ethical concerns, other professionals view higher fees for general forensic work, and for court or deposition testimony in particular, as fair compensation.

Another task is to determine if retaining counsel has access to sufficient money to properly fund the psychologist's work on the case. In some cases, the defendant or plaintiff may enter the case with limited funds to pay an expert. If the expert is hired by the plaintiff, it is preferable to avoid signing a "letter of protection" prepared by retaining counsel. This is essentially a lien against the potential proceeds from the case. We consider this to be a professionally risky tactic, because it undermines the expert's claim of neutrality by making the expert an interested party in the outcome of the matter: if the plaintiff does not prevail, the expert may not get paid at all (Specialty Guidelines for Forensic Psychologists: Committee on Ethical Guidelines for Forensic Psychologists, 1991).

In many cases, experienced forensic mental health professionals require a retainer that is roughly the cost of the initial case review or evaluation. This may be essentially a deposit that the expert bills against until those funds are exhausted, whereupon the retaining lawyer and expert may agree that additional monies will be provided as the case progresses.

Requests for Essential Documents

Referring counsel is usually the source of most of the documents to be reviewed by the expert in a civil rights case. In the referral conversation or shortly thereafter, the expert should ask the referring counsel to provide pertinent documents. These begin with a copy of the plaintiff's claim, the defendant's answers, interrogatories (answers to specific written questions posed by one of the parties), and depositions (sworn testimony

BEWARE
Do not agree to financial compensation that may be effectively contingent upon the outcome of the case.

taken by one of the parties from anyone who may have information relevant to the case or who may be called as a witness). Depending upon the extent to which discovery has progressed, these depositions may include those taken from the plaintiff, the defendant(s), witnesses to the alleged civil rights violations, and the plaintiff's family members.

Copies of medical records are also essential, even if the plaintiff has not claimed physical harm was caused by the alleged civil rights violations. These records may contain information about prior treatment for emotional disorders that could constitute preexisting conditions. Also, the medical records may contain information about physical correlates of the emotional disorders sometimes experienced by plaintiffs in civil rights cases. Records from the plaintiff's family doctor or nurse may reflect prescriptions for antidepressant or sleep medications, which may point to underlying emotional disorders.

Psychiatric or psychological records are also critical, especially if the plaintiff was in treatment during or following the alleged civil rights violations. To the extent that the mental health professional recorded the plaintiff's ongoing reactions to workplace events, these records may provide contemporaneous information concerning symptoms.

If the plaintiff served in the military, those records may be helpful. Although military records are sometimes hard to acquire, they may reveal prior disciplinary problems, or may support the plaintiff's claim that he excelled in the military and received rapid promotion and frequent awards.

The plaintiff's employment records are also critical. These should be inclusive and should cover all available jobs. Records from prior jobs may provide some evidence of the plaintiff's job stability or instability, of prior on-the-job problems, or of performance excellence. From the job in which the plaintiff is claiming discrimination, the records provide an idea of the worker's job performance, prior job ratings, and other essential information. These records may also contain mention of the incident(s) in question, providing at least what was recorded at the time as the issues that led to the complaint.

BEST PRACTICE
Always request pertinent documents from retaining counsel prior to evaluation. Relevant documents may include some or all of the following:

- Depositions
- Medical records
- Psychiatric or psychological records
- Military records
- Employment records
- Financial records

The plaintiff's financial records provide an empirical basis for understanding how the plaintiff allocated time and resources before and after the alleged civil rights violation. These should include tax returns for at least three years before the alleged civil rights violation and for the period following it. Credit card records may provide a more fine-grained picture of the plaintiff's functioning. For example, if the records reveal that the plaintiff and her husband went out to dinner about twice a month before the on-the-job problem, but have been out only once in the year following the alleged harassment, this could reveal a loss of interest in previously appreciated activities, which may be related to the alleged civil rights violation.

Before the Evaluation

Schedule the Appointment

The expert should set the appointment at a time convenient for the party and for the expert. It is sensible to set aside more time for the evaluation than the expert believes necessary so as to ensure that everything is accomplished. In situations in which the expert is employed by the defendant, it may be difficult for the expert to get permission to see the plaintiff for additional time beyond what was initially requested. This is particularly likely in Rule 35–mandated examinations, in which the plaintiff is ordered to be evaluated by the court. In cases in which the plaintiff appears to be especially fragile, such as situations in which the person was recently psychiatrically hospitalized or attempted suicide, it may be practical to schedule a series of short appointments rather than two or three sequential days for the evaluation.

A good practice is to provide forms, including informed consent, a personal-history form to be filled out by the party, and other permissions, to the party before the day of the evaluation. These may be provided directly to the plaintiff or, in the case of an evaluation requested by the defendant, they should be sent to the plaintiff's counsel so that they may be reviewed prior to forwarding them to the plaintiff. This way, if the plaintiff's counsel objects to any of the proposed forms or procedures, the expert and the lawyers may work out these details before the scheduled evaluation. For example, if it is the psychologist's intent to audio- or videotape the interview and testing, the plaintiff's counsel may object to her client's responses being recorded in a form that could be used against her at a later proceeding. It is also opportune to provide the plaintiff's counsel with a letter concerning informed consent. In the next section we discuss this procedure.

BEST PRACTICE
Always allow more time than you think is necessary to evaluate the plaintiff, and provide all necessary paperwork to relevant parties at least one day before the scheduled evaluation.

Review All Relevant Documents

Prior to the evaluation, the expert should review depositions of the plaintiff and other witnesses to the alleged civil rights violation. This review will provide an account of the events beyond that contained in the formal legally framed complaint and other documents. In the course of a review of work-related and medical records and other case documents, the expert may want to prepare a timeline of the key relevant events. This time sequence will help orient the expert during the plaintiff's interview and will encourage more relevant questions during the interview.

Determine Relevant Issues for Evaluation

A review of all of the foregoing information should allow the expert to determine the issues on which to focus the evaluation. A determination of these issues will begin with the referral questions, which will generally provide the parameters for the evaluation. However, within these parameters, the expert may want to include issues that were raised in the case documentation. For example, if the interrogatories indicate a two-year interval during which the plaintiff was unemployed, the evaluator may want to make a note to ask what happened during that interval. In some cases, the evaluator may want to develop a general outline of questions to ask, or even specific questions to use in the interview. This task may add significant time to the preparation for the interview, but may produce a more complete interview and allow the expert to engage more fully with the examinee rather than focus on constructing the next interview question.

Determine What Tests Will Be Used

Tests are primarily used in forensic evaluations to help formulate hypotheses that may be validated or discarded by multiple measures, and to address various hypotheses that have been formed on other bases. Either way, the goal is to generate hypotheses that can be supported or falsified in order to draw conclusions about the plaintiff (Greenberg, 2003; Greenberg, Otto, & Long, 2003; Heilbrun, 2001; Heilbrun, Marczyk, & DeMatteo, 2002).

A number of tests are commonly applied in workplace cases. Perhaps the most commonly used test in civil cases is the Minnesota Multiphasic Personality Inventory–2 (MMPI-2). The MMPI-2 has been more thoroughly normed and validated than many others and can differentiate between persons who have mental health problems and those who do not (Butcher & Miller, 1999). Next is the Wechsler Adult Intelligence Scale–3rd edition (WAIS-III, which has been supplanted by the WAIS-IV: Psychology Corporation, 2008a). Third in frequency is the Millon Clinical Multiaxial Inventory–3rd edition (MCMI-III: Millon, 1994).

Standardized actuarial instruments, where they apply, should be used rather than projective tests such as the Rorschach Ink Blot Test that are more projective and tests that rely on a checklist approach are less likely to withstand scrutiny and to meet the *Daubert-Kumho* criteria to establish legal reliability. Psychologists should be cautious regarding a self-report inventory consisting of 18 to 24 items composing the Sexual Experiences Questionnaire (SEQ), designed to measure the prevalence of sexual harassment

(Fitzgerald & Schullman, 1983). A 16-item version known as the SEQ-L was developed for Latina women (Cortina, 2001), and a version for male workers was developed (Waldo, Berdahl, & Fitzgerald, 1998). In *EEOC v. Dial* (2003), expert evidence on the outcomes of the SEQ was excluded because of reliability and validity problems with the scale. The validity of this test was questioned primarily on the basis of lack of standardization (many versions exist, each with different wording and numbers of items) and definitional issues (Gutek, Murphy, & Douma, 2004).

The likelihood is strong that psychologists who are consulted in workplace discrimination cases will predominantly be conducting assessments of culturally and linguistically diverse clients; women; gay, lesbian, bisexual, and transgendered clients; and persons with intellectual and psychiatric disabilities. In selecting tests for use in the assessment, psychologists should consider the limitations of tests developed on the basis of Western and male Caucasian populations. The areas of major concern to consider are:

- Norms (the test may not be normed on ethnic or gender populations or groups similar to the plaintiff);
- Content of the items (may not be culturally appropriate);
- Psychometric properties (the reliability and validity may not be assessed on the basis of populations to which the plaintiff belongs);
- Administration process (the procedure may be foreign to the clients and may contaminate the results);
- Client's acculturation (some clients may be similar to the mainstream population, and others may be very different, based on different acculturation levels);
- Language barriers.

A number of psychological tests are not suitable for use with examinees who are from diverse cultural or linguistic groups, for various reasons, including cultural differences in adaptive behavior (Marsella et al., 1996). Assessment via other methods (e.g., observation, collateral information, and other culturally fair tests) may need to be considered. Caution should be exercised when test results are interpreted, to make appropriate adjustments for the specific background of the client. For example, in the case of psychologically disabled clients, previous trauma and adversities may have an impact on their cognitive functioning (along with many other limitations of the tests).

Preparation for the evaluation will include the selection of the specific tests to be used in this evaluation (see Heilbrun, 2001). Two general kinds of tests may be employed: cognitive measures and personality/emotional functioning measures. Whether to use cognitive tests such as the Wechsler Adult Intelligence Scale–IV (Psychological Corporation, 2008a) or the Wechsler Memory Scale–IV (Psychological Corporation, 2008b) is usually determined by an indication of problems experienced by the plaintiff in thinking or information-processing and plausible attribution for these difficulties to the alleged civil rights violation. These measures permit more direct assessments of impairments of concentration, attention, speed of processing, and short- and long-term memory. The results of cognitive tests, if compared to the levels of functioning prior to the alleged harassment, may provide direct indications of loss of functioning, which would contribute to the plaintiff's damages.

Tests of emotional functioning are required to determine the psychological impact of discriminatory events. The MMPI-2 is the most widely used paper-and-pencil personality-assessment measure and has an extensive literature base (c.f., Pope, Butcher & Seelen, 2000; or MMPI-2 Restructured Clinical (RC): Tellegen et al., 2003; Tellegen et al., 2006; Tellegen, Ben-Porath, & Sellborn, 2009). It is well validated for most uses, and can provide information concerning the claimant's current functioning. The psychometric properties include a well-developed measure of random responding, irrelevant responding, exaggeration, and minimization. These response style measures will assist in determining the accuracy, not only of the claimant's responses on the MMPI-2, but the general assessment (Rogers & Bender, 2003). The weakness of the MMPI-2 in this context is the general elevation in the profiles that occurs because the claimant feels unhappy, or dysphoric.

The Personality Assessment Inventory (PAI) (Morey, 1996, 2007) is a well-designed general measure and produces quite useful results. This test contains measures of item consistency, negative impression management, and positive impression management, all of which assist in determining one's response style. The measures of post-traumatic reactions are more fine-grained, and DSM-IV Axis II measures are well-validated. Common Axis II disorders include personality disorders and intellectual disabilities (mental retardation). The inclusion of subtler exaggeration measures adds to this instrument's accuracy. The PAI is shorter than the MMPI-2 and requires a somewhat lower reading level, which makes it more useful for claimants who have learning disabilities or lower levels of education. Like other self-report techniques, the PAI is limited by what the patient knows and can express in a test format. If the plaintiff has not made a connection between a work-related trauma and his recent tendency to want to stay home all the time, he may not list this as a symptom, thus reducing the effectiveness of the instrument.

The MCMI-III is designed for patient populations and is designed to identify Axis II disorders. The first feature is often a problem in employment discrimination evaluations because the claimant may not have a mental health treatment history, in which case the patient norms will not apply. Also, the focus on Axis II disorders has the disadvantage of misidentifying some kinds of reactions—principally post-traumatic reactions—as an Axis II disorder, rather than post-traumatic avoidance or hypervigilance. The MCMI-III has been hailed as a useful measure in forensic settings (Dyer, 2005, 2008), but it has also been harshly criticized for its methods of construction and scaling, and its validity in forensic settings questioned (Bagby, Gillis, & Rogers, 1991; Hynan, 2004; Rogers, Salekin, & Sewell, 1999; Schoenberg et al., 2004). In particular, the MCMI-III personality-disorder scales are not gender-neutral (Hynan, 2004). Validity of the measure for some personality disorders, which is its supposed strength, is low. For these reasons, we do not recommend use of the MCMI-III in civil rights cases.

The Rorschach Ink Blot Test has had its share of harsh critics (Grove et al., 2002; Hilsenroth & Stricker, 2004; Wood et al., 2002). Owing partly to this criticism, recent research on the measure has resolved many of the identified problems (Gacono et al., 2008; Weiner, 2007). One advantage in using the Rorschach is that it is an indirect measure of symptoms and problems, which are generally not under the control of the claimant. In the context of exaggeration or minimization, it can provide a more accurate ongoing measure of functioning.

The expert may also choose to use a specific measure of traumatic emotional reactions such as the Trauma Symptom Inventory (TSI; Briere, 1995) or the Detailed Assessment of Post-traumatic Stress (DAPS; Briere, 2001). If the plaintiff is claiming that the civil rights violation was traumatic, these measures may allow a more direct comparison of the plaintiff's symptoms with those of established patient populations.

Tests of malingering are an essential part of the assessment (Rogers, 2008). If a cognitive assessment is part of the anticipated package, use of a test such as the Tombaugh Test of Memory Malingering (TOMM; Tombaugh, 1997) or the Validity Indicator Profile (VIP; Frederick, 1997) can be helpful. Assessment of exaggeration in the context of the tests of emotional functioning may be accomplished by using the validity measures built into tests like the MMPI-2 (Pope, Butcher, & Seelen, 2000) or PAI. In addition, specific malingering measures such as the Structured Interview of Reported Symptoms (SIRS; Rogers, 1992) may be useful.

On the Day of the Evaluation

General Approach to Meeting with Evaluee

Ideally, the person arriving at the psychologist's office should be treated respectfully, no matter the referral source or the reason for evaluation. In every case, the person should be treated with professionalism, courtesy, and helpfulness. These attitudes should be evident in the behavior of, not only the psychologist, but any staff members who interact with the person. The space for testing should be quiet, comfortable, and appropriately modified for

Table 4.1 | Summary of Tests and Structured Interviews

Name of test	Abbreviation	Test focus	Strengths	Weaknesses
Minnesota Multiphasic Personality Inventory–2	MMPI-2	Well-validated measure of current functioning	Measures: • random and irrelevant responding • exaggeration • minimization	• Elevation in profile if claimant is dysphoric • Poor at specifying personality disorders • Not specific at determining nature of traumatic reaction
Personality Assessment Inventory	PAI	General measure	• Measures response style • Good measure of post-traumatic reactions and Axis II disorders • Useful for claimants with learning difficulties or lower education	• Limited by evaluee's self-knowledge
Millon Clinical Multiaxial Inventory–III	MCMI-III	Designed for patient populations	• Designed to identify Axis II disorders	• Mental health treatment history often lacking in employment discrimination cases (∴patient norms do not apply) • Misidentifies post-traumatic reactions and hypervigilance as an Axis II disorder • Gender differences in personality disorder scales

Table 4.1 | Summary of Tests and Structured Interviews (*Continued*)

Name of test	Abbreviation	Test focus	Strengths	Weaknesses
Rorschach	Rorschach		• Indirect measure of symptoms and problems • Can provide more accurate measure of functioning in context of exaggeration or minimization	Relationship of scores to specific events is not well established
Trauma Symptom Inventory	TSI	Specific measure of traumatic emotional reactions	• Direct comparison of claimant's symptoms to established patient populations	
Tombaugh Test of Malingering	TOMM	Test of effort in cognitive tasks	Excellent screener. Failures signal need for more assessment	
Structured Interview of Reported Symptoms	SIRS	Specific measure of malingering	Although many results are "indeterminate," finding of malingering is usually conclusive	
Acute Stress Disorder Test		Predicts post-traumatic stress disorder		
Clinical Assessment of PTSD Scale–Structured Interview	CAPS	Best measure for PTSD	Validated in Veterans Administration	

people with disabilities. Within reasonable parameters, the evaluee should be able to take breaks and have access to a telephone to call their lawyer with questions. Water and perhaps other beverages should be available to the person. Although there are some aspects of the evaluation process that may prove upsetting to the person, particularly the interviews, every effort should be made to make the evaluation process at least a neutral one, rather than a harrowing, stressful experience.

Informed Consent

In almost every case, it is appropriate to begin the evaluation process with a face-to-face meeting with the evaluee to obtain his or her informed consent. This process is required by APA Ethical Standards:

> 3.10 Informed Consent
>
> (a) When psychologists conduct research or provide assessment, therapy, counseling, or consulting services in person or via electronic transmission or other forms of communication, they obtain the informed consent of the individual or individuals using language that is reasonably understandable to that person or persons except when conducting such activities without consent is mandated by law or governmental regulation or as otherwise provided in this Ethics Code (APA, 2002, p. 1065).

Forensic psychiatrists have a similar guideline:

> At the outset of a face-to-face evaluation, notice should be given to the evaluee of the nature and purpose of the evaluation and the limits of its confidentiality. The informed consent of the person undergoing the forensic evaluation should be obtained when necessary and feasible. If the evaluee is not competent to give consent, the evaluator should follow the appropriate laws of the jurisdiction (American Academy of Psychiatry and the Law, 2004).

Guidance on the requirement for informed consent in forensic evaluations has been provided by several commentators (Knapp &

VandeCreek, 2001; Pope, Butcher, & Seelen, 2000; Rogers, 1987). As noted in the ethical standards we discussed, in some criminal proceedings in which the evaluation is done in accordance with a court order, simple notification may be sufficient to meet the ethical standard. However, in civil rights cases, a full informed-consent procedure is required, and best practice mandates that the consent be memorialized in a written and signed document.

In civil rights cases, this process provides an occasion for the expert to discuss the evaluation procedures with the evaluee and to answer any questions that the person may have about the evaluation. When properly done, the informed-consent dialogue allows the evaluee to become more comfortable, and may alleviate his or her anxiety before formal evaluation procedures begin. To comply with the "law of no surprises" (Behnke, Perlin, & Berrnstein, 2003), the expert must provide the evaluee with information about all the important things that will ensue in the course of the evaluation.

We advocate an approach that recognizes that the expert may lack sufficient knowledge about the law, the evaluee, the plaintiff's case, and other legal matters to properly provide complete informed consent (Foote & Shuman, 2006). To remedy these deficits, the expert must initiate an informed-consent process to which the evaluee's counsel will contribute by providing further information about the proposed evaluation.

The lawyer can supply information responsive to the following questions: *What is the purpose of the evaluation? What are the potential uses of the information? Will the information be admissible in court? How will this information advance or frustrate the litigant's case? What form will the results take? Will a report be completed? Will the litigant be able to review the report? What are the legal consequences of terminating the evaluation?*

The expert and the lawyer will both address some issues: *What is the role of the evaluator? Will the litigant be provided with feedback about the report? Who will have control over the data after the evaluation is completed? Who will be privy to results? What are the limitations on confidentiality? Will opposing counsel see the evaluation results?*

The expert will be primarily responsible for providing the following information: *What form will the results take? Will a report be completed? Will the litigant be able to review the evaluation report? How may the litigant exercise his or her right to terminate the evaluation at any time? How will an untimely evaluation termination affect the test's validity? How will untimely evaluation termination affect scheduling? Who will be told about the decision to terminate? How may a litigant exercise his or her right to consult counsel? What are the evaluation procedures? Does the expert have the litigant's permission to interview collateral informants? What are the potential emotional harms from the evaluation procedure?*

Although ethical standards do not require that informed consent be written (Standard 3.10d, APA, 2002), it is usually most appropriate to use a form that the evaluee reads and signs to document the informed consent process (samples are provided by Pope, Butcher, & Seelen, 2000; and Foote & Shuman, 2006). Some psychologists use a form in which each paragraph requires initials by the evaluee, so that the expert has a record that proves the evaluee at least read each element of the consent before signing the form.

Once the preparatory information is in place, the evaluating expert is ready to begin gathering and organizing the data to form the basis of their opinion in the case in response to the referral question(s). To assist in this task, we recommend managing and structuring the information gathered to conform to a five-stage model of assessment of causation of psychological injuries (Foote, 2009). This is not a new model, but one that integrates elements of the existing standard of practice. In the next chapter, we describe the five-stage model and how it is applied in a workplace discrimination case.

BEST PRACTICE

You are required to provide the evaluee with informed consent prior to the evaluation. Informed consent should be written and should provide information about the purpose of the evaluation and how the data obtained will be subsequently used.

Conclusions

Starting at the time of referral, the examining psychologist keeps in mind the need to maintain a neutral stance as regards the conclusions of the evaluation. By gathering information from multiple sources and interacting with the evaluee in a professional and ethical manner, the examining psychologist begins the evaluation process on a solid basis.

Data Collection 5

The process of psychological evaluation in a civil workplace-discrimination case must focus on the basic legal issues, which in part center on damages to the plaintiff attributable to the actions of the defendant. In this situation, the concept of *proximate cause* is critical. This concept allows that the cause in question (such as the alleged sexual discrimination) may be just one of the causes of a result (such as a phobic reaction). However, in order for an event or series of events to be the *proximate* cause of damages, it must be the case that the damages would not have occurred "but for" the alleged workplace event. That is, proximate cause requires a clear connection between the damages and the alleged workplace event(s), even if other contributors to the final outcome occur before, during, or after the alleged causative event.

The problem in applying this principle to employment discrimination cases is that the plaintiff has a life outside of the allegedly discriminatory workplace. The plaintiff had a childhood, and a prior work and relationship history. At the time of the alleged discrimination, the plaintiff had relationships with family and friends. Other events occurred on the job, both good and bad, that had nothing to do with the focus of the lawsuit. Following the alleged bad acts of the defendants, the plaintiff had other things going on in his or her life, any of which may have been the source of emotional distress. These examples illustrate the complexity that faces the expert when attempting to assess damages in civil rights cases.

In order to deal with this complexity, we propose five phases of assessment that correspond with three phases or periods in the plaintiff's life and two intervals in which the damages are

INFO

The Five-Stage Model of Assessment addresses:

1. The period before the alleged discrimination
2. The period during the alleged discrimination
3. The period after the alleged discrimination
4. The claimant's current status
5. Future damages

addressed—at the time of assessment and projecting future damages. This model addresses the existing standard of practice by bringing together explication of causation and a careful determination of damages. The first of the three phases addresses: (a) the period before the alleged discrimination commenced; (b) the period during the discrimination, and (c) the period following the discrimination. The evaluator may apply a range of tools to this process, including testing, interviews, interviews of third parties, and document review. These produce an assessment at the time of the evaluation (the fourth stage) that brings all the factors into play and rules out causes unrelated to the alleged discrimination. The final phase is one in which the evaluator determines whether damages (if any) will have an impact on the post-adjudication functioning of the evaluee. The purpose of the model is to provide a method for systematically ascertaining all the sources of the plaintiff's problems, with a focus on accounting for problems and symptoms produced by nondiscriminatory events.

Some commentators have discussed different patterns of causation. For example, Melton et al. (2007) discussed a protocol prepared by Ebaugh and Benjamin that sees five different alternative types of causation patterns. First, the alleged trauma may be the sole cause of the emotional injury. Second, the alleged trauma may be a major precipitating factor in causing the emotional reaction. In this case, the emotional disorder may be subclinical or latent, and would be activated by the events in question. Third, the alleged trauma may be an aggravating factor that causes an existing disorder to become more severe. Fourth, the alleged trauma may be a minor factor in the context of a well-developed mental disorder, causing the existing disorder to become somewhat more severe. Fifth, the alleged traumatic events may be unrelated to the emotional disorders (Melton, et al., p. 420).

Our perspective differs from this in some ways, as we see nondiscriminatory events entering into the damages equation in four ways. First, the life problem may simply be caused by events unrelated to the alleged discriminatory action. For example, a plaintiff may have had an automobile accident, which could account for any depression or PTSD seen in the plaintiff. Second, the plaintiff may have had an ongoing problem that began before the alleged discrimination. For example, the plaintiff may have an ongoing major depressive disorder, recurrent, which waxes and wanes independently of events in the workplace. The assessment of that problem at the time of the evaluation may just reveal symptoms that had multiple origins separate from the focus of the lawsuit. Third, the plaintiff may have had an ongoing disorder at the time of the alleged discriminatory action, which was exacerbated by the events that occurred on the job. For example, a woman with an unresolved PTSD stemming from a prior sexual assault may experience later sexual harassment as more troubling and disabling. Events that cause the erosion of social support may also contribute to the development of symptoms not attributable to the alleged discrimination. Fourth, to the extent that supervisors and coworkers cause the plaintiff to experience emotional reactions that engender estrangement and disconnection from their family and friends, the discrimination may indirectly affect a number of other life functions, including physical health. In this chapter, we review the factors that should be addressed in the first three stages of this analysis. In the next chapter, we will provide an outline of procedures for determining both causation and compensable present and future damages in Stages 4 and 5.

Events Predating the Discrimination Allegations

In this section, we discuss the many causes of mental disorders and problem patterns that have their origins in childhood or are otherwise likely to occur earlier in a person's life. We provide as examples child sexual abuse, chronic mental disorders, and acute stress disorder or PTSD. These are the problems that serve as a basis for determining the causation of problems that the claimant attributes to the alleged discrimination. Also, by establishing a "day before" baseline, one that accurately represents the level of functioning of the claimant on the "day before" the alleged discrimination, the evaluator establishes a baseline of comparison for any increases or decreases in functioning that occur following the onset of the alleged discrimination. For example, anxiety, nervousness, headaches, memory problems, and concentration problems are often reported as consequences of workplace discrimination. Base rates in the normal population for these symptoms range from 20% to 62% (Lees-Haley & Brown, 1993).

Child Sexual Abuse

Child sexual abuse is a relatively frequent event in the lives of both men and women. If one uses the criterion of direct physical contact between the perpetrator and the victim, approximately 6.8% to 28.1% of women (Finkelhor et al., 1990; Stein et al., 1988) and 6.8% to 17.3% of men (Fromuth & Burkhart, 1987; Urquiza & Capra, 1990) were abused as children.

Considerable research has documented the impact of child sexual abuse upon adults (e.g., Briere & Runtz, 1988; Dhaliwal et al., 1996; Fromuth & Burkhart, 1987; Horowitz et al., 2001; Polusny & Follette, 1995; Roesler & McKenzie, 1994; Sparato et al., 2004; Ullman, 2007). This research indicates that a history of abuse is a risk factor for the development of childhood mental and conduct disorders. For adults, a history of abuse in childhood increases the risk of a host of adult disorders, including affective disorders, sexual dysfunction, anxiety disorders (particularly PTSD), substance abuse disorders, acting-out disorders, and personality disorders (Horowitz et al., 2001; Kessler,

INFO

A history of child sexual abuse may contribute to an increased vulnerability to harassment and victimization as an adult.

Davis, & Kindler, 1997; Sparoto et al., 2004). A history of physical, sexual, or emotional abuse also places people at risk for subsequent victimization of various sorts (Hamilton, 1989; Humphrey & White, 2000; Maker, Kemmelmeier & Peterson, 2001). Because of this probability of revictimization, people who are victims of child sexual abuse may be more vulnerable as targets of sexual harassment (Foote & Goodman-Delahunty, 2005).

Chronic Mental Disorders

A recent series of studies has determined that some mental disorders are relatively common in the general population (Kessler et al., 2005; Kessler et al., 2005; Kessler & Merikangas, 2005). Anxiety disorders are most frequent, and 28% of the U.S. population has had an anxiety disorder at some time in their lives. Phobias afflict many, with 12.5% having a specific phobia and 12.1% reporting symptoms of social phobia. Panic disorders occur in 4.7% of the general population. Recent research indicates that, in the context of some traumas, such as motor vehicle accidents, 20%–25% of victims develop acute stress disorder, and of those, about 60%–75% develop PTSD (Bryant & Panesetis, 2005; Forbes, et al., 2007; Holevia and Terrier, 2001; Moulds & Bryant, 2006). Generalized anxiety disorder occurs in 5.7% of the population, and separation anxiety disorder in 5.2% (Kessler et al., 2005).

Affective disorders are also frequent. Overall, 20.8% of the general American population has experienced an affective disorder. Major depressive disorder afflicts 16.2% (Kessler et al., 2003). Data from an extensive study (Kessler et al., 2005) indicate that dysthymia is much less frequent as a life experience, with 2.5% of the population reporting that diagnosis. Bipolar disorders are also rare, with 3.9% of the population suffering from these severe mood changes at some time in their lives.

Approximately 15% of the population has had a problem with alcohol or drugs at some time in their lives. Alcohol abuse is the most common substance abuse disorder, with 13.2% reporting this problem at some time in their histories. The more serious alcoholism (alcohol dependence) is less common, with 5.4% reporting alcohol addiction. Drug abuse and drug dependence are somewhat less common, with rates of 7.9% and 3.0%, respectively.

Epidemiologists have determined that some psychological disorders tend to occur together, a phenomenon called *comorbidity*. How this arises is not always the same for all individuals, because all we really know from the comorbidity of two disorders is that they tend to occur in the same individual at the same time. Researchers are working to tease out whether one disorder causes the other, or whether both disorders may spring from the same cause or group of causes. Whatever the cause–effect relationship, comorbidity is important for forensic mental health professionals to understand when evaluating the history of an employment-discrimination plaintiff. Understanding that two disorders tend to occur together may prompt the evaluating expert to inquire about the presence of other disorders that occur commonly with one that is already identified. Our evaluation model emphasizes changes in function that occur as a consequence of civil rights violations. In many cases, the party may experience more loss of function as a result of a comorbid condition than from symptoms related to the primary diagnosis (Kessler et al., 1995).

In some civil rights cases, particularly those involving sexual harassment, the plaintiff alleges that what happened on the job was in some way emotionally traumatic. Although some scholars contend that this trauma often produces PTSD (e.g., Avina & O'Donohue, 2002), others (Foote & Goodman-Delahunty, 2005) have maintained that most sexual harassment cases do not result in a full PTSD diagnosis, in part because the events that occur in the workplace are not severe enough to threaten the individual's "personal integrity" as required by criterion A (Simon, 2003) of the DSM-IV listing for PTSD (American Psychiatric Association, 2000). However, the absence of all the criteria for the PTSD diagnosis does not mean that the plaintiff did not suffer an emotionally traumatic

BEST PRACTICE

Knowledge of comorbidity is critical when performing a workplace-discrimination evaluation. Victims of workplace discrimination may experience more severe harm as a result of comorbid conditions.

event, and they may even evince sufficient symptoms of the disorder to otherwise meet the diagnosis. In this case, it is the examining expert's job to inquire into the presence of these symptoms, and to determine the impact of the traumatic events upon the plaintiff's functioning. The PTSD literature will help guide this exploration.

PTSD is fairly common in the non-treatment population of the United States, with a prevalence of about 7% (Kessler, et al, 1995). Research (Kessler et al., 1995) has shown that of these individuals, comorbidity is almost the rule, with the majority of people with a PTSD diagnosis also meeting criteria for another Axis 1 disorder. This is true for 88.3% of men and 79% of women. A substantial proportion meets criteria for two or more other disorders. In one study (Kessler et al., 1995), 59% of men and 43.6% of women with PTSD met the criteria for three or more disorders. On the basis of the findings by Kessler et al., (1995), for men the most common comorbid disorders were: alcohol abuse/dependence (51.9%); major depression (47.9%); conduct disorder (43.3%); and drug abuse/dependence (34.5%). For women the most common comorbid disorders were: major depression (48.5%); simple phobia (29%); social phobia (28.4%); alcohol abuse/dependence (27.9%); and drug abuse/dependence (27.9%).

Stage 2: Events That Occurred at About the Same Time as the Alleged Discrimination

In this section, we examine the multiple origins of stress and symptoms that might have occurred at about the same time as the alleged harassment. We review stressors originating in family life, the workplace, the claimant's social network, and their physical health.

Family Life–Generated Stressors

Plaintiffs in civil rights cases usually have families, and most families have problems at one time or another. For example, the family may have a change in financial status caused by imprudent investments

INFO

History of domestic abuse increases the probability that a woman will be sexually harassed.

or bankruptcy. Aging parents or the return of children after their failed relationships may stretch the worker's finances and crowd their house. Domestic violence is a major societal problem. Nearly 25% of American women report being raped and/or physically assaulted by a current or former spouse, cohabiting partner, or date at some time in their lifetime, according to the National Violence Against Women Survey, conducted from November 1995 to May 1996 (Tjaden & Thoennes, 2000). Based upon what we know about revictimization, this would increase the probability that a woman would be a simultaneous target of sexual harassment and victim of domestic violence (Rosen & Martin, 1998).

Health Problems

Like anyone else, the plaintiff may experience some physical illnesses that have nothing to do with what is happening on the job. For example, some health problems, like diabetes, have been implicated as correlates of mental disorders, particularly depression (Golden et al., 2008). Other chronic conditions, particularly chronic pain disorders (Demmelmaier, Lindberg, Asenlof & Denison, 2008) are related to a host of psychological outcomes. These physical illnesses may create anxiety, or provide an alternative basis of causation for observed symptoms or problems.

INFO

Physical illnesses unrelated to work can contribute to problems such as anxiety and depression and may provide an alternative explanation of causation of harm in workplace-discrimination claims.

On-the-Job Stressors Unrelated to Alleged Discrimination

As corporations change and go through mergers and restructuring, employees experience changes in assignments, job locations, coworkers, and supervisors, along with many other working conditions. Because of these changes, employees may experience stressors that can cause serious emotional reactions for them. For example, an involuntary reduction in status caused by restructuring may make the worker feel unappreciated and depressed.

Workers also may experience consequences based upon their own performance. If a worker is ill-suited for a position, or is unqualified for a job and is getting constant feedback of poor performance, this may give rise to unhappiness related to work that has nothing to do with discrimination in the workplace (Barsade & Wiesenfeld, 1997; National Institute for Occupational Safety and Health, 2000; Northwestern National Life Insurance Company, 1991, 1992; Princeton Survey Research Associates, 1997; Vagg & Spielberger, 1998). In the evaluation of plaintiffs, it is sometimes difficult to tease out the cause and effect in situations in which the worker is receiving negative performance appraisals. This negative feedback may actually be based on the worker's performance, and the worker may attribute the poor ratings to discriminatory activity by the employer. In contrast, the employer may be using poor ratings as a way of retaliating against the worker for complaining about discrimination or harassment.

Erosion of Social Support

Research (e.g., Ginzburg et al., 2008; Haden & Scarpa, 2008; Semmer et al., 2008) has determined that functioning social support is critical to enabe a normal person to weather life's stresses. If events that occur in the non-work life of the plaintiff erode social support, such as a divorce or a serious family disagreement, the worker's ability to cope with on-the-job stressors may be reduced. Suppose a worker has been dealing with an antagonistic boss who is nondiscriminatory in the way that he demeans and disparages his employees. When this single parent's only child leaves home, the worker's ability to cope with an otherwise barely tolerable workplace may be compromised. If one

BEWARE It can be difficult to determine whether an employee received poor performance appraisals based on actual performance or because of employer discrimination.

consequence of the alleged discrimination is to decrease the base of support for the complainant, then this may be a basis for additional pecuniary damages.

Stage 3: Post–Alleged Discrimination Events

Many of the events just described that can occur at the same time the worker alleged discrimination could also occur following the alleged unlawful discriminatory actions. For example, financial problems may arise, especially if the worker is discharged for reasons that have nothing to do with the alleged discrimination. Job changes that do not reflect retaliation may arise, with associated stresses.

In addition, the very act of claiming discrimination often has consequences in the workplace that do not reflect malicious intentions of supervisors or coworkers, but are natural responses following receipt of a complaint. For example, it is predictable that if a worker has complained of discrimination, his supervisors might be more careful about how they treat that person in the future. Treatment of a worker with "kid gloves" produces changes in the work climate for that worker.

A complaint may also adversely affect the worker's relationships with coworkers. For example, in the case of a woman making a sexual harassment complaint, our experience indicates that three kinds of coworker response can be predicted. Some will believe that the worker's complaint is false and defames a man who everyone knows would never do such a thing. Others have probably observed the supervisor's harassment or have themselves been targets and admire the complainant for her courage to complain. A third group may desire the status quo before the complaint and simply want to go to work each day without drama. If a supervisor is transferred or discharged following a complaint, some workers who were his friends or who admired the way he did his job will regard this as unjust. Whatever happens to the supervisor, coworkers may view the complaining worker in a different light. She may be seen as overly paranoid, as a troublemaker, or as someone trying to beat the system with a false complaint.

Applying the First Three Stages of the Model

In framing the evaluation, the expert should keep in mind the first three stages, taking care to gather information about relevant aspects of the claimant's history and presentation in light of competing explanations for the plaintiff's symptoms. This structure may also be applied in stages 4 and 5 when the expert is compiling information for testimony or a report. In those contexts, the use of a sequential analysis of symptom development and problem description can ground the evaluation. This framework may also be a straightforward way of discussing evaluation results with a trier of fact: the judge or jury. The analysis using the model begins with a review of available documentation, which sheds light on all of the first three stages, and provides a database for forming final conclusions and projections in the final two stages. This model reflects the standard of practice in the field because it brings together the elements that must be presented to a trier of fact: a full explication of the injury to the party, and the cause of that injury.

Document Review

General Considerations about Records

As noted in Chapter 4, the evaluator will already have requested necessary documents from retaining counsel or received appropriate releases from the plaintiff in order to request those records directly from the source. A review of these documents provides a template for developing a chronology of the plaintiff's life. For example, school records may help map the person's geographic location and reflect their general ability to function in well-understood contexts. This chronology is an essential tool for understanding cause-and-effect relationships. For example, if the worker has a work-related problem soon after an on-the-job event, this may point to the impact of workplace harassment or discrimination. If, on the other hand, the changes in job performance follow an episode of domestic violence or the incarceration of the plaintiff's child, the determination of causation may be more complicated.

BEST PRACTICE
Use relevant documents to construct a chronology of the plaintiff's life. Past life events (on the job or off) can help you determine causation of harm.

A review of documentation should focus on discriminatory cause-and-effect hypotheses. Remember, however, that the documents that are reviewed were not usually written to provide information for complaints in a lawsuit. Rather, they were usually gathered in the course of business, as part of a routine health history, or as records of military service. As such, they may not contain the precise information needed to substantiate or to refute the plaintiff's complaints.

In general, the evaluator should review records for evidence of emotional disorders. These may include sleep disorders, symptoms of depression (sadness, anhedonia), anxiety symptoms, or rapid weight changes. These symptoms may represent preexisting or coexisting disorders that must be differentiated from the problems caused by the alleged discrimination.

Other sources of trauma should be highlighted in the record review, especially those consistent with criterion A of the DSM-IV diagnosis for PTSD. Motor vehicle accidents, sexual trauma, and crime victimization are unfortunately not uncommon, and are likely to mark the history of the average civil rights plaintiff. Less common is trauma from combat or natural disasters. In reviewing military or civil records, care should be taken to document exposure to these traumas. For example, a worker claiming to have had combat-related emotional reactions should have military records that reflect her placement in a combat zone.

The record review should also consider information about other major disruptions in the plaintiff's life. For example, legal documents related to a divorce or records of a bankruptcy may provide on paper a measure of the plaintiff's losses at a particular time. If these events occurred during the alleged discrimination or in the interval between those events and the evaluation, then they may account for some or all of the observed symptoms.

Health records are often a mixed bag. In the midst of records of routine physicals, rhinoviruses, and broken bones may be notations concerning sleep disorders and anxiety attacks. Stress-related illnesses like irritable bowel syndrome or headaches may also reflect reactions to on-the-job problems. In some cases, these medical problems may be the first indication that the worker is no longer coping adequately with on-the-job events, even if the worker or the medical professional do not recognize that early indicator. It may only be through a retrospective review that the forensic evaluator is able to recognize these early symptoms.

Mental health records may also reflect preexisting problems that continue into the time frame of the alleged discrimination. Even if the worker was in treatment at the time of the alleged acts of discrimination, the records may provide contemporaneous documentation of the plaintiff's complaints. These records can be a valuable resource in cases in which the accounts of events from the defendant and the plaintiff differ significantly ("he said/she said" cases). If the mental health treatment began after the lodging of the claimant's complaints, the evaluator must be wary of the plaintiff's use of this treatment to document damages. This may especially be the case in situations in which the plaintiff's counsel made the referral for psychological or psychiatric treatment. If psychiatric treatment with psychotropic medications is part of the person's history, the evaluator may want to research the side-effects of the medication to determine if these may have had some impact upon the worker's functioning on the job.

If the plaintiff served in the military, those records may provide a unique view of the individual in specific contexts. As noted in this chapter, a history of combat or combat-related trauma may provide an understanding of the impact of serious traumatic events. In less exigent circumstances, how the worker adapted to the highly structured life of the armed services can provide a picture of the person's adaptability and basic levels of motivation. For example, failure to achieve rank in an orderly fashion may reflect poor performance or an inability to get along with supervisors or fellow service members. A history of judicial punishments such as courts martial, or nonjudicial punishments such as Article 15 or Captain's Mast, may be a reflection of impulsivity or anger-management problems. The nature of the service person's discharge is also important. If it is anything but "honorable," this may reflect very serious problems in the military; or if it is under some sort of disability, the basis may indicate serious preexisting problems. With an increasing number of women serving in the military and in combat zones, the substantially higher rate of sexual assault and harassment of service women than their civilian counterparts must be considered (Bostock & Daley, 2007; Katz, Bloor, Cojucar & Draper, 2007; Murdoch, Pryor, Polusny & Gackstetter, 2007; Pryor, 1995; Roessler & McKenzie, 1994; Valente & Wright, 2007). Although military records may not reflect these complaints, the presence of the records may prompt this avenue of inquiry so these probabilities can be explored at a suitable occasion in a later interview. The presence of these problems or preexisting conditions will be accounted for in the "day before" analysis, and may constitute preexisting conditions unrelated to the alleged employment discrimination or conditions that may be exacerbated by subsequent on-the-job events.

Legal Documents

Sworn documents such as deposition transcripts, and quasi-sworn documents such as responses to interrogatories, are not necessarily more accurate than other documents. However, lawyers often give them more credence, so the expert should be familiar with them. As with many other documents, depositions are often taken for purposes other than gathering information about damages in a civil case. In general, depositions are designed to lead to the discovery of other information, documents, or witnesses or to delimit or "nail down" specific facts. Once those statements are taken in sworn testimony, they may later be used by the deposing lawyer to impeach the same witness in trial. However, lawyers only rarely ask the questions that a forensic mental health evaluator would ask of a witness. This means that the expert reading a deposition may often be frustrated by the question not asked or the followup not pursued. However, these sources of sworn testimony frequently serve as anchor points for the expert when later conducting the clinical interview, at which point the expert can assess the credibility of the interviewee. By reading these documents before the interview, the interviewer will have the opportunity to clarify conflicts while the evaluee is in the office, rather than just noting those differences in the later report. In many cases, apparent contradictions are more a product of the manner of questioning than an attempt on the part of the evaluee to lie or evade questions.

BEST PRACTICE
Review all legal documents related to the case prior to the evaluation. This gives you the opportunity to clarify any conflicting information at the time of the interview.

Conducting Interviews with Claimants

Interview Style

The interviewer should bring to bear all his or her professional skills to help the claimant feel comfortable during the interview. This is especially important in situations in which the evaluator is working for the opposing party, usually the defendant(s) in the case. It has been the authors' experience that employment discrimination cases often cause claimants to become defensive, angry, and suspicious in their interactions with just about everyone in the case. Ethical practice would suggest that the evaluator should not do anything to abrogate the informed consent (Shuman, 1993). The evaluator cannot become the claimant's therapist or best friend. Rather, a pleasant, professional attitude on the part of the evaluator can defuse defensiveness or anger on the part of the evaluee, and establish a more productive interview.

The most common question asked in the interview should be "What happened next?" The interviewer should begin with open-ended questions that cover the claimant's relevant history. It is usually most effective to advise the claimant that, in order to understand what happened on the job, it is first essential to gain a grasp of the person's life. Beginning at birth and going forward can provide this context. This background provides essential information for the first of the three stages in the evaluation model. The chronology should be completed up until the day before the beginning of the alleged employment discrimination. At that point, the evaluator should review and draw together the critical aspects of the claimant's history.

BEST PRACTICE
Begin the interview by asking open-ended questions about the claimant's history. Construct a chronology up until the day before the alleged discrimination took place.

Claimant's History

The claimant's history is an essential and rich basis for forensic conclusions, and should include the many elements described in the paragraphs that follow. These elements should all be covered as part of a standard-of-practice clinical history, although the order may be a matter of personal preference or a reflection of the interpersonal flow of the clinical interview.

A full medical history to that point should be obtained in the interview. In particular, the evaluator should ask questions about any hospitalizations for any reason. The interviewer should inquire whether the claimant had any chronic diseases such as diabetes or high blood pressure, when those problems started, and how they affected the person's life. In particular, the claimant should be asked if any hospitalizations occurred in relation to any workplace events. That is, was hospitalization prompted by an accident in the workplace? Did the worker seek medical attention following a blowup with a supervisor?

Next, the interviewer should inquire about the claimant's mental health history. Has the worker ever seen a psychologist, psychiatrist, counselor, social worker, or clergy for emotional problems? The focus should center on the worker's life situation at the time the treatment was sought, including the nature and severity of the problems that prompted treatment. The examiner should inquire into diagnosis and application of treatment such as psychotropic medication and inpatient hospitalization. A history of suicide or other self-destructive behavior is part of this portion of the interview. Did those problems improve with treatment? Did any of these problems occur in relation to events in the workplace?

The claimant should next be asked about a history of trauma. This should begin with questions concerning any history of child physical, sexual, or emotional abuse. Then, questions should shift to any history of other sexual trauma such as rape or sexual assault. The interviewer should ask about interpersonal violence history, such as being a victim of an armed robbery or a battery. Because auto accidents are a common source of trauma, the claimant should be asked about any history of crashes. Interview questions may focus on injuries to the claimant or others, the death of anyone in the accident, and the need for treatment for those injuries. If injuries were sustained, the examiner would want to know the treatment provided for those injuries and the long-term outcome of those injuries. If there were no physical injuries, were there psychological consequences of the impact? As a result of the accident, did the worker have any common PTSD symptoms such as nightmares, intrusive recollections, hypervigilance, or trauma-related avoidance?

The interviewer should then inquire about substance abuse. The levels of alcohol or drug use before the alleged discrimination will clarify the "day before" analysis, as will a discussion of any serious consequences of drug or alcohol use such as physical illness, interpersonal problems, and legal difficulties or on-the-job problems. In some cases, substance use patterns may change after the alleged discrimination begins, and such changes should be discussed. Did the worker have any on-the-job problems such as excessive sick leave or tardiness, coming to work drunk or hung over, or becoming intoxicated during offsite business occasions such as working dinners or office parties? Has the person had any treatment for alcohol problems? Has there been any period in this interval when the person did not drink? Similar questions may be asked about the use of illegal drugs such as marijuana or cocaine, or prescription drug abuse.

The marital and relationship history of the claimant is the next area of inquiry. This should begin with questions concerning the claimant's teen years and carry forward to the present. In this phase of the interview, the interviewer should focus on any marital or relationship problems that may have occurred in the interval before or during the time when the job-related difficulties appeared. In particular, how many marriages or long-term relationships has the worker had? Is there a history of divorce or separation in these relationships? Does the worker report any history of infidelity? Was the worker involved in a violent relationship? In prior jobs, did work generate marital or relationship problems?

The claimant's military history is the next topic of the interview. This should begin with questions concerning the considerations that entered into the person's decision to enter the military. The claimant should be asked to provide an overview of their military service: basic training, advanced training, duty stations, and changes in military grade over the course of the service. A discussion of the training received in the military and the presence of combat experience in the claimant's military history creates an opportunity to discuss their experience of traumatic events in that time frame. Were there any experiences of discrimination, sexual assault, or sexual harassment by superiors or fellow service members? (See section below on assessing instances of discrimination in prior employment.) In the course of the military service, was the person ever a subject of judicial or nonjudicial punishment (e.g., Captain's Mast, Article 15, court martial)? The interviewer may ask about the circumstances of the claimant's discharge from military service, whether the discharge was less than honorable, and if so, about the events leading up to the less-than-honorable result. At the time of discharge, was the person considered disabled? Has the claimant ever applied for disability benefits based on the military service? If so, what was the result of that claim?

The claimant's vocational history is an essential part of the employment discrimination interview (Foote, 2003; Foote & Goodman-Delahunty, 2005). Although the evaluator should already have a complete collection of available employment records, the claimant should be able to add additional information about previous jobs—in particular, the names of the employers, the nature of the employers' businesses, and the nature of the work environments. For example, in a large industrial concern, did the claimant work in the office, on the manufacturing floor, in the receiving room, or in a similar location? What was the name of the job the person filled? What were the duties associated with that position? What hours did the claimant work? What was the nature of the work schedule (e.g., were split, swing, or night shifts part of the schedule)? With whom did the claimant work? For example, how many coworkers did he or she have? How close was the supervision by superiors? The interviewer will want to ask about the interpersonal environment of the workplace, including how the worker got along with others in this job, and the presence in the workplace of any people with whom the person had special difficulty. The history of the worker's performance ratings and pay increases should be reviewed. If the worker had on-the-job problems, the inquiry should focus on the history of disciplinary actions such as a suspension or leave without pay. If the worker has left the workplace, the examiner needs to know the circumstances of the termination of service.

Related to the vocational history are inquiries concerning the worker's prior history of discrimination or harassment. The interviewer will begin these questions by focusing on the nature of the job in question (which may have already been recorded in their vocational history). The following questions will focus on what happened at the time of the alleged discrimination and the events that followed. These are essentially the same questions you will later ask about the alleged discrimination in the current case, which will be detailed in the following section. In addition, the interviewer should inquire: What were the circumstances of your exit from that job? Did you file a complaint about the discrimination after you left the job?

The interview should then center on the work the person was doing at the time of the alleged discrimination. Related to this portion of the interview is a discussion of the claimant's history with the defendant organization, including factors that attracted the worker to the job in the first place. The conditions of the employment are an important area of inquiry, including the locations, hours, and duties of the job; the people who were the coworkers and supervisors; and the chain of command. The expert needs to explore the defendant organization's practices and policies concerning discrimination, including training provided about discrimination, mechanisms for dealing with discrimination complaints; and explore the claimant's impression of the organization's

BEST PRACTICE

When inquiring about the claimant's personal history, be sure to address the following areas:

- Medical history
- Psychiatric history
- Trauma history
- History of substance abuse
- Marital and relationship history
- Military history
- Vocational history (including prior history of discrimination or harassment)

attitude toward discrimination. Did that attitude differ from their stated policy?

When discussing the workplace in which the alleged discrimination took place, a history of any prior difficulty with coworkers or supervisors should be gathered, including any impression that supervisors or coworkers held grudges against the claimant. The claimant may have had difficulty in some aspects of the job. At this point, inquiry into problems at home or with the claimant's family should be elicited. The presence and extent of social support networks should be explored, as well as the presence of ongoing health problems, and changes in substance use.

The Claimant's Account of Discrimination

Before specific questions begin, the claimant should be asked open-ended questions such as, "Can you describe what happened on the job?" Following this relatively free narrative, a more specific account of the events should yield very specific information: when the discrimination began; who was responsible for those actions; the role of the defendants in the discriminatory conduct, and their role as supervisors or coworkers. Next, the interviewer should gather details of the alleged discrimination: the first events that, even in retrospect, constituted discriminatory conduct; whether the claimant recognized those acts as discrimination at the time; and the presence of any witnesses to the conduct. The interview should include questions about the claimant's reactions to the alleged discrimination. Probative questions include: "Did you say or do anything to stop the discrimination? Did you tell the person discriminating against you not to do it again? Did you complain to a supervisor? Did you tell anyone? If you did complain, what, if anything, was done about your complaint?" If the claimant indicates that the discrimination occurred more than once or over a long period, details concerning the subsequent instances should be covered. This discussion should focus on any aspects of the alleged discrimination that were especially upsetting or disturbing, and whether the worker changed anything about his or her working conditions, including hours, days worked, or work location. For example: " Did the discrimination occur again? When, and where? What was your immediate reaction to these events? Did you find anything that happened in the course of the discrimination to be especially upsetting or disturbing? Did you change anything about your working conditions (hours, days worked, duties, work location)?" Questions focusing on common reactions to discrimination may follow. These might include questions such as, "Did any of your attitudes about your work or your feelings about work change? Did you have any changes in your sleep patterns or appetite? Did you have any changes in your relationships with family members? Did you have any changes in your intimate relationships? Did you develop any new medical problems in the weeks or months following the beginning (or single incident) of the discrimination?"

If the worker left the job, whether the person was laid off, was fired, or quit may have important clinical as well as legal implications. If the worker is claiming constructive discharge, a history of events that the worker believes forced him or her out of the job should be discussed. The events that led the worker to file the complaint should be covered, as well as the organization-based complaint procedure, EEOC, or state Fair Employment Practices organization complaint used by the worker. The outcome of those complaints and the circumstances of hiring a lawyer should also be explored. If the worker believes that he or she was subjected to retaliation, questions should focus on the nature of any adverse action[s] by the employer.

Events that have occurred since the worker left the job are the next area of inquiry. Changes in the worker's personal life, deaths among family and friends, and changes in relationships with family members should be covered. The development of any new health problems, if not evident from the medical records, should be addressed at this time.

The course of problems the worker attributes to the alleged discrimination is the next area of focus. For instance: "Of the problems that you relate to what happened on the job, have they gotten better, worse, or stayed the same? Have you sought treatment from a medical or mental health provider? If so, when did you seek that treatment? What are your current symptoms or problems you relate to the discrimination? Describe an average day from the time you get up until you go to sleep. Please describe your functioning in each of these activities of daily living: personal hygiene; household chores; reading activities; use of electronic equipment; social activities; family responsibilities; community/religious activities; exercise regimen; vacations; sleep/wake cycle; eating habits, with any weight gain or loss; recreational activities, especially as restricted or changed; driving activities; financial management; doctor's visits; work or work-related activities; and academic pursuits," (Foote, 2007; Vore, 2005).

Checklist for claimant interview

1. Personal history
   - Full medical history
   - Psychiatric history
   - History of past trauma and/or abuse (including child abuse, sexual assault, interpersonal violence, and other traumatic events, such as car accidents)
   - Substance abuse (alcohol and drug use prior to current workplace problems)
   - Marital and relationship history
   - Military history
   - Vocational history (including prior history of discrimination or harassment)
2. Events surrounding alleged discrimination:
   - Events and circumstances at the time of the alleged discrimination (e.g., type of work the claimant was doing, hours and duties, relationship with coworkers and supervisor, difficulties with coworkers or supervisors before the discrimination began)
   - Concurrent issues in non–work life that were causing the claimant problems or concerns

- Claimant's account of the discrimination, including:
  - The nature of the discrimination (specific details about alleged events)
  - The claimant's responses to the discrimination (e.g., talked to others, approached supervisor; and emotional reactions to discrimination)
  - Changes in the claimant's working conditions or attitude to work (if they left their job, was it voluntary or were they fired?)
  - Changes in areas of the claimant's life outside work (e.g., changes in sleep, appetite, or intimate relationships)
  - Reason for filing complaint
  - Whether the claimant accessed treatment
  - The claimant's current level of functioning

Collateral Information

Current standards of practice (Heilbrun et al., 1994; Heilbrun, Warren, & Picarello, 2003) dictate that the evaluator conduct interviews with people who have information concerning the worker's history and status. As it is advisable (though not essential) for the evaluator to obtain the permission from the claimant for some of those interviews, the authors of this book suggest that the evaluator use a form to obtain formal permission from the claimant for the collateral interviews with friends and family. This same form may also contain the names and phone numbers of those potential sources of information. There are several reasons for this. First, the names and phone numbers of friends and family members must usually be obtained from the claimant. Second, if the claimant is asked to contact those individuals and advise them that the evaluator will be calling them for a telephone interview, the collaterals are much more likely to cooperate. Third, the evaluator runs the risk of a lawsuit or a board complaint if contact is made with a collateral party and otherwise-confidential information is conveyed in the course of that interview. In many cases, it is difficult to conduct a collateral interview without disclosing at least the context of the interview.

BEST PRACTICE

Psychologists are advised to obtain permission from the claimant to conduct collateral interviews with third parties who have information about the claimant's work history and status.

On the other hand, it may also be helpful to conduct interviews with others whom the claimant may not name. These may be former or current coworkers or supervisors, vendors, customers, or others known to the defendant[s]. For that reason, it may be advisable to also request the names of potential collateral sources from the defendant.

Collateral Interviews

Collateral interviews may be conducted face-to-face or by telephone. In either context, it is advisable to obtain informed consent from the person to be interviewed prior to the onset of the conversation. In a face-to-face situation, the evaluator may use a simplified, written informed consent form, advising the person about the context of the interview and the purposes the information will be used for, including the parameters of confidentiality. In the case of a telephone interview, the same information should be conveyed to the source, and the evaluator should obtain verbal informed consent before proceeding. As in all contexts, no recording should be made without the explicit permission of the claimant (see "Ethical Principles of Psychologists and Code of Conduct," American Psychological Association, 2002, Code of Conduct 4.02).

The collateral interview should begin with questions about the history of the relationship between the claimant and the collateral individual. Then it should discuss the claimant's status prior to the onset of the alleged discrimination. The interview should next focus on the time interval during which the discrimination was allegedly occurring. Did the claimant discuss the discrimination with the collateral person as it was occurring? What changes did the collateral observe in the course of the alleged discrimination, or, in the case of a single event, in the immediate aftermath of this event? What has the collateral observed in the claimant's functioning in the last year? Is the source aware of any other adverse events in the claimant's life in the relevant period? How would the source describe the claimant's current activities of daily living (use list in earlier section)?

BEST PRACTICE

Be sure to obtain informed consent from all the individuals you intend to interview.

Psychological Testing

Another aspect of best practice for forensic evaluations is the use of psychological testing. This source of information permits a comparison of the scores or results of the individual with those of specific clinical and normative populations, and also allows a more rigorous comparison of some aspects of the individual to their other skills or characteristics. Testing also provides an objective metric of symptom exaggeration or minimization. The preceding chapter provides considerations for choosing tests in employment discrimination cases.

In the examination, care should be taken to administer the tests according to the test manual, to maintain congruence between the data gathered in the employment discrimination evaluation and the database for that instrument. In the cognitive assessment, conditions should be established to allow the claimant to produce optimal performance. Careful observations of test behavior are important in this context because much may be revealed about how the claimant is approaching the evaluation process and work-related tasks in general. A cooperative attitude may suggest that the data are useful and valid, while a disputatious attitude may show a more general approach to dealing with others in situations of conflict.

The evaluator should focus on using tests that allow for inferences regarding the claimant's current level of functioning, the underlying basis for impairments in functioning, and drawing lines of causation between these and the claimed wrongs in the plaintiff's case. Although the commonly used MMPI-2, the newly developed MMPI-RF, and PAI may allow for these uses, care should be taken in applying patient norms to the data from employment cases if the plaintiff is not a therapy patient or is not complaining of a mental disorder resulting from the alleged discrimination. The evaluator should be aware of the potential for misinterpreting an individual's behavior in a very difficult life situation as psychopathology. For example, if the claimant is contending that the employer has engaged in retaliation, it is quite likely that scales from the tests may show elevations on scales reflecting paranoid thinking, even though the claimant may actually be experiencing people conspiring to do them harm (see Foote & Goodman-Delahunty, 2005, for a more extensive discussion).

Conclusions

The *evaluation interval* is the time when the evaluator will gather all the information concerning the first four phases of the claimant's case. In the history from the claimant and collaterals and the available documents, the evaluator will collect information concerning the claimant's status before the alleged discrimination, during the discrimination, and in the interval between the end of the alleged discrimination and the time of the evaluation. At this point, the claimant's current status is assessed through the interviews and testing. This provides a snapshot of the claimant's current functioning and a benchmark for comparison to the claimant's pre-discrimination status. A thorough exploration and understanding of the claimant's current status is critical, as it serves as a basis for the evaluator to make predictions about how the claimant will fare in the months and years following the evaluation. In Chapter 6, we will review ways to process and interpret this information.

Interpretation 6

By the time the record review, client and collateral interviews, and testing are complete, the evaluator has a wealth of information about the claimant. The next task of the evaluator is to integrate these data to address the referral question. The five-phase model discussed earlier in Chapter 4 will be the evaluator's guide for this task. The evaluator must consider several issues before beginning the interpretation.

First, with a few exceptions, it is not the evaluator's job to determine whether discriminatory conduct actually occurred in contravention of any antidiscrimination laws. Although some research exists that may apply to liability issues (Foote & Goodman-Delahunty, 2005), this exploration is not a topic covered in this volume. For many reasons, the determination of liability is ultimately the domain of the trier of fact and requires considerations and information that are usually not available to the examining expert. Second, before beginning this interpretation, the evaluator should remain cognizant of her or his duty to maintain objectivity and balance in the assessment. Nowhere is this approach to the task more important than in the interpretation of the data generated in an evaluation. The evaluator should approach the data without any goal in mind other than to clearly understand the experience of the claimant in the context of the workplace situation and to apply that understanding to the legal issues implicated in the referral question. Third, as part of this commitment to balance, evaluators must open their minds to a range of outcomes. Evaluators will encounter cases in which the worker's claims have little or no basis in fact, and the evaluator is presented with a malingerer with a fabricated emotional disorder. Some claimants

BEST PRACTICE
Before beginning interpretation:

- Remember that it is not your job to determine whether discrimination conduct actually occurred; this is for the court to decide
- Maintain your objectivity
- Consider all possible outcomes

have not experienced discrimination, yet claim they have, but have not experienced any discernable emotional disorder. Other claimants will have experienced discrimination in some form, and may have fared well in spite of actual discrimination. Others will have experienced discrimination and will have developed serious emotional disturbance as a result. In some cases, after reviewing all the data, the evaluator may determine that, despite the claimant's apparently genuine belief that the alleged discrimination is the source of a host of their life's problems, in fact, some or all of the difficulties did not arise from that source but from a cause unrelated to the alleged discriminatory conduct of the employer.

In the process of sorting through the mountain of data generated by a comprehensive evaluation, the legal principle of *relevance* is critical one (Gagliardi & Miller, 2008). As embodied in Federal Rule of Evidence 401, "'Relevant evidence' means evidence having any tendency to make the existence of any fact that is of consequence to the determination of the action more probable or less probable than it would be without the evidence." This means that in the course of reviewing the information in the case, the evaluator should focus on the information that sheds light upon the legal issue in the case, particulary factors pertaining to damages.

The evaluation model we use incorporates a requirement for balance that other models may lack. This approach forces the evaluator to entertain alternative explanations for the data throughout the assessment process (Goodman-Delahunty & Foote, 2009). In considering all the other things going on in the claimant's life and in assessing the presence of preexisting and ongoing mental disorders, the evaluator may have greater assurance that the final conclusions of the evaluation take into account both information favorable to the plaintiff's case, and data that would favor the defendant's perspective.

In this section, we will discuss how the five-stage model may be applied to data interpretation in employment discrimination cases. We review each of the five stages, and discuss how to identify and integrate the important data from those separate time intervals. The final section of this chapter will focus on assimilating the data to inform relevant legal conclusions. Table 6.1 summarizes the issues addressed in this chapter.

Application of the five-stage model permits the evaluating expert to assess both causation and the nature and scope of injuries and damages, as these are separate legal issues (Goodman-Delahunty & Foote, 1995). The emphasis as we examine each of first three of the five phases is on causation. It is only when we examine the worker at the time of the assessment or in the interval between the assessment and the trial that the damages may be fully assessed.

Stage One: Status of the Plaintiff the "Day Before" the Alleged Discrimination

The first job of the evaluator is to determine the claimant's status prior to the onset of the alleged discrimination. Review of the medical, vocational, and mental health records will provide an idea of the "trajectory" of the claimant's life. The trajectory is the direction and quality of the claimant's life as determined by aggregating these sources. This will be augmented by the data from interviews with the claimant and collateral parties.

One problem in assessing the status of the worker before the onset of the alleged discrimination centers on the possibility that a retrospective evaluation of their status may be less reliable. This concern was illustrated in a small sample in which retrospective assessments of individuals who were not in litigation were compared with those of a group in litigation (Williams, Lees-Haley, & Djanogly, 1999). Both groups were asked to estimate their well-being at a point in time a number of years before the date of the interview, and to rate themselves on a number of dimensions. Then they estimated their status on the interview date. The non-litigation group rated their well-being at the earlier time point in

Table 6.1 Five-Stage Model of Legal Causation to Determine Damages for Psychological Injuries

Stage	Time period	Causation issue	Injury	Legal damages
I	Day before	• Preexisting conditions: –Continuous –For later exacerbation Vulnerability	• Baseline for day before • Functioning	Preexisting conditions non-compensable
II	During discrimination	• Rule-outs: –Work stress –Family problems –Financial Illness	• Injury onset • Natural history of discrimination-caused disorders • Co-morbidity	• Temporary damages that improved before trial, and "garden variety damages"
III	Following discrimination	• Rule-outs: –Financial changes not caused by discrimination –Family problems, etc. –Litigation stress	• Onset of injuries caused by reprisal • Onset of fallout of wrongful discharge	• Temporary damages that improved before trial, and "garden variety damages"
IV	Assessment date/trial interval	• Assessment of current symptoms/problems of claimant: –Emotional –Cognitive –Interpersonal –Work status • Rule out malingering/exaggeration • From perspective of causation: –Determine what is attributable to discrimination. Include exacerbation of pre-existing conditions –What is left is injury attributable to discrimination.	• Functional analysis (see flow chart) • Consequences of discrimination: –Physical –Social –Psychological –Workplace • Hedonic damages	• Legally compensable damages • Loss of function (I minus IV)

Table 6.1 Five-Stage Model of Legal Causation to Determine Damages for Psychological Injuries (*Continued*)

Stage	Time period	Causation issue	Injury	Legal damages
V	Future		• Identify future needs for treatment • Project loss of work capacity in ensuing years	**Pecuniary** • Cost of future treatment • Lost future income based on impaired work capacity **Non-pecuniary** • Future pain and suffering • Projected loss of function over time: –Physical –Social –Psychological –Workplace • Probability of improvement or deterioration?

about the same range as their current status, a generally mid-range score. In contrast, the litigation group rated their well-being at the earlier date as much better than did the non-litigation group, and, unsurprisingly, their current status as much poorer. This outcome suggested that, for those in litigation, hindsight bias may influence retrospective self-reports of well-being in a way that inflates that worker's rating of well-being on the "day before," exaggerating the degree of loss when that rating is compared to the worker's current status. This unconscious tendency is one reason why documentary data are so vital at this stage of the analysis. Whereas a claimant may characterize his or her status the day before alleged discrimination as "happy-go-lucky," medical records may show treatment for depression, vocational

BEWARE Hindsight bias may cause the claimant to exaggerate his or her sense of well-being before the alleged discrimination, as well as the degree of loss after. Collateral interviews can help present a more balanced view of the discriminatory event.

records may demonstrate functional deficits in the workplace, and neighbors may indicate that the worker appeared constantly unhappy.

To overcome the limitations of reliance on self-reports which may be biased by hindsight, collateral interviews are critical sources of information. Because the plaintiff will often nominate collateral parties for the evaluator to interview, care must be exercised to scrutinize potential biases of the parties in favor of the plaintiff, or perceptions that what happened to the claimant was morally wrong, leading to a desire to support the claimant as much as possible. Subtler biases may also be at work. The large body of research on memory indicates that it is selective and prone to modification based upon present knowledge and concerns (e.g., Loftus, Feldman, & Dashiell, 1995). Other research has raised concerns about the accuracy of retrospective accounts from collateral witnesses. One neuropsychologist hypothesized: "Where relatives have already judged the patient's current personality adjustment to be extremely poor, they are likely to underestimate pre-morbid levels of personality pathology (e.g., "Well, compared to how difficult he is now, Henry was an angel before the car wreck!") (Sweet, 1999, p. 69). As applied to the discrimination context, information that the plaintiff has experienced workplace harassment or retaliation may cause a friend or family member to view the claimant's current status as more impaired, and the claimant's prior status as better than it was. The point is that data from collateral sources must be processed with the same degree of scrutiny as any other self-report data.

BEST PRACTICE

Be sure to conduct collateral interviews in order to get a clearer picture of the effect the alleged discrimination had on the claimant. Third parties can be biased, however, so it is important to process collateral data with the same scrutiny as you did the claimant's self-report.

Test data may assist in assessing the level of a claimant's "day before" functioning. If cognitive measures are used in the assessment, it is critical to determine the worker's level of functioning before the alleged discrimination. One well-respected method for analyzing pre-injury intellectual status was developed by neuropsychologists at the University of Oklahoma in the form of the OPIE, the Oklahoma Pre-morbid Intelligence Estimate (Krull, Scott, & Scherer, 1995). Using a combination of weighted current test scores and demographic variables, this methodology has proven to be reliable in determining the intellectual functioning of the person prior to the events that might reasonably produce changes in cognitive function (Langeluddecke & Lucas, 2004; Schoenberg et al., 2003). Although this measure was designed and validated with brain injuries, which often leave some functions such as vocabulary intact, it also provides an estimate of functioning prior to emotionally disabling events. In this application, there may be concern that verbal functions are more vulnerable to emotional disorders, so this measure may underestimate the pre-morbid functioning of the plaintiff in a discrimination case.

With respect to personality assessment, research has indicated that personality traits tend to be stable, even in the context of trauma or other untoward events (Millon & Davis, 1996). For example, if the MMPI-2, PAI, or MCMI-III shows evidence of narcissistic or hysteroid traits, it is likely that some of those traits were manifest on the "day before." If the evaluator finds evidence of sufficient criteria to diagnose a personality disorder, this may also point to a stable personality pattern. In the normal scope of discrimination litigation, a two- to three-year span may pass from the time of the alleged discrimination to the time of the evaluation by the psychologist. According to the DSM-IV (American Psychiatric Association, 2000), the time span for development of a personality disorder is nominally five years, and the clock starts after the person turns 18. This timeframe, along with the fact that personality disorders are generally not produced by discrimination or other trauma, indicates that, if a personality disorder is assessed, it was probably present prior to the alleged workplace discrimination.

The presence of a preexisting personality disorder may have significant impacts upon the reactions of the individual to workplace events. In some cases, the personality disorder may have played a role in preexisting work-related problems, as is discussed in more detail in the next section. Second, similar to personality traits, a personality disorder may predispose an individual to react

INFO

If assessment reveals the claimant has a personality disorder, it is likely that the disorder was present before the alleged discrimination occurred.

to workplace events in a more extreme manner. For example, someone with a borderline personality disorder may be thrown into a severe paranoid reaction if he experiences harassment or adversity in the workplace. Or, a person with paranoid features may react to reprisal with a severe, almost psychotic response. Third, a personality disorder may interfere with an individual's mobilizing social support. For example, a person with an avoidant or schizoid pattern may have few friends who can be counted on for counsel or help during a work-related crisis.

By the end of the data interpretation task for the first phase, the evaluator should have a clear idea of several aspects of the claimant's functioning. The first is the presence of any ongoing mental disorder. This may be evident in the description of the worker's symptoms or, even better, a diagnosis by a physician or mental health professional.

Second, the evaluator must determine the presence of impairments that may have existed on the "day before." Although the evaluation of impairments occurs in the context of the diagnostic process, the presence of a psychiatric diagnosis does not necessarily imply that the person suffered impairments in functioning. For example, depression often produces impairments in work functioning in the form of increased absences and lower productivity (Wang et al., 2004). However, because individuals differ significantly in their reactions to depression, a given person may carry a depressive disorder diagnosis but still function well in most aspects of her life in work, family, and community situations. In contrast, she may not have a clearly diagnosed condition, but still have some major problems in functioning evident in repeated work-related problems, repeatedly failing relationships, or ongoing difficulties in maintaining housing.

Third, the evaluator should be aware of the presence of one or more vulnerabilities to the development of emotional problems.

In addition to the presence of an emotional disorder, a history of various traumas and losses may make the individual more vulnerable to the impact of a stressor (Beichtman et al., 1992; Dhaliwal et al., 1996; Jumper, 1995; Neumann et al., 1996; Paolucci, Genuis, & Violato, 2001; Polusny & Follette, 1995). Considerable research indicates that the experience of prior trauma can increase the probability that an individual will suffer later harassment and other negative and exploitative events (Arata, 2000; Briere & Runtz, 1987; Dansky et al., 1996; Roesler & McKenzie, 1994). In addition, some research (Cherry, 1984) suggests that when workers have a number of demands on their time and energy, the addition of harassment or discrimination may be much more difficult to tolerate.

This analysis is critical in providing the basis for later assessment of damages. A thorough knowledge of the worker's functioning before the alleged discrimination is the qualitative and quantitative basis for later subtraction of the claimant's level of functioning at the time of assessment (Stage 4). The extent to which the evaluator is able to establish this baseline accurately will determine the extent to which the final analysis will be helpful to the judge and jury.

Stage Two: Status of the Plaintiff During the Alleged Discrimination

Discriminatory events vary in duration as well as intensity. In some cases, particularly hostile workplace environment or harassment cases, the discrimination may occur on only one occasion or on several occasions over a short time. Other sorts of discrimination, such as discrimination based on disparate salary or conditions of employment, may occur over a longer period. In either case, other events are likely to occur in a time proximate to the events upon which litigation is focused.

In interpreting the influence of events that occur during the alleged discrimination, the evaluator may find it helpful to compile a chronology. A comprehensive sequence of events facilitates the determination of cause-and-effect relationships. This timeline may be assembled from the history gathered from the client in the

BEST PRACTICE
It can be helpful to construct a timeline of events that occurred during the alleged discrimination. It should include, not only the events that occurred on the job, but off-the-job events as well.

interview, from collateral interviews, and from documentary sources such as personnel and medical records. If discrete off-the-job events occurred, such as a domestic violence incident or automobile accident, police records may help document the timing of those events. If the claimant was in treatment at the time of the alleged discrimination, therapy records may capture accounts of both discrimination-related stressors as well as those arising from family or other sources.

As noted in Chapter 3, one primary impact of employment discrimination is on the worker's ability to continue to function in the workplace. Interview, documentary, and collateral information should focus on his or her work-related functioning. Signs of erosion to work commitment such as increased sick leave, days without pay, or tardiness may be evidence of the impact of discrimination.

Although the temporal proximity of events and reactions is often a strong clue to causation, such obvious connections are not always evident. One factor clouding these connections is that individuals are often capable of tolerating significant distress before showing evidence of emotional breakdown (Buchanan & Fitzgerald, 2008). While the claimant's subjective emotional status may be deteriorating, an observer may believe that he is holding up well, and showing no obvious signs of distress. It may only be after a protracted period or after a series of discriminatory events that the worker begins to show the signs of strain and becomes objectively symptomatic. Or, as in the case of one study (Buchanan & Fitzgerald, 2008), when the worker experiences a combination of racial and sexual discrimination, the worker is more likely to reach a "tipping point" at which symptoms become overwhelming.

In the analysis of the impact of an employer's alleged discriminatory acts, it is often difficult to distinguish the things that are a result of the behavior of the worker from those that are consequences of the employer's actions. In some cases, the analysis becomes complex. For example, a worker who believes he is the target of racial discrimination may become depressed and upset about what he perceives as unfair treatment. Because of this depression, he may start taking sick days and showing lackluster performance when he is on the job. If his supervisor takes note of this negative change in her subordinate's work performance and first counsels the worker, then reprimands him when his performance worsens, the natural consequences of the worker's behavior may result in real-world consequences that have the impact of increasing the severity of the employee's emotional reactions. If the supervisor's actions were perceived by the employee to be punitive and excessive in relation to the worker's work problems, the supervisor's actions may be a basis for a retaliation or reprisal claim by the worker. In this case, sorting out cause and effect may be quite difficult.

At the end of the analysis of the claimant "during the discrimination," the evaluator should have a clear idea of a number of aspects of the case. First, the evaluator should be able to draw a clear timeline of alleged discriminatory acts on the part of the employer or coworkers. Second, the evaluator should have examined out-of-work events, such as family problems or health issues, which may themselves prove troublesome to the worker. Third, the evaluator should know what on-the-job stressors existed during that interval—cutbacks, transfers, supervisory changes, etc., which may cause stress in the workplace. Fourth, the evaluator should have a clear idea about which symptoms the worker claims to have developed as a result of the alleged discrimination. Fifth, the evaluator should have learned whether the worker sought some sort of support or mental health treatment for these problems.

In the analysis of the discrimination interval, the evaluator may observe injuries or problems that became apparent, but resolved by the end of this interval. For example, a worker may have difficulty adjusting to changes in the workplace caused by a hostile work environment. However, the hostile work environment may have stopped either as a result of the worker's complaint or a cause extraneous to her activities. Once the hostile work environment stops, the worker may return to normal functioning. If this is the case, the worker has experienced "pain and suffering," but may

INFO

At the end of the assessment of the claimant during the time of the alleged discrimination, you should be have a clear idea of the following:

- The timeline of events
- Any off-the-job events that may have served as risk factors
- Any on-the-job stressors
- The symptoms caused by the discrimination
- Whether or not the claimant sought help or support for these symptoms

have sustained no permanent damages. The evaluator should take note of these temporary damages, as these may be compensable.

Stage Three: Status of the Plaintiff Following the Alleged Discrimination

Forensic evaluations are rarely sought within a few weeks or months following the end of the alleged discrimination; often several years have passed before the evaluation occurs. In this interval, a number of post-discrimination events will have occurred, and many of those events can affect a claimant in a way that alters the outcome of the forensic evaluation.

Exposure to workplace discrimination may leave a claimant in one of several different circumstances. First, he may be fired by the employer, and part or all of the discrimination case may focus on wrongful discharge or some other civil rights claim related to involuntary departure from the workplace. Recall that hiring and firing are regarded as critical actions in employment law. Non-hire and discharge as a result of discrimination are a basis for a civil rights case. In some cases, firing may be a form of retaliation by the employer following some action of the worker to initiate a legally protected activity, such as whistle-blowing, making a complaint about perceived discrimination, or filing a lawsuit.

The second alternative is that the worker left the workplace for reasons unrelated to the civil rights claim. In our experience, this is rare in employment discrimination cases. In a fluctuating economy, the employer may find it necessary to reduce the workforce to conserve funds. Even in situations in which the employer submits that the layoff of the worker was totally unrelated to any of the worker's protected activities, the worker may claim that those ostensible business-related rationales are only *a pretext* for retaliation.

Third, the worker may quit the job, claiming that involuntary quitting is the only course of action she could take because the job situation had deteriorated to such an extent that she had no other option. This is called "constructive discharge" because the worker's actions may be *construed as a discharge* when the worker is exposed to "working conditions so difficult that a reasonable person in the employee's position would feel compelled to resign" (*Rupp v. Purolator Courier Corp.,* 1994). When the claimant is making a case of constructive discharge, the evaluator may be required to determine the contemporaneous working conditions both from the subjective perspective of the claimant, and, as much as possible, the objective circumstances, as reflected in employment documents and the testimony of coworkers and supervisors.

In addition to involuntary discharge, the worker may experience other forms of retaliation. For example, one worker was moved from a corner office to one that was previously a broom closet. Another who worked in a sales position and was paid on commission was given different hours, which did not allow him to connect with as many potential customers as he had prior to the alleged retaliation.

In many cases, when retaliation occurs, it produces emotional reactions akin to those arising when an individual feels attacked by others, and becomes very distrustful of those around him. This reaction bears a close resemblance to paranoid symptomology, the difference being that, in the former case, the employer really wishes bad things for the worker. When analyzing employment discrimination data, it is critical to determine the presence of paranoid traits prior to the onset of the alleged retaliation, and whether those traits were present in other aspects of the claimant's life. For example, a chronically paranoid person is unjustifiably suspicious of others, will have been unable to sustain good long-term relationships, will harbor chronic resentment and grudges, and is likely to be excessively jealous in her intimate relationships. In contrast, the worker experiencing reprisal is more likely to recognize that friends are still trustworthy, and that his intimates are still faithful.

Another consideration in evaluating a claimant as part of a legal action is the impact of the legal action itself upon the claimant (see discussion of litigation stress in Chapter 3). One commentator (Weissman, 1991) noted that being a plaintiff in litigation is inherently stressful. Particularly in workplace litigation, plaintiffs may feel like they, rather than the defendants, are on trial (Streseman, 1995). Frequent meetings with their lawyers, confrontational depositions, taxing mediation sessions, and preparation for trial can all take their toll on plaintiffs. This is especially the case when the plaintiff claims that the alleged discrimination was traumatic in some way. Repeated confrontation with the events surrounding the alleged discrimination can retraumatize her, or delay healing from those events. In addition, the process of litigation and the usual waiver of psychotherapist-patient privilege that occurs during this process may weaken or nullify the positive impact of psychotherapy if the person is seeing a mental health practitioner.

Stage Four: Status of the Plaintiff on the Day of the Assessment

In the assessment, the goal of the evaluator is to develop a clear idea of two critical aspects of the civil rights case: causation and damages. By the end of the first three stages, alternative sources of the claimant's distress should be identified, and the nature of the damages that now exist should be clear. A critical part of the data interpretation process is developing an understanding of the impairments of functioning caused by the alleged discrimination. This determination is a result of a number of different decisions made by the evaluator in the course of the data analysis (see Figure 6.1).

First, in addition to evaluating causation issues, the evaluator needs to develop a clear picture of the symptoms and other

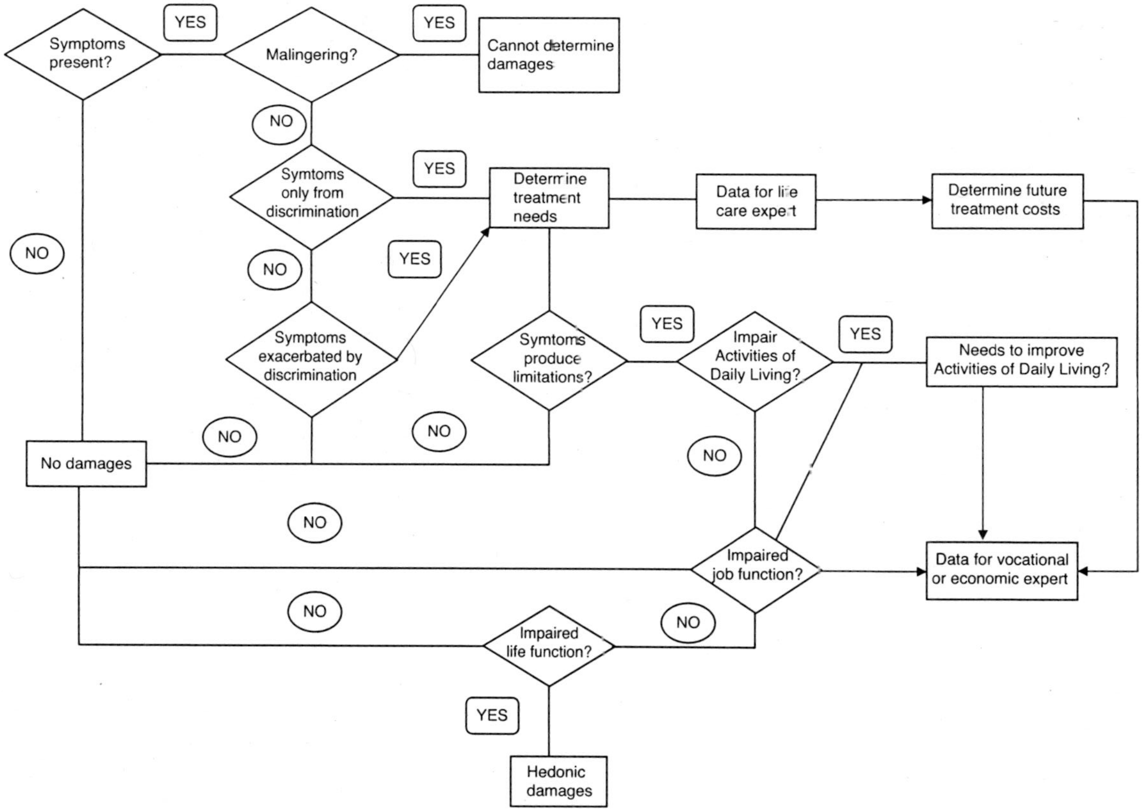

Figure 6.1 Flow Chart for Determining Damages in Phase V

emotional problems currently revealed by the plaintiff. The data from the testing will provide a lead for this process, in that the personality assessment should delineate the presence of one or more emotional disorders. In addition, in the interview the claimant will have described his or her current symptoms and problems. Collateral interviewees will provide information from observers.

Although the diagnostic process may produce sufficient symptoms or clusters of symptoms to conjoin with the DSM-IV diagnostic schema, providing a diagnosis is not essential, or even advisable. This is for several reasons. First, the provision of a diagnosis does not necessarily supply causation. Even though some diagnoses, such as PTSD, do require certain prerequisites, in the particular discrimination case, the causation may not be the basis for the lawsuit. Second, provision of a diagnosis does not determine the limitations produced by that condition (see below). Third, diagnoses can often confuse or distract a jury. Unlike insurance systems, the justice system does not revolve around diagnosis. However, lawyers on both sides of the case will often seize upon a diagnosis and make much more or less of it than would a mental health professional.

Second, the evaluator must make a determination about whether the symptom or problem is a result of the alleged discrimination. If it was caused by the alleged discrimination, then the assessment moves on to a more fine-grained analysis. If the symptom or problem was not a direct result of the alleged discrimination, then the question still remains as to whether the claimant had a preexisting condition that was exacerbated by the alleged discrimination. If it was not, then that symptom is eliminated as a basis for damages in the case. If it was, then the process moves to a determination of impairment.

BEWARE
Even if symptoms are present during assessment, you should avoid diagnosing the claimant with a disorder. Provision of a diagnosis does not prove causation of harm and can confuse and distract a jury.

A symptom becomes relevant when it interferes with one or more relevant life activities. A worker may have a mental disorder or emotional problem that does not produce impairment in relevant life activities. For example, an obsessive-compulsive person might function quite well in a detail-oriented occupation such as auditor, and may have structured her life in such as way that the symptoms do not cause other problems.

BEST PRACTICE

When assessing damages, be sure to examine the impact of the claimant's symptoms on his activities of daily living (ADL)—the routine daily activities that must be accomplished in order to function in the world such as taking care of personal hygiene, completing household chores, and paying bills.

To begin in this assessment of damages, examine the impact of the symptom on activities of daily living (ADL). These are routine daily activities that an individual must accomplish in order to function in the world. Although a number of lists of ADL have been published, Vore (2005) provides a list that includes the following: personal hygiene; household chores; reading activities; use of electronic equipment; social activities; family responsibilities; community/religious activities; exercise regimen; vacations; sleep/wake cycle; eating habits, with any weight gain or loss; recreational activities, especially as restricted or changed; driving activities; financial management; doctor's visits; work or work-related activities; and academic pursuits. If a claimant is unable to perform one or more as a result of symptoms or problems caused by the alleged discrimination, then the person has usually suffered a serious disability.

The next decision point is a determination of whether the impairment in one or more ADL also interferes with functioning in the workplace. For example, an impairment of social functioning may interfere with relationships both with family and with coworkers. If the ADL impairment also interferes with work function, then proceed to assess his work functioning.

Even if ADL do not show impairment from the discrimination-caused symptoms, the claimant may still experience work-related dysfunction as a result of those symptoms. In this case, the evaluator should look at several areas of functioning to determine if work-related impairments exist. First, examine whether the worker makes it into the workplace at all. As noted in Chapter 3, experiences of workplace harassment and strain often cause individuals to withdraw from work, avoid going to work, or to evidence increased absenteeism (Darr & Johns, 2008; Willness, Steel, & Lee, 2007). In addition, some disorders, particularly depression and sleep disturbances, cause significant absenteeism from work.

Even if the worker is able to report to work, sleep problems may cause frequent tardiness, a cause for reasonable discipline from an employer. Impaired workers who get to work on time may still experience impairments of attention and concentration that slow their work and result in mistakes. Depression or other conditions may likewise slow their work, and if the job has requirements for high levels of production, impairments of pace may be a problem. Increased suspiciousness or anger may interfere with social relationships on the job. The evaluator should be alert for any of these impairments of work function observed by the claimant, coworkers, or other collaterals.

If the worker does not have significant impairment of ADL and of work-related functioning, there still may be compensable damages related to discrimination. In this case, does the impairment affect an activity that impacts the claimant's "quality of life"? If so, then this impairment may be a basis for hedonic damages. These are compensable damages to the ability of the claimant to enjoy aspects of her life that she did before. For example, a worker may have developed agoraphobia as a result of alleged discrimination. If that worker used to enjoy vacations and camping and no longer does either of those things as a result of the disorder, then the worker may claim hedonic damages.

What the Stage 4 Interpretation Process Should Yield

By the time the interpretation process is complete, the evaluator should have several aspects of the case clearly in mind. This does not imply that some aspects of the case may not still remain a mystery. In almost every case, especially employment cases, the evidence is equivocal: the female worker says that her employer propositioned her; the Native American employee claims that her coworker used a racial slur; a male employee of a beauty salon claims that his female boss did not send him customers because she did not like men. In each of these cases, it is neither within the evaluator's power, nor is it the evaluator's job, to determine if the discrimination that was alleged actually occurred. If the evaluation yielded evidence of psychological impairments that would reasonably result from the alleged discrimination, the evaluator is in no position to say that, just because these injuries are not uncommon in employment cases, the discrimination probably occurred, which is ascribing to the *post hoc, ergo propter hoc* fallacy (see Pope, 2009). The most that the evaluator may conclude is that if the finder of fact determines that the discrimination occurred, then these reactions would be reasonable in that circumstance and would be reasonably assumed to be caused by the discrimination. If the finder of fact determines that no discrimination occurred, then the evaluator should be prepared to explore reasons that these symptoms may have appeared absent that discrimination. An assessment of malingering should be a routine part of the evaluation.

Adherence to DSM-IV guidelines

As noted earlier, the evaluator need not provide a diagnosis in order to determine the presence of damages in a discrimination case, and, in some cases, the provision of a diagnosis may generate confusion. However, when a diagnosis is used, the evaluator should take into account these considerations. In many countries around the world, the *International Classification of Diseases, Injuries, and Causes of Death,* 10th rev. (ICD-10-CM: World Health Organization, 2007) is used for diagnoses. In North America, the *Diagnostic and Statistical Manual of Mental Disorders* (DSM) is used. In interpreting any symptoms displayed by or reported by the plaintiff, the consulting expert should adhere to the approach set forth in the *Diagnostic and Statistical Manual–IV* (American Psychiatric Association, 2000).

Notably, diagnostic criteria for PTSD vary between the DSM-IV and the ICD-10-CM. Given that this is a common diagnosis in civil claims, it is important to review the common categories that overlap with PTSD, such as acute stress disorder.

Malingering and Exaggeration

Malingering is defined as conscious fabrication or gross exaggeration of the symptoms experienced (Rogers, 1997). Three forms of malingering have been distinguished by researchers:

- Pure malingering—complete fabrication of symptoms, along with the possible fabrication of traumatic experiences
- Partial malingering—gross exaggeration of existing symptoms or reporting of remitted symptoms as ongoing, along with the possible exaggeration of aversive experiences
- False imputation—intentional and false attribution of symptoms to a traumatic event (Resnick, 1997)

Although research support for the notion of compensation neuroses (neurotic symptoms fabricated as a basis for monetary compensation) is scant, many lawyers and judges subscribe to the view that a key element that influences the recovery of compensatory damages is plaintiffs' propensity to exaggerate their emotional distress. Accordingly, some commentators (e.g., Binder and Rohling, 1996) assert that the plaintiffs who receive higher awards are those who did not exaggerate, and whose testimony about the impact of the discrimination on the plaintiff's life was corroborated by other lay witnesses. Thus, the evaluating expert who conducts a mental health assessment must determine whether the plaintiff is malingering or faking the symptoms. Multiple measures, rather than reliance on a single test for this purpose, are recommended (Heilbrun, Rogers, & Otto, 2002).

In part, this assessment will turn on the response style of the plaintiff or the test-taking attitude displayed by the plaintiff during the evaluation. Four response styles were distinguished by Heilbrun (2001): (1) reliable, honest; (b) malingering in the form of exaggeration to claim symptoms are worse than they are ("fake bad"); (c) defensive

BEST PRACTICE

It is your job as the evaluator to determine whether or not the plaintiff is malingering or faking or exaggerating symptoms.

to the point that symptoms experienced are denied or minimized ("fake good"); (d) irrelevant, not engaged. Subsequently, Heilbrun and colleagues added two more response styles (Heilbrun, Warren, & Picarello, 2003, p. 71): (e) uncooperative, in which the individual responds minimally or not at all to assessment questions; and (f) impaired, in which the individual experiences communication deficits that may be the result of the young age of the plaintiff, or of thought and speech disorganization, intellectual deficits, or memory problems.

Although some commonly applied psychological tests like the MMPI, contain subscales, such as the L, F, and K scales, that may serve as indicators of malingering, some research has created extensive doubts about the validity of these measures (e.g., Nicholson & Martelli, 2006). Subsequent studies have tended to confirm their validity, however (e.g., Bianchini et al., 2008; Tsuchima & Tsuchima, 2009). The Structured Interview of Reported Symptoms (Rogers, 1992) is helpful in detecting malingering faking of psychotic symptoms.

If malingering did not occur, then you may find other sources of the problems. Absent alternative sources, you must be prepared to say that the evaluation left some questions unanswered, and that, even after bringing to bear all the tools in the psychologist's toolbox, you cannot make a determination.

Critical Findings

When the evaluator can make a determination, then three things should be known. First, the expert should have a clear understanding of the symptoms and problems of the claimant. Second, the expert should know and understand the causation of those symptoms. Third, the expert should be able to describe the functional impairments produced by those symptoms, both in the workplace and in other aspects of the worker's life.

Legally compensable damages will fall into four general realms. The first is at the level of physical problems manifested by the worker. As indicated in Chapter 3, the claimant may develop psychophysiological reactions, such as ulcers, or may have a stress-related increase in an existing disorder, such as high blood pressure.

INFO

Legally compensable damages can fall into one or more of the following categories:

1. Physical problems
2. Impairments in social functioning
3. Psychological problems
4. Work-specific symptoms

Second, the worker may experience impairments in his social functioning. Social avoidance, increased anger, or paranoid thinking can all be consequences of discrimination, and may be manifested in both work and social settings. Psychological reactions, such as depression, anxiety, and other conditions, can interfere with a host of functions, including attention and concentration, persistence in work tasks, keeping a consistent and adequate pace of work, and other aspects critical to functioning in the workplace. Finally, there may be some problems or symptoms that are only shown in the workplace, and, in some cases, in a particular workplace. For example, if the worker was humiliated by a supervisor in a context of a racially hostile work environment, she may have difficulty returning to that workplace. Or, a worker may also have impairments that are not especially problematical in some out-of-work contexts such as occasional angry outbursts, but in his role as a clergyman, he may have serious difficulty.

As a final step, functional limitations are examined to provide the court and other experts with enough specific information to determine legal damages. In many cases, counsel may also employ vocational experts and economists to translate functional limitations into dollar damages. The vocational expert takes the vocational history and aptitude data and combines that with the functional limitations generated by her work to determine which jobs the claimant can and cannot do. This information, in turn, is translated into lost future earnings and other future pecuniary damages by the economist. Vocational experts and economists differ in the form of information that they prefer, and direct consultation with the other experts may be necessary in order to be able to provide useful information for the estimation of pecuniary damages.

Information concerning damages is of four general types. In the first group are the factors that relate to functioning in the workplace. These are translated into particular impaired work functions. If the evaluator can be specific about the number of work days, weeks or months that the worker has lost because of the impairment, it will make later analysis easier.

The second group relates to impaired ADL. For example, severe depression may prevent a woman from leaving her house to shop for groceries, or may impair her ability to keep track of a checking account. If the woman requires assistance in ADL, this loss may yield pecuniary damages.

Third, the claimant may have suffered impairments in other life functions. These may fall under hedonic damages. While loss of "pleasure in life" may not translate directly into monetary damages, counsel can, in argument, advise the jury of the value that these losses may be accorded, and juries may be given an instruction to compute hedonic damages.

Fourth, the worker may experience emotional distress and discomfort that constitute pain and suffering damages. Although the law considers these to be "non-pecuniary" damages, the court will consider them compensable to an extent judged by the judge or jury. It is not the evaluator's job to assign a dollar value to, say, a sleep disorder. Rather, it is the evaluator's role to describe these continuing unpleasant experiences in terms that the judge and jury can understand and in such a way that the lawyers can argue about their value. All these determinations will provide sufficient information for the Stage Five analysis.

Stage Five: Status of the Plaintiff in the Future

At the end of Stage Four, the evaluator should have a clear idea of the current level of functioning of the claimant. At this point, in some cases, the evaluator may be asked to project future damages for that person. Most obvious among these predictable expenses caused by the discrimination are future treatment costs. For example, a severely depressed claimant may require regular psychiatric treatment with antidepressants for the next five years. A claimant with post-traumatic symptoms may require a course of treatment to reduce avoidance and re-experiencing symptoms (e.g., Zayfert et al., 2005). The evaluator should take care to avoid open-ended conclusions such as, "If things remain as they are, the complainant will require therapy for an undetermined amount of time," but should specify the likely period that treatment is required: for example, "for the next five years." A severely impaired person may require a case manager to provide assistance for daily tasks such as house cleaning, shopping, or doing household or auto repairs. In addition the claimant may be required to refrain from working for a finite period. For example, if the worker was so impaired that treatment was necessary before returning to work, this lost future work period would constitute a basis for pecuniary damages. The claimant may be unable to work full-time for some period, or may need a period of "work hardening" prior to returning to full-time employment. In either case, pecuniary damages would be computed on the basis of these changes in work capacity.

In addition, the worker may continue to suffer from non-pecuniary damages in the form of continuing pain and suffering. While placing a value on these negative experiences is part of the lawyer's job, the expert may be able to provide information about the nature and degree of suffering that the worker may experience in coming years. In some contexts, traumatic reactions may continue even after the worker leaves the workplace.

Implicit in all these future projections is a question about whether the individual's condition is projected to improve or to deteriorate. In many cases, improvement is expected because of the natural history of some mental disorders, such as PTSD, which many times shows significant spontaneous recovery (Kessler et al., 1995). However, if a condition is expected to

BEST PRACTICE

When asked to speak to future damages, take care to provide specific and detailed conclusions. For example, specify the period of time the claimant may need treatment (if treatment is needed).

increase in severity over time, then those damages would be expected to generate increasing mental health costs over coming years.

Conclusions

At the completion of the evaluation, the job of determining causation and damages is the focus of the evaluator's work. The process of determining causation is necessarily primary, since the emotional reactions that were not attributable to the alleged workplace discrimination do not figure further into the evaluation equation. It is only the reactions that the evaluator can, within a reasonable probability, attribute to the workplace discrimination that will be considered as a basis for functional limitations and compensable damages.

The second job is to take the diagnosable mental impairments and emotional reactions and translate them into functional impairment. That translation is not easy, and it requires the evaluator to identify particular life or work functions that the worker can no longer do, or must do with some degree of disability. Then those must be placed into the worker's particular work context, most often the job that was done at the time of the alleged discrimination. Also, the worker may have suffered impairments that affect only non-work functions, such as home and leisure activities. These impairments and problems may fall into the category of hedonic damages and pain and suffering, which may also be a basis for monetary damages. Finally, the evaluator will consider the costs of future treatment, both psychotherapeutic and psychotropic.

Once the data analysis and compilation are completed, preparation of a written report can commence.

7 Report Writing and Expert Testimony

Psychological evaluation reports in employment discrimination cases are governed by two Federal Rules of Civil Procedure (2007). The first rule applies to reports in the context of disclosures of expert testimony prior to trial (Mueller & Kirkpatrick, 2007). Federal Rule of Civil Procedure 26(a) (2), Disclosure of Expert Testimony, contains provisions regarding the disclosure and discovery of expert reports. Well in advance of the trial date, the plaintiff in the case, through his or her legal counsel, is obliged to provide information to the defendant and to the court concerning expert evidence that will be proffered in court. This disclosure is part of the discovery process, which will allow the defendant to thoroughly examine the plaintiff and to pursue further discovery to rebut the plaintiff's claims and bolster their defense case. This rule requires the plaintiff to identify the expert by name and to supply a written copy of the expert's report. This report must be prepared and signed by the expert witness and must contain:

> (i) a complete statement of all opinions the expert will express and the basis and reasons for them; (ii) the data or other information considered by the witness in forming his opinion; (iii) any exhibits that will be used to summarize or support them; (iv) the witness's qualifications including a list of all publications authored in the previous ten years; (v) a list of all other cases in which, during the previous four years, the witness testified as an expert at trial or by deposition; and (vi) a statement of the compensation to be paid for this study and testimony in the case.

The second circumstance in which an expert report must be submitted is when an expert is hired by the defendant/employer.

This evaluation comes within the scope of Federal Rule of Evidence 35 and is related to the procedures compelling an evaluation of the plaintiff. Compelled evaluations typically arise in workplace discrimination claims when the defendant obtains the leave of the court to order an individual, usually the plaintiff, to undergo a psychological evaluation. The rule in general states:

> The court where the action is pending may order a party whose mental or physical condition—including blood group—is in controversy to submit to a physical or mental examination by a suitably licensed or certified examiner. The court has the same authority to order a party to produce for examination a person who is in custody or under its legal control.

A later section, Rule 35(b) (1), provides that a written copy of the report must be provided to the party or person examined.

- Request by the Party or Persons to be examined. The party who moved for the examination, must, on request, deliver to the requestor a copy of the examiner's report, together with like reports of all earlier examinations of the same condition. A request may be made by the party against whom the examination order was issued or by the person examined.
- Contents. The examiner's report must be in writing and must set out in detail the examiner's findings, including diagnoses, conclusions, and results of any tests.

However, in actual practice, even in the context of the Federal Rules, counsel for the plaintiff has much more latitude regarding the provision of a report than does counsel for the defendant. In most jurisdictions, the plaintiff's counsel may refer his or her client for a confidential forensic mental health evaluation that comes within the scope of attorney work-product. In this case, the results of the evaluation are protected from disclosure by the attorney-client privilege. If the results of the evaluation are not useful or favorable to the goals of the plaintiff in his or her legal action, counsel for the plaintiff may instruct the evaluating expert not to write a report or may ask the evaluating expert to continue to hold the evaluation confidential, and not disclose its existence or contents to anyone.

Only very rarely have U.S. courts allowed an expert who was retained by a legal counsel on behalf of a plaintiff to give evidence when that expert was not identified by counsel as a testifying expert for that party at trial. At times, opposing counsel has attempted to obtain reports or to compel the testimony of retained, but not testifying, experts (*Baki v. B. F. Diamond Const. Co.*, 1977; *Perry v. W. S. Darley & Company*, 1971; Shuman, 2005, contains a more extensive discussion). The applicable legal threshold to be met before courts will order disclosure of a consulting expert is a demonstration of "exceptional circumstances under which it is impracticable for the party seeking discovery to obtain facts or opinions in this same subject by any other means" (Mueller & Kirkpatrick, 2007; Federal Rule of Civil Procedure 26[b][4], 2007). A proposed amendment to Rule 26, scheduled to go into effect in December, 2010, will obviate discovery of draft expert reports and prohibit discovery of expert-attorney communications by extending the attorney work-product protection to any report or disclosure under Rule 26(a); namely, communications about the expert's compensation, and facts, data, or assumptions provided by the attorney and considered by the expert in forming an opinion (Beyler, 2007).

Notwithstanding the option that plaintiff's counsel can consult an evaluating expert and avoid having to call this expert to testify, the evaluating expert should nevertheless proceed in all evaluations as though trial testimony will eventually be part of the psychologist's duties. A focus on the preparation of a report to serve as a basis for in-court testimony will keep the expert attuned to the need to write clearly to produce a report and expert conclusions that will be of use to the court and the parties and can withstand cross-examination at trial.

Evaluation Report

A forensic mental health evaluation must address several goals in the context of workplace discrimination cases. These goals are common to the production of an expert report in most forensic contexts. A commendable general resource and overview of critical features in expert report preparation pertinent in forensic mental health examinations was published by Heilbrun (2001). Further guidance comes from research conducted on the content of expert reports. For example, eight common errors that experts commit in assessing impairments and disabilities were identified by Schultz and Stewart (2008):

- Focus on results of standardized tests and clinical assessments although these do not bear much on occupational issues and performance abilities and so may be unhelpful;
- Fail to distinguish impairment from disability;
- Assume a linear relationship between the impairment level and occupational disability level. The more important issue is whether the workplace context is source of trauma. In discrimination cases, these will be closely related;
- Fail to address one or more relevant occupational issues; e.g.,
    - Loss of capacity to return to former position
    - Loss of earning capacity
    - Duration of disability
    - Potential return to work date and schedule (e.g., graduated return, part-time, full-time)
    - Need to change position
    - Accommodation for disability
    - Whether the plaintiff is employable
- No comparison of disability before and after discrimination;
- No distinction made between the plaintiff's perception of disability vs. objective assessment of disability;

- Role of pain;
- Motivation of the plaintiff to recover or to return to work is not discussed.

There is no established length for an expert report, and its length will vary with the complexity of the case. Some employment discrimination cases are fairly straightforward single events. Others are extremely complex and involve multiple claims, multiple parties, and witnesses to many events over an extended period of time. The amount of detail to be reported will vary accordingly, even if the reporting on any particular aspect is concise. In most employment discrimination cases, the evaluator should anticipate that a detailed and lengthy report will be required. An emphasis on detail is vital because the evaluating expert has access to unique information based upon the interview, testing, and record review. By virtue of his or her access to information that no other expert or lay witnesses will possess, the expert is obliged to set forth the findings in a detailed manner that will facilitate later inquiry and testimony.

In many instances, high levels of detail are required because the expert may be restricted from testifying orally about issues or matters that were not fully discussed in the written report and disclosed to the court and the opposing part before the trial. This procedure and evidentiary rule forces the expert to err on the side of including more details and describing issues in more depth than will actually be the basis for testimony in order not to unduly restrict the potential for testimony at a later date in court. To avoid being constrained from presenting detailed explanatory information in court, the expert must avoid writing a report that is too short or too sketchy. This level of detail must also be in keeping with the "best evidence" rule for inclusion of information, i.e., information that is both relevant and non-prejudicial.

BEST PRACTICE
Be sure your reports are detailed and balanced. The length of your report should depend on the facts and complexity of the case.

The expert report is usually written for lay audiences. To accomplish the appropriate clarity of expression when writing the report,

BEST PRACTICE
It can be helpful to include direct quotes from the claimant in the report. Be sure to avoid paraphrasing and do not report quotes out of context.

the evaluator should imagine that the person reading the report does not necessarily understand anything about the law of employment discrimination, nor about psychology, psychological testing, or any other aspect of the psychologist's expertise. The evaluator should avoid using technical terms, or, when technical terms are required, should provide a definition or explanation that is accessible to lay readers. The expert must define each term in such a way that the average reader will be able to understand them.

Most typically, reports do not include an extensive list of scholarly references. However, if literature is cited and scholarly materials are referred to in completing the report, those resources should be noted and a list of those references added to the report.

The authors of this book believe that a useful technique is to incorporate extensive quotes in the expert report, drawing on notes made during the interview that captured the direct words and comments spoken by the examinee. This will provide the reader a sense of how the claimant communicates in his or her own words about experiences or reactions relevant to any psychological injuries. The evaluator should take care to place each of these quotations in context and to avoid using quotations in such a way as to confuse the reader or misstate the intent of the claimant in making the original statement. The evaluator should note whether any inconsistencies in recollection fall within normal expected variation.

Although the order of the information presented in the report may vary from one case to another, the report should be divided into comprehensible sections. There are three main sections in a report: (a) preliminary details regarding

BEST PRACTICE
Divide the report into the following sections:

1. preliminary details
2. core information
3. summary and conclusions

the evaluation; (b) the core information forming the basis of the assessment upon which the expert opinion is based; and (c) the summary and conclusions of the expert. The report must provide clear recommendations about possible treatment and return-to-work options.

Preliminary Information Regarding the Evaluation

At the outset, the first section of identification alerts the reader as to who was examined, and usually includes the person's name and birth date. Section two itemizes the test procedures employed in conducting the evaluation by listing dates of all formal tests administered, the titles of all documents reviewed, names of all persons with whom collateral interviews were conducted, and the dates and duration of all interviews. The third section on the referral states who provided the referral and specifies the essential referral questions. These may be quoted directly from a letter from the referring counsel. In section four, a summary is provided of the informed-consent procedures employed in the course of the evaluation. Section five includes details of behavioral observations by the evaluator and the evaluator's impressions of mental status of the evaluee at the time of the evaluation interview. These topics may comprise separate sections if either of the subsections is lengthy. However, they often jointly provide a picture of the complainant for the reader that allows the reader to construct a mental picture of the examinee's appearance and response to the evaluator in the course of the interview. A standard mental status description will include orientation and nature of speech to provide a snapshot of the claimant's presentation as a point of comparison for later evaluators.

History of the Claimant

The major body of the report will consist of the claimant's history, which may be divided into subsections. The history will usually be presented chronologically, starting with the childhood of the claimant, including developmental features, any history of child abuse,

BEST PRACTICE

It is best to provide a separate, detailed section on the claimant's employment history rather than integrate this information into the personal history section of the report.

and an educational chronology from childhood through later educational experiences. This section should also address any history of family problems known to the plaintiff, such as a history of depression or other mental disorders. A section on the evaluee's employment history should probably be a separate detailed section in the context of a workplace discrimination claim, rather than be integrated into the personal history narrative. This topic offers an opportunity to discuss the plaintiff's problems, if any, in previous jobs, and antecedents in that person's career that may influence responses to alleged discriminatory events.

The claimant's mental health history may constitute a separate section of the report if it is extensive. Otherwise, these details can be integrated into the overall narrative of the person's life. Similarly, the claimant's military history may warrant a separate section if it is extensive and relevant.

Claimant's Account of Discriminatory Events

A separate section in the report should always be developed for the claimant's account of the discrimination-related events. This account should provide some detail about the plaintiff's allegations, in the claimant's own words. If this history is contradicted by documentary sources or by the testimony of witnesses in the case, those contrasting accounts may be included and juxtaposed within this section. In accordance with the five-stage model, the narrative should include a series of paragraphs that define the client's status on the "day before" the onset of the alleged discrimination. The "day before" analysis should be as complete as possible in integrating medical, collateral, and employment information to provide a clean picture concerning the claimant's status on the day before the alleged discrimination began. This should include any description of ongoing mental disorders or diseases that may be present, any medical problems the claimant was grappling with, any ongoing family or marital problems, and ongoing employment difficulties.

The next section should include a detailed account of the plaintiff's perspective on what happened in the workplace. Direct quotations from the plaintiff are often helpful in providing the reader a clear idea of what the plaintiff believes occurred or contends happened in the workplace. This narrative should be chronological and should provide specific names and other information that help the reader organize these events in time, space, and give an idea of the interpersonal relationships within the workplace. For example, the evaluator may say, "The plaintiff decided to report the events to her immediate supervisor, Mr. Randal Jones, as she believed he would help her to prevent further discrimination from taking place."

The section on discrimination should also include a report of changes in the claimant's emotional and physical status during the discrimination, if the duration was protracted. Reports of changes in family functioning may also be documented by integrating information gathered in the course of collateral interviews with other sources, such as friends, family members, or coworkers. This section of the report is the place to note any statement concerning the plaintiff's departure from the workplace and the mechanism of their work termination. For instance, if a constructive discharge is alleged, details concerning the events that the plaintiff believes compelled him or her to leave the workplace should be set forth, as well as the plaintiff's fitness for work at that time.

In accordance with the assessment model, the report should next turn to events that occurred after the plaintiff left the workplace or after the discrimination was alleged to have ceased. This section should include a detailed recitation of the plaintiff's treatment history, any changes in the job situation, and changes in her or his emotional and physical well-being that occurred in the subsequent time period.

Next, a detailed picture of the claimant's current status in terms of physical, social, psychological, and workplace functioning should be provided. As part of this summary, the claimant's daily activities should be described, along with a description of ongoing treatment he or she has received, including medications, and his or her current fitness for work and employment status.

BEST PRACTICE
Organize the information from the claimant regarding the alleged discrimination according to the five-stage model.

Results of Objective Tests

The report should then turn to a review of the psychological test data generated by the plaintiff, focusing on the legally relevant test interpretations. This is best accomplished by reporting cognitive and personality components separately. The cognitive section should set forth results of each test, placing each test score (e.g., I.Q. scores) in context by stating them in percentile terms. Include results of any measures provided to assess effort on the part of the plaintiff during the examination. Report any statements concerning the validity of the cognitive assessment in this section. If relevant, the examiner should provide examples of cultural or linguistic factors that may affect the test results. Conclude the cognitive assessment with a summary of the results as they apply in this particular case to this individual, highlighting evidence of any emotional disruption produced by emotional problems.

The personality assessment section reports the results of each of the personality assessment measures. Each subsection should include an overview of validity indicators for that measure. Invalid tests should not be discussed in detail, but the nature of the invalidity of that measure should be documented, along with the possible sources of the invalidity. For example, if the MMPI-2 is invalid because of elevated exaggeration scales (e.g., F, Fb, Fp), the report should state that "the MMPI-2 was invalid because of high scores on scales reflecting symptom exaggeration." Valid measures should be discussed in some detail, including proffered diagnoses and other information that may form the basis of the evaluator's concluding opinions. Any diagnosis should be presented in multiaxial format in conformity with the guidelines set forth in the DSM-IV. Conclude the personality assessment section with a summary that

BEST PRACTICE
It is best to report cognitive and personality test results separately in the written report.

brings together the results of all the measures as they bear on this case.

Opinions

The penultimate section of the report is the evaluating expert's opinion. This section is critical for several reasons. First, it is the only section of the report that will be read by time-limited readers, such as the judge. Second, it is the evaluator's chance to bring together information from disparate sources into one place and to frame conclusions in a comprehensive and intelligible fashion. Third, it includes statements that are critical for the legal resolution of the case. Empirical research on forensic reports shows that the most common weakness is the failure to specify the reasoning used by the expert to reach the conclusion or opinion offered. In other words, information about the way that disparate items of information were integrated, evaluated, and weighed is often lacking (Wettstein, 2005).

At the outset, the summary should include a disclaimer concerning the limitations of the data in the case. The evaluator should specify limitations to the data forming the basis for her or his opinions, such as the inability to contact certain acknowledged collateral sources, problems in gathering or interpreting test data because of particular aspects of the case complexity, language and cultural factors, and other influences. These limitations should be stated honestly to guide the reader in interpreting the summary section of the report.

The summary should integrate all the information presented in the report in a concise form that directly addresses the referral questions. This is best accomplished by repeating the referral questions at the beginning of the section and providing a short answer to each referral question, followed by the details that informed the response to each question. For example, one referral question might be: "Did Ms. Jones suffer emotional distress as a result of the alleged discrimination at Mega Foods Corporation?" The evaluator's response might be, "Ms. Jones alleges she experienced discrimination at Mega Foods Corporation, and the evaluation

BEST PRACTICE
The statement of opinion should be concise and followed by a brief description of the data that generated the opinion.

indicates that she experienced a severe emotional response to the sexual harassment and wage discrimination in that setting."

In a compensatory damages case, the specific events that contributed to the injury should be noted. The causative events can be designated as "substantial contributing factors" or "predominant contributing factors," as appropriate. Specific events that contributed to a condition must be concisely enumerated. Such examples might include, "Increased workload following the absence of a colleague on maternity leave," or "Complainant lodged divorce proceedings against partner four weeks before the discrimination complaint was filed," or "Conflict with supervisor over delayed annual leave." In a civil rights case tried in a tort setting, a statement about proximate cause is necessary. That is, you should indicate how the injuries of the plaintiff were fully or partially caused by the actions of the defendant(s). The summary systematically sets forth each of the major results of the evaluation and the supporting data that inform that result or conclusion. The most important aspect of the data to discuss is the complainant's functionality. Research on expert reports has revealed that a common deficit is failure to connect the results of tests or diagnoses to functional impairments (Young, Kane, & Nicholson, 2007). As was noted in Chapter 6, the analysis of function and the impact of functioning caused by any emotional disorder observed in the complainant are far more important legally than the diagnosis per se. The plaintiff who has no discernible recognized diagnosis may nonetheless be suffering from disability as a result of on-the-job discrimination. It may simply be the case that these problems do not constellate into a recognized diagnosis encompassed within the DSM-IV. This emphasis on functionality provides data in a form that is useful for other experts, particularly employment and vocational experts, concerning the value of that loss of function in terms of future employment and other pecuniary damages. Discussion of loss of function, if it is evident, allows other experts to utilize the report as a basis for their professional opinions.

Future Damages

The final section of the assessment addresses Stage 5 of the model: the claimant's prognosis and needs for future treatment or intervention. This section may include some figures based on estimated costs of those interventions, if the evaluator has enough information concerning those issues. This final section should also include some statement about the probable efficacy of the proposed interventions, and some opinion concerning the claimant's long-term status.

The report should conclude with a statement to the effect that the evaluator has based the opinions expressed in the report only on information currently available and may expand on the report or amend it based upon new information. This statement is especially important in the case of Rule 26(a) evaluations (the federal rule that mandates the time frame and contents of the plaintiff's expert's report), which may be prepared early in a case; and additional information is quite likely to be provided prior to trial. In such circumstances, the evaluator will want leave to amend the report following a review of the additional information.

A well-structured and detailed report may reduce the need for detailed and lengthy depositions and will provide all parties with a road map of the evaluator's testimony in court. Although a detailed report from the evaluator provides opposing counsel with ammunition for cross-examination, in our experience, the detail aids the discovery process and allows the parties to be better prepared for trial.

Testimony

The expert is likely to offer testimony at two points in time in a civil case: deposition and trial. The purpose of a deposition is to provide a record of the examining expert's findings so that opposing counsel has an opportunity to question the expert about what will later be stated in court. A deposition is sworn testimony recorded by a court reporter, usually in the presence of only the plaintiff's counsel and defense counsel, and the parties to the litigation who opt to attend. In some jurisdictions, both the plaintiff

Table 7.1 Model Forensic Report Structure on Causation of Workplace Psychological Injuries

Section	Title of section	Contents
I	PREAMBLE	**Preliminary information about the evaluation**
1	Identification	• Name of evaluee • Date of birth of evaluee
2	Sources of information	• Names of test procedures and date of administration • Titles of all documents reviewed • Names of persons interviewed; date and duration of interview
3	Referral	• Name of party seeking evaluation • Referral question(s)
4	Informed consent	
5	Behavioral observations and mental status of evaluee	• Description of orientation of evaluee to examination • Communication capacity of evaluee, speech style, etc.
II	ASSESSMENT	**Details of components forming the basis of the expert opinion**
6	History of evaluee	• Childhood and development, presence and history of child abuse • Educational background • Family history • Employment history • Military history, if applicable • Physical and mental health history

Table 7.1 Model Forensic Report Structure on Causation of Workplace Psychological Injuries (*Continued*)

Section	Title of section	Contents
7	Account of discrimination	• Status the "day before" the alleged onset • Description of alleged discriminatory events • Reports of any changes in emotional and physical status • Description of status following the end of the discrimination, treatment history, changes in job situation, emotional and physical status
8	Current status of evaluee	• Describe claimant's physical, social, psychological, and workplace functioning. • Claimant's daily activities • Ongoing treatment, medications • Current job status
9	Results of objective psychological testing	• Cognitive components • Personality components • Effort by evaluee • Validity test results • Results summary and emotional problems of evaluee, if any
10	Summary	• Limitations of the data • Answers to referral question(s) and bases for opinion • Functioning of evaluee and the impact on functioning of any emotional disorder • Summary of loss of functioning
III	OPINION	Expert opinion on referral questions
1	Future damages	• Prognosis and needs for future treatment or intervention • Long-term prospects
2	Caveats	• Limitations on opinions

INFO

In a civil case, the expert is likely to provide testimony at deposition and trial.

and defendant employer will be present when the expert's deposition is taken. Statements made in the course of a deposition may be used to impeach the testimony of the evaluator at trial.

Deposition testimony is often pivotal in a case. First, it may serve as a basis for mediation or settlement negotiations. Second, the deposition is an occasion for opposing counsel to test the mettle of the evaluator, and to determine the depth of the evaluator's knowledge on the topic and the extent to which that the expert may be vulnerable to challenges on expertise or sufficiency of data. Reports that are incomplete and unresponsive to the referral questions may make the evaluator look like an easy target for cross-examination. Third, the deposition creates a record for later use in the event that the expert witness is unavailable for *viva voce* (in-person) testimony in court. In cases in which this is likely, the parties and the expert will know this beforehand, and will arrange for the deposition to be videotaped.

Because the deposition is a critical point in the trial, the evaluator should devote significant time to prepare for the deposition, reviewing all of the records, test data and interview notes. Having a current and facile grasp of the data will not only bolster the evaluator's self confidence, but also his or her credibility. The evaluator should be prepared for more direct, confrontational, and occasionally hostile questioning from the deposing counsel. In the absence of a jury, some lawyers feel free to use all their intimidation skills to reduce the confidence and effectiveness of the evaluator-witness. Recall that, in most cases, the only enduring record of the deposition will be a transcript, so some aspects of voice and gesture are lost to the reader, whereas they may be very real to the expert. By the same token, remembering that the only record of the deposition is likely to be a written one, the expert should ensure that answers are made in complete sentences, use formal speech, and avoid jargon. The evaluator should always ask to review and sign the deposition. This review is an occasion for correcting transcription errors. In some jurisdictions, the expert may also correct factual or interpretive errors in answers in the record. This should be done sparingly, as excessive corrections may necessitate additional depositions.

INFO

Deposition testimony:

- may serve as a basis for mediation or settlement negotiations
- is a chance for opposing counsel to test the expert and determine the depth of his knowledge
- creates a record for later use in the event that the expert witness is unavailable to testify in court

Court testimony is the other venue for conveying opinions and findings in civil rights cases. Recall that civil rights cases rarely go to trial. In our experience, those that do are often complicated, with findings that favor both sides of the case. In these situations, counsel may advise the client that a judge or jury can more effectively decide the matter than the parties in mediation.

Trial testimony involves some theater. Brodsky, in his volumes on expert evidence by forensic psychologists (Brodsky, 1991; 1999; 2004), provided advice that is informative to even the most experienced and confident expert witness. In civil rights cases, it is important for the evaluator to remember that the expert's role is usually not central to the case. In most cases, the determination of liability is central, and the psychologist's role to explicate damages is less significant.

The evaluator may want to outline the five-stage model in presenting the results of the evaluation to the jury. This approach is straightforward and makes intuitive sense to lay persons, and it allows the evaluator to deal with competing explanations of the data. By discussing preexisting conditions, problems that were contemporaneous with the alleged discrimination, and events that occurred after the discrimination

BEST PRACTICE

The goal of testimony is to present conclusions or opinions as well as the data and inferences on which those conclusions and opinions were based.

ended, the evaluator can demonstrate that consideration was given to alternative theories of causation. This model also allows the distinction to be drawn between injuries that are transitory and those that contribute significantly to the claimant's current status.

Conclusions

Oral testimony in depositions, administrative proceedings, or in court is an occasion for the evaluator to integrate the information presented in the written report in a way that is most useful to finders of fact. While this may be the most challenging aspect of the evaluator's job, it is also the venue in which the claimant, the job context, and the actions of the defendant come into sharpest focus. In this final role, the evaluator may contribute materially to the determination of the outcome of the case. This important phase of work in an employment discrimination case is where the careful efforts of all the stages of the case come to fruition.

From the moment that the referral was received, the expert has taken care to retain balance in gathering and reviewing data. Those processes have been careful and thorough. Problems in testimony often (and embarrassingly) occur when data has not been gathered; when questions have not been asked. When all the available and relevant information has been reviewed, however, and put together in a way that combines the expertise of the psychologist with the unique aspects of the plaintiff, the workplace, the defendants and the legal setting, expert testimony is much more useful to the judge and jury. Well-prepared and well-founded testimony is also much less vulnerable to cross-examination.

References

Abel, R. (2006). General damages are incoherent, incalculable, incommensurable, and inegalitarian (but otherwise a great idea). *DePaul Law Review, 56,* 53–329.

Agabi, C.E., & Wilson, J.P. (2005). Trauma, PTSD and resilience: A review of the literature. *Trauma Violence, Abuse, 6,* 195–216.

Agnew, R. (2001). Building on the foundation of general strain theory: Specifying the types of strain most likely to lead to crime and delinquency. *Journal of Research in Crime and Delinquency, 38(4):* 319–362.

Allen, R.J., Brunet, A., & Roth, S.S. (2006). An external perspective on the nature of noneconomic compensatory damages and their regulation. *DePaul Law Review, 56,* 1249–1278.

Almeida, D.M., Neupert, S.N., Banks, S.R., & Serido, J. (2005). Do daily stress processes account for socioeconomic health disparities? *The Journals of Gerontology Series B: Psychological Sciences and Social Sciences, 60,* 34–39.

American Academy of Psychiatry and the Law (2004). *Ethics guidelines for the practice of forensic psychiatry.* Retrieved August 23, 2009, from https://www.aapl.org/ethics.htm.

American Medical Association (2007). *Guides to the evaluation of permanent impairment,* 6th ed. Chicago, IL: Author

American Psychiatric Association (2000). *Diagnostic and statistical manual of mental disorders* (4th ed., text rev.). Washington, D.C.: Author.

American Psychological Association (2002). Ethical principles of psychologists and code of conduct. *American Psychologist, 57,* 1060–1073.

Americans with Disabilities Act of 1990, 42 U.S.C.A. §12101 et seq. (West 1993).

Americans with Disabilities Amendment Act of 2008 (2009). Pub. Law 110–325.

Andary, L., Stolk, Y., Klimidis, S. (2003). *Assessing mental health across cultures.* Australian Academic Press, Bowen Hills.

Antilla, S. (2002). *Tales from the boom-boom room: Women v. Wall Street.* Princeton, NJ: Bloomberg Press.

Aquino, K., & Thau, S. (2009). Workplace victimization: Aggression from the target's perspective. *Annual Review of Psychology, 60,* 717–741.

Arata, C.M. (2000). From child victim to adult victim: A model for predicting sexual revictimization. *Child Maltreatment: Journal of the American Professional Society on the Abuse of Children, 5(1):* 28–38.

Avina, C., & O'Donohue, W. (2002). Sexual harassment and PTSD: Is sexual harassment diagnosable trauma? *Journal of Traumatic Stress, 15(1)*: 69–75.

Avraham, R. (2006). Putting a price on pain-and-suffering damages: A critique of the current approaches and a preliminary proposal for change. *Northwestern University Law Review, 100,* 87–120.

Badgett, M.V.L., & Frank, J. (Eds.) (2007). *Sexual orientation discrimination: An international perspective.* London: Routledge.

Bagby, R.M., Gillis, J.R., & Rogers, R. (1991). Effectiveness of the Millon Clinical Multiaxial Inventory Validity Index in the detection of random responding. *Psychological Assessment: A Journal of Consulting and Clinical Psychology, 3,* 285–287.

Barling, J., Kelloway, E.K., & Frone, M.R. (Eds.) (2005). *Handbook of work stress.* Thousand Oaks, CA: Sage.

Barsade, S., & Wiesenfeld, B. (1997). *Attitudes in the American workplace III.* New Haven, CT: Yale University School of Management.

Bastian, L.D., Lancaster. A.R., & Reyst, H.E. (1996). *Department of Defense 1995 sexual harassment survey.* Arlington, VA: Defense Manpower Data Center.

Bauss, C. (2009). Response by Carol Bauss to Bornstein and Schwartz. *The Jury Expert, 21(2)*: 39–40.

Behnke, S.H., Perlin, M.L., & Bernstein, M. (2003). *The essentials of New York mental health law: A straightforward guide for clinicians of all disciplines.* New York: W.W. Norton & Co.

Beiner, T.M. (2005). *Gender myths v. working realities: Using social science to reformulate sexual harassment law.* New York: New York University Press.

Beitchman, J.H., Zucker, K.J., Hood, J.E., daCosta, G.A., Akman, D., & Cassavia, E. (1992). A review of the long-term effects of child sexual abuse. *Child Abuse & Neglect, 16(1)*: 101–118.

Bell, D.A. (2004). *Silent covenant:* Brown v. Board of Education *and the unfulfilled hopes for racial reform.* Oxford University Press.

Bergman, M.E., & Drasgow, F. (2003). Race as moderator in a model of sexual harassment: An empirical test. *Journal of Occupational Health Psychology, 8,* 131–145.

Berrey, E. (2009). Sociology finds discrimination in the law. *Contexts, 8,* 28–32.

Beyler, K. (2007). Expert testimony disclosure under Federal Rule 26: A proposed amendment. *John Marshall Law Review, 41,* 117–159.

Bianchini, K.J., Etherton, J.L., Greve, K.W., Heinly, M.T., & Meyers, J.E. (2008). Classification accuracy of MMPI-2 validity scales in the detection of pain-related malingering. *Assessment, 15,* 435–449.

Binder, L., & Rohling, M.L. (1996) Money matters: A meta-analytic review of the effects of financial incentives on recovery after closed-head injury. *American Journal of Psychiatry, 153,* 7–10.

Binder, R.L. (1992). Sexual harassment: Issues for forensic psychiatrists. *Bulletin of the American Academy of Psychiatry and Law, 20,* 409–418.

Bingham, C., & Gansler, L.L. (1999). *Class action: The story of Lois Jenson and the landmark case that changed sexual harassment law*. New York: Random House, Inc./Doubleday.

Blanchard, E.B., Hickling, E.J., Taylor, A.E., Buckley, T.C., Loos, W.R., & Walsh, J. (1998). Effects of litigation settlements on posttraumatic stress symptoms in motor vehicle accident victims. *Journal of Traumatic Stress, 11*(*2*)*:* 337–354.

Blanck, P. (2005). *Disability rights*. Burlington, VT: Ashgate.

Blanck, P. (2008). "The right to live in the world": Disability yesterday, today, and tomorrow. *Texas Journal on Civil Liberties and Civil Rights, 13*(*2*)*:* 369–403.

Bond, M.A., Punnett, L., Pyle, J.L., Cazeca, D., Cooperman, M. (2004). Gendered work conditions, health, and work outcomes. *Journal of Occupational Health Psychology, 9,* 28–45.

Borgida, E., & Fiske, S.T. (2008). *Beyond common sense: Psychological science in the courtroom*. Oxford: Wiley-Blackwell.

Bornstein, B.H. (1998), From compassion to compensation: The effect of injury severity on mock jurors' liability judgements. *Journal of Applied Social Psychology, 28,* 1477–1502.

Bornstein, B.H. (2009, Feb). Physical v. mental pain: A legal double standard? *Monitor on Psychology, 40*(*2*)*:* 18.

Bornstein, B.H., & Schwartz, S.L. (2009). Injured body, injured mind: Dealing with damages for psychological harm. *The Jury Expert, 21*(*2*)*:* 33–39.

Bornstein, B.H., Weiner, R.L., Schopp, R.F., & Willborn, S.L. (2008). *Civil juries and civil justice: Psychological and legal perspectives.* New York: Springer.

Bostock, D.J., & Daley, J.G. (2007). Lifetime and current sexual assault and harassment victimization rates of active-duty United States Air Force women. *Violence Against Women*, *13*, 927–944.

Bradford, G.E. (2001, May/June). Dissecting Missouri's requirement of "reasonable medical certainty." *Journal of the Missouri Bar, 57*(*3*). Retrieved June 7, 2009, from http://www.mobar.org/journal/2001/mayjun/index.htm.

Bresticker, B., & Fitzgerald, L. (2005). The feasibility and need for creating a presumed emotional distress damage in sexual harassment litigation. Unpublished manuscript.

Briere, J. (1995). *Trauma Symptom Inventory professional manual.* Odessa, FL: Psychological Assessment Resources.

Briere, J. (2001). *Detailed Assessment of Posttraumatic Stress* (*DAPS*). Odessa, FL: Psychological Assessment Resources.

Briere, J., & Runtz, M. (1987). Post sexual abuse trauma: Data and implications for clinical practice. *Journal of Interpersonal Violence, 2,* 367–379.

Briere, J., & Runtz, M. (1988). Symptomatology associated with childhood sexual victimization in a nonclinical adult sample. *Child Abuse & Neglect, 12,* 51–59.

Bright, D.A., & Goodman-Delahunty, J. (2010, in press). Mock juror decision making in a civil negligence trial: The impact of gruesome evidence, injury severity and information processing route. *Psychiatry, Psychology and Law..*

Brodsky, C.M. (1976). *The harassed worker.* Lexington, MA: Lexington Books.

Brodsky, S.L. (1991). *Testifying in court: Guidelines and maxims for the expert witness.* Washington, D.C.: American Psychological Association Books.

Brodsky, S.L. (1999). *The expert expert witness: More maxims and guidelines for testifying in Court.* Washington, D.C.: American Psychological Association Books.

Brodsky, S.L. (2004). *Coping with cross-examination and other pathways to effective testimony.* Washington, D.C.: American Psychological Association Books.

Brown, A.J. (Ed.) (2008). *Whistleblowing in the Australian public sector: Enhancing theory and practice of internal witness management in public sector organisations.* Canberra: ANU EPress.

Brown, B.B., & Seymour, R.L. (1998). Analysis & perspective: Sexual harassment: Dialogue on the Supreme Court's decisions in Ellerth and Faragher. *Equal employment law update.* Washington, D.C.: U.S. Bureau of National Affairs.

Brun, J.P., & Kedl, E. (2006). Filing a psychological harassment complaint in the workplace: A difficult history. *Industrial Relations, 61(3):* 381–407.

Bryant, R.A. (2005a). Assessing individuals for compensation. In D. Carson & R. Bull (Eds.), *Handbook of psychology in legal contexts* (pp. 89–107). Oxford, UK: Oxford University Press.

Bryant, R.A. (2005b). Predicting posttraumatic stress disorder from acute reactions. Journal of Trauma and Dissociation, *6*(2): 5–15.

Bryant, R..A., & Guthrie, R.M. (2007). Maladaptive self-appraisals before trauma exposure predict posttraumatic stress disorder. *Journal of Consulting and Clinical Psychology, 75(5):* 812–815.

Bryant, R.A., & Harvey, A.G. (2003). The influence of litigation on maintenance of posttraumatic stress disorder. *Journal of Nervous and Mental Disease, 191*, 191–193.

Bryant, R.A., Moulds, M.L., & Guthrie, R.M. (2000). Acute stress disorder scale: A self-report measure of acute stress disorder. *Psychological Assessment, 12*(1): 61–68.

Bryant, R.A., & Njenga, F.G. (2006). Cultural sensitivity: Making trauma assessment and treatment plans culturally relevant. *Journal of Clinical Psychiatry. 67(2):* 74–79.

Bryant, R.A., & Panasetis, P. (2005). The role of panic in acute dissociative reactions following trauma. *British Journal of Clinical Psychology, 44*, 489–494.

Buchanan, N.T., & Fitzgerald, L.F. (2008). Effects of racial and sexual harassment on work and the psychological well-being of African

American women. *Journal of Occupational Health Psychology, 13*(2): 137–151.

Burgess, D.J., Ding, Y., Hargreaves, M., van Ryn, M., & Phelan, S. (2008). The association between perceived discrimination and underutilization of needed medical and mental health care in a multi-ethnic community sample. *Journal of Health Care for the Poor and Underserved, 19*, 894–911.

Burns, S.E. (1995). Issues in workplace sexual harassment law and related social science research. *Journal of Social Issues, 51,* 193–207.

Burstein, P. (1992). Affirmative action, jobs and American democracy: What has happened to the quest for equal opportunity? *Law and Society Review, 26*(4): 901–922.

Bush, S.S., Connell, M.A., & Denny, R.L. (2006). *Ethical practice in forensic psychology: A systematic model for decision making.* Washington, D.C.. American Psychological Association.

Butcher, J.N., & Miller, K.B. (1999). Personality assessment in personal injury litigation. In I.B. Weiner & A.K. Hess (Eds.), *The handbook of forensic psychology* (pp. 140–166). New York: John Wiley & Sons.

Carter, R.T. (2007). Racism and psychological and emotional injury. *The Counseling Psychologist, 35*, 13–105.

Chan, D.K-S., Bun Lam, C., Yee Chow, S., Fai Cheung, S. (2008). Examining the job-related, psychological and physical outcomes of workplace sexual harassment: A meta-analytic review. *Psychology of Women Quarterly, 32,* 362–376.

Chang, W.C. (1996). Toward equal opportunities: Fairness, values and affirmative action programs in the US. *Journal of Social Issues, 52*(4): 93–98.

Charuvastra, A., & Cloitre, M. (2008). Social bonds and posttraumatic stress disorder. *Annual Review of Psychology, 59*, 301–328.

Chen, Z., Williams, K.D., Fitness, J., & Newton, N.C. (2008). When hurt will not heal: Exploring the capacity to relive social and physical pain. *Psychological Science, 19,* 789–795.

Cherry, N. (1984). Women and work stress: Evidence from the 1946 birth cohort. *Ergonomics, 27,* 519–526.

Clark, R., Anderson, A., Clark, V.R., & Williams, D.R (1999). Racism as a stressor for African Americans. *American Psychologist, 54,* 805–816.

Clarke, M., Lewchuk, W., de Wolff, A., & King, A. (2007). "This just isn't sustainable": Precarious employment, stress and workers' health. *International Journal of Law and Psychiatry, 30*, 311–326.

Clermont, K.M., & Schwab, S.J. (2009). Employment discrimination plaintiffs in federal court: From bad to worse? *Harvard Law and Policy Review, 3,* 103–132,

Cocchiarella, L., & Andersson, G. (2001) *Guides to the evaluation of permanent impairment* (5th ed.). Chicago, IL: American Medical Association.

Colker, R. (2005). *The disability pendulum: The first decade of the Americans with Disabilities Act.* New York: New York University Press.

Colvin, A.J.S. (2007). Empirical research on employment arbitration: Clarity amidst the sound and fury? *Employee Rights and Employment Policy Journal, 11*(2): 1–36.

Committee on Ethical Guidelines for Forensic Psychologists (1991). Specialty guidelines for forensic psychologists. *Law and Human Behavior, 15*(6): 655–665.

Connell, M. (2007). Ethical issues in forensic psychology. In R.J. Jackson (Ed.), *Learning forensic assessment* (pp. 55–72). New York: Routledge, Taylor & Francis Group.

Cook, P.J., Jones, A.M., Lipari, R.N., & Lancaster, A.R. (2005). *Service academy sexual harassment and assault survey*. Arlington, VA: Defense Manpower Defense Center.

Corbie-Smith, G., Frank, E., Nickens, H.W., & Elon, L. (1999). Prevalences and correlates of ethnic harassment in the U.S. Women Physicians' Health Study. *Academic Medicine, 74*, 695–701.

Cortina, L.M. (2001). Assessing sexual harassment among Latinas: Development of an instrument. *Cultural Diversity and Ethnic Minority Psychology, 7*(2): 164–181.

Cortina, L.M., Magley, V.J., Williams, J.H., & Langhout, R.D. (2001). Incivility in the workplace: Incidence and impact. *Journal of Occupational Health Psychology, 6*, 64–80.

Crangle, C.E. (2007). Gender equity at Stanford University. In F.J. Crosby, M.S. Stockdale & S.A. Ropp (Eds.), *Sex discrimination in the workplace: Multidisciplinary perspectives* (pp. 60–82). Oxford, UK: Blackwell.

Creamer, M., O'Donnell, M.L., & Pattison, P. (2004). The relationship between acute stress disorder and posttraumatic stress disorder in severely injured trauma survivors. *Behaviour Research and Therapy, 42*, 315–328.

Crosby, F.J. Stockdale, M.S., & Ropp S.A. (Eds.) (2007). *Sex discrimination in the workplace: Multidisciplinary perspectives.* Malden, MA: Blackwell.

Curcio, A.A. (1988). Rule 412 laid bare: A procedural rule that cannot adequately protect sexual harassment plaintiffs from embarrassing exposure. *University of Cincinnati Law Review, 67*, 125–183.

Dansky, B.S., Brady, K.T., Saladin, M.E., Killeen, T., Becker, S., & Roitzsch, J. (1996). Victimization and PTSD in individuals with substance use disorders: Gender and racial differences. *American Journal of Drug and Alcohol Abuse, 22*(1): 75–93.

Dansky, B.S., & Kilpatrick, D.G. (1997). Effects of sexual harassment. In W. O'Donohue (Ed.), *Sexual harassment: Theory, research, and treatment* (pp. 152–174). Boston: Allyn & Bacon.

Darr, W., & Johns, G. (2008). Work strain, health and absenteeism: A meta-analysis. *Journal of Occupational Health Psychology, 13*(4): 293–318.

Dawson, E., Anderson, M.G., & MacCoun, R.(1999). Goal conflict in juror assessments of compensatory and punitive damages. *Law and Human Behavior, 23*(3): 313–330.

Deitch, E.A., Barsky, A., Butz, R.M., Chan, S., Brief, A.P., & Bradley, J.C. (2003). Subtle yet significant: The existence and impact of everyday racial discrimination in the workplace. *Human Relations, 56,* 1299–1324.

Demmelmaier, I., Lindberg, P., Åsenlöf, P., & Denison, E. (2008). The associations between pain intensity, psychosocial variables, and pain duration/recurrence in a large sample of persons with nonspecific spinal pain. *Clinical Journal of Pain, 24,* 611–619.

Dhaliwal, G.K., Gauzas, L., Antonowicz, D.H., & Ross, R.R. (1996). Adult male survivors of childhood sexual abuse: Prevalence, sexual abuse characteristics, and long-term effects. *Clinical Psychology Review, 16,* 619–639.

Dipboye, R.L., & Collela, A. (Eds.) (2005). *Discrimination at work: Psychological and organizational Bases.* Mahwah, NJ: Lawrence Erlbaum Associates.

Dyer, F.J. (2005). Forensic application of the MCMI-III™ in light of current controversies. In R.J. Craig (Ed.), *New directions in interpreting the Millon™ Clinical Multiaxial Inventory-III [MCMI-III™],* (pp. 201–223). Hoboken, NJ: John Wiley & Sons, Inc.

Dyer, F.J. (2008). Using the Millon Inventories in forensic psychology. In T. Millon & C. Bloom (Eds.), *The Millon inventories: A practitioner's guide to personalized clinical assessment* (2nd ed., pp. 177–195). New York: Guilford Press.

Einarsen, S., & Raknes, B. (1997). Harassment in the workplace and the victimisation of men. *Violence and Victims, 12,* 247–263.

Einarson, S., Hoel, H., Zapf, D., & Cooper, C.L. (Eds.) (2003). *Bullying and emotional abuse in the workplace. International perspectives in research and practice.* New York: Taylor & Francis.

Ennis, E., Vrij, A., & Chance, C. (2008). Individual differences and lying in everyday life. *Journal of Social and Personal Relationships, 25,* 105–118.

Federal Rules of Civil Procedure (2007). Retrieved June 17, 2009, from http://www.law.cornell.edu/rules/frcp/

Feigenson, N. (2001). *Legal blame: How jurors think and talk about accidents.* Washington, D.C.; American Psychological Association.

Finch, B.K., Kolody, B., & Vega, W.A. (2000). Perceived discrimination and depression among Mexican-origin adults in California. *Journal of Health and Social Behavior, 41,* 295–313.

Finkelhor, D., Hotaling, G., Lewis, I.A., & Smith, C. (1990). Sexual abuse in a national survey of adult men and women: Prevalence, characteristics, and risk factors. *Child Abuse & Neglect, 14,* 19–28.

Fiske, S.T., & Borgida, E. (2009). Providing expert knowledge in an adversarial context: Social cognitive science in employment discrimination cases. *Annual Review of Law and Social Science, 4,* 123–148.

Fitzgerald, L.F. (2003). Sexual harassment and social justice: Reflections on the distance yet to go. *American Psychologist, 58(11):* 915–924.

Fitzgerald, L.F., & Collinsworth, L.L. (2007). (Un)common knowledge: The legal viability of sexual harassment research. In E. Borgida & S. Fiske, eds. *Beyond Common Sense: Psychological Science in the Courtroom.* (pp. 103–125). Boston: Blackwell Publishing.

Fitzgerald, L.F., Drasgow, F., Hulin, C.L., Gelfand, M., & Magley, V.J. (1997). Antecedents and consequences of sexual harassment in organizations: A test of an integrated model. *Journal of Applied Psychology, 82*, 578–589.

Fitzgerald, L.F., Drasgow, F., & Magley, V.J. (1999). Sexual harassment in the Armed Forces: A test of an integrated model. *Military Psychology, 11*, 329–343.

Fitzgerald, L.F., & Schullman, S.L. (1993). Sexual harassment: A research analysis and agenda for the 1990s. *Journal of Vocational Behavior, 42*, 97–109.

Fitzgerald, L.F., Swan, S., & Fischer, K. (1995). Why didn't she just report him? The psychological and legal implications of women's responses to sexual harassment. *The Journal of Social Issues, 51*, 117–138.

Fitzgerald, L.F., Swan, S., & Magley, V.J. (1997). But was it really sexual harassment? Legal, behavioral, and psychological definitions of the workplace victimization of women. In W. O'Donohue (Ed.), *Sexual harassment: Theory, research, and treatment;* (pp.5–28). Boston: Allyn & Bacon.

Foote, W.E. (2003). Forensic evaluations in Americans with Disabilities Act cases. In A.M. Goldstein (Ed.), *Handbook of psychology, Volume 11, Forensic psychology* (pp. 279–300), New York: John Wiley & Sons.

Foote, W.E., & Goodman-Delahunty, J. (1999). Same-sex harassment: Implications of the *Oncale* decision for forensic evaluations of plaintiffs. *Behavioral Sciences & the Law, 17*, 123-139.

Foote, W.E., & Goodman-Delahunty, J. (2005). *Evaluating sexual harassment: Psychological, social, and legal considerations in forensic evaluations.* Washington, D.C.: American Psychological Association.

Foote, W.E., (2009) Fundamentals of Forensic Evaluation in Civil Rights and Tort Cases. A workshop conducted for the Maine Forensic Evaluators, Augusta, Maine. July, 2009.

Foote, W.E., & Shuman, D.W. (2006). Consent, disclosure, and waiver for the forensic psychological evaluation: Rethinking roles of expert and lawyer. *Professional Psychology: Research and Practice, 37*(5): 437–445.

Forbes, D., Creamer, M., Phelps, A., Bryant, R., McFarlane, A., Devilly, G.J., Matthews, L., Raphael, B., Doran, C., Merlin, T., & Newton, S. (2007). Australian guidelines for the treatment of adults with Acute Stress Disorder and Post-Traumatic Stress Disorder. *Australian and New Zealand Journal of Psychiatry, 41*, 637–648.

Frederick, R. (1997). *The Validity Indicator Profile manual.* Minneapolis, MN: National Computer Systems.

Fromuth, M.E., & Burkhart, B.R. (1987). Childhood sexual victimization among college men: Definitional and methodological issues. *Violence & Victims, 2(4)*: 241–253.

Fullbright & Jaworski L.L.P. (2008). *Fifth annual litigation trends survey findings: Directions and dynamics.* Retrieved on June 5, 2009, from: http://www.fulbright.com/mediaroom/files/2008/Fulbright-FifthLitTrends.pdf.

Gacono, C.B., Evans, F.B., Kaser-Boyd, N., & Gacono, L.A. (2008). *The handbook of forensic Rorschach assessment.* New York: Routledge/Taylor & Francis Group.

Gagliardi, G.J, & Miller, A.K. (2008). Writing forensic psychological reports. In R. Jackson (Ed.) *Learning forensic psychology.* Mahwah, NJ: Lawrence Erlbaum Associates.

Gee, G., & Walsemann, K.M. (2009). Does health predict the reporting of racial discrimination or do reports of discrimination predict health? Findings from the National Longitudinal Study of Youth. *Social Science & Medicine, 68(9)*: 1676–1684.

Gilbert, G.M. (2007). *Compensatory damages and other remedies in federal sector employment discrimination cases* (3rd ed.). Arlington, VA: Dewey Publications, Inc.

Ginzburg, K., Wrensch, M., Rice, T., Farren, G., & Spiegel, D. (2008). Breast cancer and psychosocial factors: Early stressful life events, social support, and well-being. *Psychosomatics: Journal of Consultation Liaison Psychiatry, 48*, 407–712.

Glasø, L., Nielsen, M.B., Einarsen, S., Haugland, K., & Matthiesen, S.B. (2009). Grunnleggende antagelser og symptomer på posttraumatisk stresslidelse blant mobbeofre [A study of basic life assumptions and Post-Traumatic Stress Disorder among victims of workplace bullying]. *Tidsskrift for Norsk Psykologforening, 46*, 153–160.

Glomb, T.M., Munson, L.J., Hulin, C.L., Berryman-Fink, C., & Drasgow, F. (1999). Structural equation models of sexual harassment: Longitudinal explorations and cross-sectional generalizations. *Journal of Applied Psychology, 84*, 14–28.

Glomb, T.M., Richman, W.L., Hulin, C.L., & Drasgow, F. (1997). Ambient sexual harassment: An integrated model of antecedents and consequences. *Organizational Behavior and Human Decision Processes, 71*, 309–328.

Goodman, J., & Croyle, R.C. (1989). Social framework testimony in employment discrimination cases. *Behavioral Sciences & the Law, 7*, 227–241.

Goodman-Delahunty, J. (1999). Civil law: Employment and discrimination. In R. Roesch, S.D. Hart, & J.R.P. Ogloff (Eds.), *Psychology and law: The state of the discipline* (277–337). New York: Kluwer/Plenum.

Goodman-Delahunty, J., & Foote, W. (1995). Compensation for pain, suffering and other psychological injuries: The impact of *Daubert* on employment discrimination claims. *Behavioral Sciences & the Law, 13,* 183–206.

Goodman-Delahunty, J., & Foote, W.E. (2009). Forensic evaluations advance scientific theory: Assessing causation of harm. [In special issue on case-based theory building.] *Pragmatic Case Studies in Psychotherapy, 5,* 38–52.

Goodman-Delahunty, J., & O'Brien, K. (2009a). *Jury perceptions of psychological workplace injuries.* Unpublished manuscript, Charles Sturt University, NSW, Australia.

Goodman-Delahunty, J., & O'Brien, K. (2009b). *A comparison of lay and expert knowledge of psychological workplace injuries.* Unpublished manuscript, Charles Sturt University, NSW, Australia.

Gold, L.H. (2004). *Sexual harassment: Psychiatric assessment in employment litigation.* Washington, D.C.: American Psychiatric Publishing, Inc.

Goldenhar, L.M., Swanson, N.G., Hurrell, J.J., Ruder, A., & Deddens, J. (1998). Stressors and adverse outcomes for female construction workers. *Journal of Occupational Health Psychology, 3(1):* 19–32.

Goldenhar, L., Williams, L.J., & Swanson, N.G. (2003). Modelling relationships between job stressors and injury and near-miss outcomes for construction labourers. *Work & Stress, 17,* 218–240.

Golden, S.H., Lazo, M., Carnethon, M., Bertoni, A.G., Schreiner, P.J., Roux, A.V.D., Lee, H.B., Lyketsos, C. (2008). Examining a bidirectional association between depressive symptoms and diabetes. *Journal of the American Medical Association, 299(23):* 2751–2759.

Goldman, B.M., Gutek, B.A., Stein, J.H., Lewis, K. (2006). Employment discrimination in organizations: Antecedents and consequences. *Journal of Management, 32(6):* 786–830.

Greenberg, S. (2004, April). *Psychological consultation in personal injury cases.* Paper presented at the American Academy of Forensic Psychology. New Orleans, LA.

Greenberg, S.A. (2003). Personal injury examinations in torts for emotional distress. In A.M. Goldstein (Ed.), *Handbook of psychology: Forensic psychology,* vol. 11 (pp. 233–257). Hoboken, NJ: John Wiley & Sons Inc.

Greenberg, S.A., Otto, R.K., & Long, A.C. (2003). The utility of psychological testing in assessing emotional damages in personal injury litigation. *Assessment, 10(4):* 411–419.

Greenberg, S.A., & Shuman, D.W. (1997). Irreconcilable conflict between therapeutic and forensic roles. *Professional Psychology: Research and Practice, 28(1):* 50–57.

Greenberg, S.A., & Wheeler, J.G. (2004). Forensic psychological examinations in personal injury cases: Empirical haves and have nots. *Journal of Forensic Psychology Practice, 4(1):* 79–95.

Greene, E. (2000). Compensating plaintiffs and punishing defendants: Is bifurcation necessary? Law & Human Behavior, *24,* 187–205.

Greene, E., & Bornstein, B. (2000). Precious little guidance: Jury instruction on damage awards. *Psychology, Public Policy and Law, 6(3):* 743–768.

Greene, E., & Bornstein, B. (2003). *Determining damages: The psychology of jury awards.* Washington, D.C.: American Psychological Association.

Greene, E., Downey, C., & Goodman-Delahunty, J. (1999). Juror decisions about damages in employment discrimination cases. *Behavioral Sciences & the Law, 17*, 107–121.

Greene, E., & Goodman-Delahunty, J. (1995). Diagnosis of psychological impairment in employment discrimination claims. *Behavioral Sciences & the Law, 13,* 459–476.

Gregory, R.E. (2001). *Age discrimination in the American workplace: Old at a young age.* New Brunswick, NJ: Rutgers University Press.

Griffith, E.H. (2007). A forensic and ethics-based view of Carter's "Racism and psychological and emotional injury." *The Counseling Psychologist, 35*, 116–125.

Grove, W., Barden, R., Garb, H., & Lilienfeld, S. (2002). Failure of Rorschach- Comprehensive-System-based testimony to be admissible under the *Daubert/Kumho* standard. *Psychology, Public Policy and Law, 8*, 216–234.

Gunnarsdottir, H.K., Sveinsdottir, H., Gunnar Bernburg, J., Fridriksdottir, H., & Tomasson, K. (2006). Lifestyle, harassment at work and self-assessed health of female flight attendants, nurses and teachers. *Work: A Journal of Prevention, Assessment and Rehabilitation, 27*(2): 165–172.

Gutek, B.A., & Koss, M.P. (1993). Changed women and changed organizations: Consequences of and coping with sexual harassment. *Journal of Vocational Behavior, 42*, 28–48.

Gutek, B.A, Murphy, R.O., & Douma, B. (2004). A review and critique of the Sexual Experiences Questionnaire (SEQ). *Law & Human Behavior, 28*, 457–482.

Haden, S.C., & Scarpa, A. (2008). Community violence, victimization and depressed mood: The moderating effects of coping and social support. *Journal of Interpersonal Violence, 23*, 1213–1234.

Hadley, E.C., & Laws, E.J. (2008). *Federal sector sexual harassment law.* Arlington, VA: Dewey Publications.

Halligan, P.W., Bass, C., & Oakley, D.A. (2003). *Malingering and illness deception.* Oxford, UK: Oxford University Press.

Hamilton, M.J. (1989). A comparison of psychological symptoms of treated and nontreated incestuous male perpetrators. *Dissertation Abstracts International, 50*(02): 748B–749B.

Hans, V.P. (1996). The contested role in the civil jury in business litigation. *Judicature, 79,* 242–248.

Hans, V.P. (2000). *Business on trial: The civil jury and corporate responsibility.* New Haven, CT: Yale University Press.

Hans, V.P., & Albertson, S. (2003), Empirical research and civil jury reform. *Notre Dame Law Review, 78,* 1497–1523.

Harned, M.S., & Fitzgerald, L.F. (2002). Understanding a link between sexual harassment and eating disorder symptoms: A mediational analysis. *Journal of Consulting and Clinical Psychology, 70*(5): 1170–1181.

Hart, H.L.A., & Honoré, T. (1959). *Causation in the law*. Oxford: Clarendon Press.

Hassell, B.L., & Perrewe, P.L. (1993). An examination of the relationship between older workers' perceptions of age discrimination and employee psychological states. *Journal of Managerial Issues, 5*, 109–120.

Heilbrun, K. (2001). *Principles of forensic mental health assessment*. New York: Luwer Academic/Plenum Press.

Heilbrun, K., Marczyk, G.R., & DeMatteo, D. (2002). *Forensic mental health assessment: A casebook* (pp. 387–406). New York: Oxford University Press.

Heilbrun, K., Rogers, R., & Otto, R.K. (2002). Forensic assessment: Current status and future directions. In J.P. Ogloff (Eds.), *Taking psychology and law into the twenty-first century* (pp. 120–147). New York: Kluwer Academic/Plenum Publishers.

Heilbrun, K., Rosenfeld, B., Warren, J.I., & Collins, S. (1994). The use of third-party information in forensic assessments: A two-state comparison. *Bulletin of the American Academy of Psychiatry & Law, 22*, 399–406.

Heilbrun, K., Warren, J., & Picarello, K. (2004). Third party information in forensic assessment. In A.M. Goldstein (Ed.), *Handbook of psychology: Forensic psychology* (pp. 69–86). Hoboken, NJ: John Wiley & Sons.

Hemingway, C.W. (1994). A review of administrative compensatory damage award decisions under the Civil Rights Act of 1991. *Federal Bar News & Journal, 41*(10): 688–704.

Hill, L.K., Kobayasji, I., & Hughes, J.W. (2007). Perceived racism and ambulatory blood pressure in African American college students. *Journal of Black Psychology, 33*, 404–421.

Hilsenroth, M., & Stricker, G. (2004). A consideration of challenges to psychological assessment instruments used in forensic settings: Rorschach as exemplar. *Journal of Personality Assessment, 83*, 141–152.

Hirsch, C.E. (2008). Settling for less? Organizational determinants of discrimination-charge outcomes. *Law & Society Review, 42*(2): 239–274.

Holeva, V., & Tarrier, N. (2001) Personality and peritraumatic dissociation in the prediction of PTSD in victims of road traffic accidents. *Journal of Psychosomatic Research, 51*, 687–692.

Holzbauer, J.J., & Berven, N.L. (1996). Disability harassment: A new term for a long-standing problem. *Journal of Counseling and Development, 74*(5): 478–483.

Hopkins, A.B. (1996). *So ordered: Making partner the hard way*. Amherst, MA: University of Massachusetts Press.

Hopkins, A.B. (2007). Opposing views, strongly held. In F.J. Crosby, M.S. Stockdale, & S.A. Ropp (Eds.), *Sex discrimination in the workplace: Multidisciplinary perspectives* (pp. 59–68). Oxford, UK: Blackwell

Horowitz, A.V., Widom, C.S., McLaughlin, J., & White, H.R. (2001). The impact of childhood abuse and neglect on adult mental health:

A prospective study. *Journal of Health and Social Behavior, 42,* 184–201.

Horowitz, I., & Bordens, D. (1990). An experimental investigation of procedural issues in complex tort trials. *Law & Human Behavior, 14,* 269–285.

Humphrey, J.A., & White, J.W. (2000). Women's vulnerability to sexual assault from adolescence to young adulthood. *Journal of Adolescent Health, 27,* 419–424.

Hynan, D.J. (2004). Unsupported gender differences on some personality disorder scales of the Millon Clinical Multiaxial Inventory-III. *Professional Psychology: Research and Practice, 35,* 105–110.

Ilies, R., Hauserman, N., Schowochau, S., & Stibal, J. (2003). Reported incidence rates of work-related sexual harassment in the United States: Using meta-analysis to explain reported rate disparities. *Personnel Psychology,* 56, 607–631.

James, K., Lovato, C., & Khoo, G. (1994). Social identity correlates of minority workers' health. *Academy of Management Journal, 37,* 383–396.

Janutis, R.M. (2008). The new industrial accident crisis: Compensating workers for injuries in the office. *Loyola of Los Angeles Law Review, 42,* 25–50.

Jensvold, M.F. (1993). Workplace sexual harassment: The use, misuse, and abuse of psychiatry. *Psychiatric Annals, 23,* 438–445.

Jumper, S.A. (1995). A meta-analysis of the relationship of child sexual abuse to adult psychological adjustment. *Child Abuse & Neglect, 19(6):* 715–728.

Kagehiro, D. (2004, Feb.). The impact of bifurcation on jury damages awards. *For the Defense, 13,* 45–48.

Kamphuis, J.H., & Emmelkamp, P.M.G. (2001). Traumatic distress among support-seeking female victims of stalking. *American Journal of Psychiatry, 158,* 795–798.

Katz, L.S., Bloor, L.E., Cojucar, G., & Draper, T. (2007). Women who served in Iraq seeking mental health services: Relationships between military sexual trauma, symptoms, and readjustment. *Psychological Services, 4,* 239–249.

Katzen, M.F. (2006). *Gender, race, and ethnicity in the workplace: Issues and challenges for today's organizations.* Santa Barbara, CA: Praeger Perspectives.

Keashly, L., & Harvey, S. (2004). Emotional abuse at work. Washington, D.C.: American Psychological Association. In S. Fox & P.E. Spector (Eds.), *Counterproductive Work Behavior* (pp. 201–236). Washington, D.C.: American Psychological Association.

Kessler, R.C., Berglund, P., Demler, O., Jin, R., Koretz, D., Merikangas, K.R., Rush, A.J., Walters, E.E., & Wang, P.S. (2003). The epidemiology of major depressive disorder: Results from the National Comorbidity Survey Replication (NCS-R). *Journal of the American Medical Association, 289,* 3095–3105.

Kessler, R.C., Berglund, P., Demler, O., Jin, R., & Walters, E.E. (2005). Lifetime prevalence and age-of-onset distributions of DSM-IV disorders in the National Comorbidity Survey Replication. *Archives of General Psychiatry, 62*(6): 593–602.

Kessler, R.C., Chiu, W.T., Dealer, O., & Walters, E.E. (2005). Prevalence, severity, and comorbidity of 12-month DSM-IV disorders in the National Comorbidity Survey Replication. *Archives of General Psychiatry, 62*(6): 617–627.

Kessler, R.C., Davis, C.G., & Kendler, K.S. (1997). Childhood adversity and adult psychiatric disorder in the U.S. National Comorbidity Survey. *Psychological Medicine, 27*(5): 1101–1119.

Kessler, R.C., & Merikangas, K.R. (2004). The National Comorbidity Survey Replication (NCS-R): Background and aims. *International Journal of Methods in Psychiatric Research, 13*(2): 60–68.

Kessler, R.C., Mickelson, K.D., & Williams, D.R. (1999). The prevalence, distribution and mental health correlates of perceived discrimination in the United States. *Journal of Health and Social Behavior, 40,* 208–230.

Kessler, R.C., Sonnega, A., Bromet, E., Hughes, M., et al. (1995). Posttraumatic stress disorder in the National Comorbidity Survey. *Archives of General Psychiatry, 52,* 1048–1060.

Kilpatrick, D.G., Dansky, B.S., & Saunders, B.E. (1994). *Sexual harassment in the workplace: Results from the National Women's Study* [monograph]. Charleston, SC: Crime Victims Research and Treatment Center, Department of Psychiatry and Behavioral Sciences, Medical University of South Carolina.

Kjellberg A. (1998). Men, work and health. In: Å. Kilbom, K. Messing, & C.B. Thorbjornsson (Eds.), *Women's health at work* (pp. 279–307). Solna, Sweden: Arbetslivsinstitutet.

Klonoff, E.A., Landrine, H., & Campbell, R. (2000). Sexist discrimination may account for well-known gender differences in psychiatric symptoms. *Psychology of Women Quarterly, 24,* 93–99.

Klonoff, E.A., Landrine, H., & Ullman, J.B. (1999). Racial discrimination and psychiatric symptoms among blacks. *Cultural Diversity & Ethnic Minority Psychology, 5,* 329–339.

Knapp, S., & VandeCreek, L. (2001). Ethical issues in personality assessment in forensic psychology. *Journal of Personality Assessment, 77*(2): 242–254.

Knox-Haly, M. (2008). *How to stop your workplace going pear shaped: Readings in HR risk mitigation.* Prahan, Victoria, AU: Tilde University Press.

Koch, W.J., Douglas, K.S., Nicholls, T.L., & O'Neill, M.L. (Eds.) (2006). Psychological injuries: Forensic assessment, treatment and law. New York: Oxford University Press.

Kovera, M.B., & Cass, S.A. (2002). Compelled mental health examinations, liability decisions, and damage awards in sexual harassment cases: Issues for jury research. *Psychology, Public Policy and Law, 8*(1): 96–114.

Krafka, C., Dunn, M.A., Johnson, M.T., Cecil, J.S., & Miletich, D. (2002). Judge and attorney experiences, practices, and concerns regarding expert testimony in federal civil trials. *Psychology, Public Policy and Law, 8(3):* 309–332.

Krieger, N. (1990). Racial and gender discrimination: Risk factors for high blood pressure? *Social Science and Medicine, 30*, 1273–1281.

Krieger, N. (1999). Embodying inequality: A review of concepts, measures, and methods for studying health consequences of discrimination. *Journal of Health and Social Behavior, 29*, 295–352.

Krieger, N. (2003). Does racism harm health? Did child abuse exist before 1962? On explicit questions, critical science, and current controversies: An ecosocial perspective. *American Journal of Public Health, 21,* 194–199.

Krieger, N., & Sidney, S. (1997). Prevalence and health implications of anti-gay discrimination: A study of black and white women and men in the CARDIA study. *International Journal of Health Services, 27,* 157–176.

Krull, K.R., Scott, J.G., & Scherer, M. (1995). Estimation of premorbid intelligence from combined performance and demographic variables. *The Clinical Neuropsychologist, 9,* 83–42.

Lapierre, L., Spector, P., & Leck, J. (2005). Sexual vs. nonsexual workplace aggression and victims' overall job satisfaction: A meta-analysis. *Journal of Occupational Health Psychology, 10*, 155–169.

Landy, F.J. (Ed.) (2005a). *Employment discrimination litigation: Behavioral, quantitative, and legal perspectives.* San Francisco: Jossey-Bass.

Landy, F.J. (2005b). A judge's view: Interviews with federal judges about expert witness testimony. In F.J. Landy (Ed.,) *Employment discrimination litigation: Behavioral, quantitative and legal perspectives.* San Francisco: Jossey-Bass.

Langeluddecke, P.M., & Lucas, S.K. (2004). Evaluation of two methods for estimating premorbid intelligence on the WAIS-III in a clinical sample. *Clinical Neuropsychologist, 18*, 423–432.

Langhout, R.D., Bergman, M.E., Cortina, L.M., Fitzgerald, L.F., Drasgow, F., & Hunter Williams, J. (2005). Sexual harassment severity: Assessing situational and personal determinants and outcomes. *Journal of Applied Social Psychology, 35*, 975–1007.

Lazarus, R.S., & Folkman, S. (1984). *Stress, appraisal, and coping.* New York: Springer.

Leal, S., & Vrij, A. (2008). Blinking during and after lying. *Journal of Nonverbal Behavior, 32(4):* 187–194.

Lees-Haley, P.R. (1988). Litigation response syndrome. *American Journal of Forensic Psychology, 6(1):* 3–12.

Lees-Haley, P.R., & Brown, R.S. (1993). Neuropsychological complaint base rates of 170 personal injury claimants. *Archives of Clinical Neuropsychology, 8*, 203–209.

Lees-Haley, P.R., Williams, C.W., Lees-Haley, C.E., Price, J.R., & Smith, J.T. (1994). Sexual harassment and emotional distress: A ranking of social-sexual behavior. *American Journal of Forensic Psychiatry, 15(4):* 5–25.

Lenhart, S.A. (2004). *Clinical aspects of sexual harassment and gender discrimination: Psychological consequences and treatment interventions.* New York: Brunner-Routledge.

Leymann, H. (1990). Mobbing and psychological terror at workplaces. *Violence and Victims, 5*, 119–126.

Lilly Ledbetter Fair Pay Act of 2009, Pub. L. No. 111–2 (2009).

Lippel, K. (1999). Workers' compensation and stress: Gender and access to compensation. *International Journal of Law and Psychiatry, 22*, 79–89.

Lippel K. (2003). Compensation for musculoskeletal disorders in Quebec: Systemic discrimination against women workers? *International Journal of Health Services, 33*(2): 253–281.

Lippel, K. (2007). Research, policy and practice in work and mental health: A multidisciplinary discussion. *International Journal of Law and Psychiatry, 30,* 269–271.Livingstone, D.R, Shanor, C.A., & Mirengoff, P.E. (2005). *EEOC litigation and charge resolution.* Washington, D.C.: Bureau of National Affairs.

Loftus, E.F., Feldman, J., & Dashiell, R. (1995). The reality of illusory memories. In D.L. Schacter (Ed.), *Memory distortions: How minds, brains, and societies reconstruct the past* (pp. 47–68). Cambridge, MA, US: Harvard University Press.

Long, B., Rouse, S.V., Nelsen, R.O, & Butcher, J.N. (2004). The MMPI-2 in sexual harassment and discrimination litigants. *Journal of Clinical Psychology, 60,* 643–657.

Magley, V.J., Hulin, C.L., Fitzgerald, L.F., & DeNardo, M. (1999). Outcomes of self-labeling sexual harassment. *Journal of Applied Psychology, 84,* 390–402.

Magley, V.J., Waldo, C.R., Drasgow, F., & Fitzgerald, L.F. (1999). The impact of sexual harassment on military personnel: Is it the same for men and women? *Military Psychology, 11*, 283–302.

Maker, A.H., Kemmelmeier, M., & Peterson, C. (2001). Child sexual abuse, peer sexual abuse, and sexual assault in adulthood: A multi-risk model of revictimization. *Journal of Traumatic Stress, 14,* 351–368.

Marin, A.J., & Guadagno, R.E. (1999). Perceptions of sexual harassment victims as a function of labeling and reporting. *Sex Roles, 41*(11–12): 921–940.

Marsella, A.J., Friedman, M.J., Gerrity, T., & Scurfield, R.M. (1996). *Ethnocultural aspects of posttraumatic stress disorder.* Washington, D.C.: American Psychological Association.

Matthiesen, S.B. (2004). When whistleblowing leads to bullying at work. *Occupational Health Psychologist, 1*(*1*): 1.

Matthiesen, S.B., & Einarsen, S. (2004). Psychiatric distress and symptoms of PTSD among victims of bullying at work. *British Journal of Guidance & Counselling, 32*(*3*)*:* 335–356.

Mayhew, C., McCarthy, P., Chappell, D., Quinlan, M., Barker, M., & Sheehan, M. (2004). Measuring the extent of impact from occupational violence and bullying on traumatized workers. *Employee Responsibilities and Rights Journal, 16(3):* 117–134.

Mays, V.M., Coleman, L.M., & Jackson, J.S. (1996). Perceived race-based discrimination, employment status, and job stress in a national sample of black women: Implications for health outcomes. *Journal of Occupational Health Psychology, 1*, 319–329.

McCaffery, E.J., Kahneman, D.J., Spitzer, M.L. (1995). Framing the jury: Cognitive perspective on pain and suffering awards. *Virginia Law Review, 81*, 341–405.

McKenzie, K. (2006). Racial discrimination and mental health. *Psychiatry, 5(11):* 383–387.

McNally, R.J., Bryant, R.A., & Ehler, A. (2003). Does early psychological intervention promote recovery from posttraumatic stress? *Psychological Science in the Public Interest, 4(2)*: 45–79.

Mehri, C. (2008, Sept.). Barriers to justice: Examining equal pay for equal work. Testimony before the Senate Judicial Committee. Retrieved June 5, 2008, from http://judiciary.senate.gov/hearings/testimony.cfm?id=3564&wit_id=7439

Melton, G.B., Petrila, J., Poythress, N.G., & Slobogin, C. (2007). *Psychological evaluations for the courts: A handbook for mental health professionals and lawyers* (2nd ed.). New York: Guilford Press.

Miceli, M.R., Near, J.P., & Dworkin, T.M. (2008). *Whistle-blowing in organizations.* Mahwah, NJ: Taylor and Francis, LEA Organization and Management Series.

Millon, T. (1994). *Millon Clinical Multiaxial Inventory Manual* (3rd ed.). Minneapolis, MN: National Computer Systems.

Millon, T., & Davis, R.D. (1996). *Disorders of personality: DSM-IV and beyond.* New York: John Wiley.

Miner-Rubino, K., & Cortina, L.M. (2007). Beyond targets: Consequences of vicarious exposure to misogyny at work. *Journal of Applied Psychology, 92(5):* 1254–1269.

Monahan, J., Walker, L., & Mitchell, G. (2008). Contextual evidence of gender discrimination: The ascendance of "Social Frameworks." *Virginia Law Review, 94,* 1705–1739.

Morey, L.C. (1996). *An interpretive guide for the Personality Assessment Inventory.* Odessa, FL: Psychological Assessment Resources.

Morey, L.C. (2007). *Personality Assessment Inventory professional manual* (2nd ed.). Lutz, FL: Psychological Assessment Resources.

Mott, N.L., Hans, V.P., & Simpson, L. (2000). What's half a lung worth? Civil jurors' accounts of their award decision making. *Law and Human Behavior, 24(4):* 401–419.

Moulds, M.L., & Bryant, R.A. (2006). The influence of distressing information on memory in acute stress disorder. *Behavioral and Cognitive Psychotherapy, 34,* 333–341.

Mueller, C.B., & Kirkpatrick, L.C. (2007). *Federal rules of evidence with advisory committee notes, legislative history, and cases.* New York: Aspen Law and Business.

Mujtaba, B.G., Cavico, F., Hinds, R.M., & Oskal, C. (2006). Age discrimination in the workplace: Cultural paradigms associated with age in Afghanistan, Jamaica, Turkey, and the United States. *Journal of Applied Management and Entrepreneurship, 11,* 17–35.

Munson, L.J., Hulin, C.L., & Drasgow, F. (2000). Longitudinal analysis of dispositional influences and sexual harassment: Effects on job and psychological outcomes. *Personnel Psychology, 53,* 21–46.

Murdoch, M., Polusny, M.A., Hodges, J., & Cowper, D. (2006). The association between in-service sexual harassment and post-traumatic stress disorder among Department of Veterans Affairs disability applicants. *Military Medicine, 171,* 166–173.

Murdoch, M., Pryor, J.B., Polusny, M.A., & Gacstetter, G.D. (2007). Functioning and psychiatric symptoms among military men and women exposed to sexual stressors. *Military Medicine, 172(7):* 718–725.

Murrell, A.J., Olson, J.E., & Frieze, I.H. (1995). Sexual harassment and gender discrimination: A longitudinal study of women managers. *Journal of Social Issues, 51,* 139–149.

National Institute for Occupational Safety and Health (2000). *Stress at work.* Washington, D.C.: U.S. Department of Health and Human Services.

Neumann, D.A., Houskamp, B.M., Pollock, V.E., & Briere, J. (1996). The long-term sequelae of childhood sexual abuse in women: A meta-analytic review. *Child Maltreatment: Journal of the American Professional Society on the Abuse of Children, 1(1):* 6–16.

Nicholson, K., & Martelli, M.F. (2006). Confounding effects of pain, psychoemotional problems or psychiatric disorders, premorbid ability structure, and motivational or other factors on neuropsychological test performance. In G. Young, A.W. Kane, & K. Nicholson (Eds.), *Psychological knowledge in court: PTSD, pain and TBI* (pp. 335–351). New York: Springer.

Nielsen, L.B., & Nelson, R.L. (Eds.) (2005). *Handbook of employment discrimination research: Rights and realities.* Amsterdam, Netherlands: Springer.

Nielsen, L.B., Nelson, R.L., & Lancaster, R. (2008). Uncertain justice: Litigating claims of employment discrimination in the contemporary United States. *American Bar Foundation Research Paper No. 08–04.* Chicago: American Bar Foundation.

Nielsen, L.B., Nelson, R.L., Lancaster, R., & Pedriana, N. (2008). *Contesting workplace discrimination in court: Characteristics and outcomes of federal employment discrimination litigation 1987–2003.* Retrieved May 20, 2009, from http://www.americanbarfoundation.org/uploads/cms/documents/nielsen_abf_edl_report_08_final.pdf.

Nordberg, P. (2009). *Daubert* on the web: *Daubert* decisions by field of expertise. Retrieved June 17, 2009, from http://www.daubertontheweb.com/psychologists.htm.

Northwestern National Life Insurance Company (1991). *Employee burnout: America's newest epidemic*. Minneapolis, MN: Author.

Northwestern National Life Insurance Company (1992). *Employee burnout: Causes and cures*. Minneapolis, MN: Author.

O'Connor, M. (2007). Expert testimony in sexual harassment cases: Its scope, limits and effectiveness. In M. Costanzo, D. Krauss, & K. Pezdek (Eds.), *Expert psychological testimony for the courts* (pp. 119–148). Mahwah, NJ: Lawrence Erlbaum Associates.

O'Donnell, M.L., Creamer, M., Bryant, R.A., Schnyder, U., & Shalev, A. (2006). Posttraumatic disorders following injury: Assessment and other methodological considerations. In G. Young, K. Nicholson, & A.W. Kane (Eds.). *Psychological knowledge in court* (pp. 70–84). New York: Springer.

O'Donnell, M.L., Holmes, A.C., Creamer, M.C., Ellen, S., Judson, R., McFarlane, A.C., Silove, D.M., & Bryant, R.A. (2009). The role of post-traumatic stress disorder and depression in predicting disability after injury. *The Medical Journal of Australia, 190*(*7*): 71–74.

Orpen, C. (1995). The effects of perceived age discrimination on employee job satisfaction, organizational commitment and job involvement. *Psychology: A Quarterly Journal of Human Behavior, 32*, 55–56.

Owens, J.M., Gomes, G.M., & Morgan, J.F. (2008). Broadening the definition of unlawful retaliation under Title VII. *Employment Responsibilities and Rights Journal, 20*, 249–260.

Palmieri, P.A., & Fitzgerald, L.F. (2005). Confirmatory factors analysis of posttraumatic stress symptoms in sexually harassed women. *Journal of Traumatic Stress, 18*(*6*): 657–666.

Paolucci, E.O., Genuis, M.L., & Violato, C. (2001). A meta-analysis of the published research on the effects of child sexual abuse. *The Journal of Psychology, 135*(*1*): 17–36.

Paul, K.I., & Moser, K. (2009). Unemployment impairs mental health: Meta-analyses. *Journal of Vocational Behavior, 74*(*3*): 264–282.

Pavalko, E.K., Mossakowski, K.N., & Hamilton, V.J. (2003). Does perceived discrimination affect health? Longitudinal relationships between work discrimination and women's physical and emotional health. *Journal of Health and Social Behavior, 43*, 18–43.

Peirce, C.S. (1931–1958). *Collected papers of Charles Sanders Peirce.* C. Hartshorne & P. Weiss (Eds.). Cambridge, MA: Harvard University Press.

Perrin, G., & Sales, B.D. (1993). Artificial legal standards in mental/emotional injury litigation. *Behavioral Sciences & the Law, 11*, 193–203.

Piotrkowski, C.S. (1998). Gender harassment, job satisfaction and distress among employed white and minority women. *Journal of Occupational Health Psychology, 3*, 33–43.

Polusny, M.A., & Follette, V.M. (1995). Long-term correlates of child sexual abuse: Theory and review of the empirical literature. *Applied & Preventive Psychology, 4*(*3*): 143–166.

Pope, K.S. (2009). *Logical fallacies in psychology: 21 types.* Retrieved June 1, 2009, from: http://kspope.com/fallacies/fallacies.php.

Pope, K.S., Butcher, J.N., & Seelen, J. (2000). *The MMPI, MMPI-2, & MMPI-A in court: A practical guide for expert witnesses and attorneys* (2nd ed.). Washington, D.C.: American Psychological Association.

Poythress, N.G. (1982). Concerning reform in expert testimony: An open letter from a practicing psychologist. *Law and Human Behavior, 6,* 39–43.

Price-Spratlen, L.P. (1995). Interpersonal conflict which includes mistreatment in a university workplace. *Violence and Victims, 10,* 285–297.

Princeton Survey Research Associates (1997). *Labor Day survey: State of workers.* Princeton, NJ: Author.

Pryor, J.B. (1995). The phenomenology of sexual harassment: Why does sexual behavior bother people in the workplace? *Consulting Psychology Journal: Practice & Research, 47*(3): 160–168.

Psychological Corporation (2008a). *Wechsler Adult Intelligence Scale-IV Technical Manual.* New York: The Psychological Corporation.

Psychological Corporation (2008b). *Wechsler Memory Scale-IV Technical Manual.* New York: The Psychological Corporation.

Raitz, A., Greene, E., Goodman, J., & Loftus, E. (1990). Determining damages: The influence of expert testimony on jurors' decision making. *Law and Human Behavior, 14*(4): 385–395.

Rehg, M.T., Miceli, M.P., Near, J.P., & Van Scotter, J.R. (2008). Antecedents and outcomes of retaliation against whistleblowers: Gender differences and power relationships. *Organization Science, 19,* 221–240.

Reina, M.V., Adya, M., & Blanck, P. (2007). Defying double discrimination. *Georgetown Journal of International Affairs, 8,* 95–104.

Report of the Special Committee ABA Section of Litigation (1990). *Jury comprehension in complex cases.* Chicago: American Bar Association.

Resnick, P.J. (1997). Malingering of posttraumatic disorders. In R. Richard (Ed.), *Clinical assessment of malingering and deception* (2nd ed., pp. 130–152). New York: Guilford Press.

Richman, J., Rospenda, K., Nawyn, S., Flaherty, J., Fendrich, M., Drum, M., & Johnson, T. (1999). Sexual harassment and generalized workplace abuse among university employees: Prevalence and mental health correlates. *American Journal of Public Health, 89,* 358–363.

Richman, J.A., Fendrich, M., Wislar, J.S., Flaherty, J.A., & Rospenda, K.M. (2004). Drinking and anxiety effects of 9/11/01 in combination with work stressors: A longitudinal cohort study. *American Journal of Public Health, 94,* 2010–2015.

Riggs, D.S., & Foa, D.B. (2009). Psychological treatment of posttraumatic stress disorder and acute stress disorder. In M.M. Anthony & M.B. Stein (Eds.), *Oxford handbook of anxiety and related disorders* (pp. 417–428). New York: Oxford University Press.

Robinson, S. (2009, Feb.). *Ostracism at work: Attributions and outcomes.* Paper presented at the Laurier School of Business and Economics, Waterloo, Canada.

Roesler, T.A., & McKenzie, N. (1994). Effects of childhood trauma on psychological functioning in adults sexually abused as children. *Journal of Nervous & Mental Disease, 182(3):* 145–150.

Rogers, R. (2002). Validating retrospective assessments: An overview of the research models. In R.I. Simon & D.W. Shuman (Eds.), *Predicting the past: The retrospective assessment of mental states in civil and criminal litigation* (pp. 287–306). Washington, D.C.: American Psychiatric Press, Inc.

Rogers, R. (1987). Ethical dilemmas in forensic psychology. *Behavioral Sciences and the Law, 5(2):* 149–160.

Rogers, R. (1992). *SIRS, Structured Interview of Reported Symptoms: Professional manual.* Odessa, FL: Psychological Assessment Resources.

Rogers, R. (1997). Structured interviews and dissimulation. In R. Rogers (Ed.), *Clinical assessment of malingering and deception* (pp. 301–327). New York: Guilford Press.

Rogers, R. (Ed.) (2008). *Clinical assessment of malingering and deception* (3rd ed.). New York: Guilford Press.

Rogers, R., & Bender, S.D. (2003). Evaluation of malingering and deception. In A.M. Goldstein (Ed.), *Handbook of psychology: Forensic psychology* (pp. xviii, 109–129). Hoboken, NJ: John Wiley & Sons

Rogers, R., Salekin, R.T., & Sewell, K.W. (1999). Validation of the Millon Clinical Multiaxial Inventory for Axis II disorders: Does it meet the *Daubert* standard? *Law and Human Behavior, 23*(4): 425–443.

Rosen, L.N., & Martin, L. (1998). Childhood maltreatment history as a risk factor for sexual harassment among U.S. Army soldiers. *Violence & Victims, 13(3)*: 269–286.

Rospenda, K.M. (2002). Workplace harassment, services utilization, and drinking outcomes. *Journal of Occupational Health Psychology, 7*, 141–155.

Rospenda, K.M., Fujishiro, K., & Richman, S.J. (2008). Workplace harassment, stress, and drinking behavior over time: Gender differences in a national sample. *Addictive Behaviors, 33*, 964–967.

Rospenda, K.M., & Richman, J.A. (2005). Harassment and discrimination. In J. Barling, E.K. Kelloway, & M.J. Frone (Eds.), *Handbook of work stress* (pp. 149–188). Thousand Oaks, CA: Sage.

Rospenda, K.M., Richman, J.A., Ehmke, J.L.Z., & Zlatoper, K.W. (2005). Is workplace harassment hazardous to your health? *Journal of Business and Psychology, 20(1)*: 95–110.

Rotundo, M., Nguyen, D., & Sackett, P. (2001). A meta-analytic review of gender differences in perceptions of sexual harassment. *Journal of Applied Psychology, 86*, 914–922.

Rudman, L.A., & Glick, P. (2008). *The social psychology of gender: How power and intimacy shape gender relations.* New York: Guilford Press.

Rupp v. Purolator Courier Corp., 45 F.3rd 440 (10th Cir. 1994).

Ryu, D., & Larkin, J.D. (2007). A gender discrimination class action from the point of view of the plaintiffs' lawyers. In F.J. Crosby, M.S. Stockdale, & S.A. Ropp (Eds.), *Sex discrimination in the workplace: Multidisciplinary perspectives* (pp. 97–106). Malden, MA: Blackwell.

Sagrestano, L.M. (2004). Health implications of workplace diversity. In M.S. Stockdale & F.J. Crosby (Eds.), *The psychology and management of workplace diversity* (pp. 122–144). Boston: Blackwell.

Sales, B.D., & Shuman, D.W. (2005). *Experts in court: Reconciling law, science and professional knowledge.* Washington, D.C.: American Psychological Association.

Salin, D. (2010, in press). The significance of gender for third parties' perceptions of negative interpersonal behaviour: Labelling and explaining negative acts. *Gender, Work, and Organization.* http://www3.interscience.wiley.com/journal/120123915/issue, DOI: 10.1111/j.1468-0432.2009.00465.x

Salisbury, J., Ginorio, A.B., Remick, H., & Stringer, D.M. (1986). Counselling victims of sexual harassment. *Psychotherapy, 23,* 316–324.

Samra, J., & Koch, W.J. (2002). The monetary worth of psychological injury: What are litigants suing for? In J.R.P. Ogloff (Ed.), *Taking psychology and law into the 21st century* (pp. 286–324). New York: Kluwer Academic/Plenum Publishers.

Sanders, J. (2006). Why do proposals designed to control variability in general damages (generally) fall on deaf ears? (And why this is too bad). *DePaul Law Review 55,* 489–515.

Satchell et al. v. FedEx Express. Case No. C 03-2659 SI; C 03-2878 SI (N.D. Ca. April 13, 2007). *Consent Decree.* Retrieved June 9, 2009, from http://www.racecaseagainstfedex.com/staticdata/Consent_Decree.pdf.

Sauter, S.L., Murphy, L.R., & Hurrell, J.J. (1990). Prevention of work related psychological disorders: A national strategy proposed by the National Institute for Occupational Health and Safety (NIOSH). *American Psychologist, 45,* 1146–1158.

Scarville, J., Button, S.B., Edwards, J.E., Lancaster, A.R., & Elig, T.W. (1999). *Armed forces equal opportunity survey.* Arlington, VA: Defense Manpower Data Center, Report No. 97-027.

Schneider, K.T., Hitlan, R.T., & Radhakrishnan, P. (2000). An examination of the nature and correlates of ethnic harassment experiences in multiple contexts. *Journal of Applied Psychology, 85,* 3–12.

Schneider, K.T., Tomaka, J., & Palacios, R. (2001). Women's cognitive, affective and physiological reactions to a male co-worker's sexist behaviour. *Journal of Applied Social Psychology, 31(10):* 1995–2018.

Schoenberg, M.R., Dorr, D., Morgan, C.D., & Burke, M. (2004). A comparison of the MCMI-III personality disorder and modifier indices with the MMPI-2 clinical and validity scales. *Journal of Personality Assessment, 82,* 273–280.

Schoenberg, M.R., Duff, K., Scott, J.G., & Adams, R.L. (2003). An evaluation of the clinical utility of the OPIE-3 as an estimate of premorbid WAIS-III FSIQ. *The Clinical Neuropsychologist, 17(3):* 308–321.

Schuller, R.A., & Klippenstine, M.A. (2004). The impact of complainant sexual history on jurors' decisions: Considerations from a psychological perspective. *Psychology, Public Policy & Law, 10(3):* 321–342.

Schultz, I.G., & Stewart, A.M. (2008). Disentangling the disability quagmire in psychological injury and law. Part 2: Evolution of disability models: Conceptual, methodological and forensic practice issues. *Psychological Injury and Law, 1,* 103–121.

Schultz, I.Z., & Brady, D.O. (Eds.) (2003). *Psychological injuries at trial.* Chicago: American Bar Association Press.

Schur, L., Kruse, D., Blasi, J., & Blanck, P. (2009). Is disability disabling in all workplaces? Workplace disparities and corporate culture. *Industrial Relations: A Journal of Economy and Society, 48(3):* 381–410.

Sebok, A.J. (2007). Punitive damages: From myth to theory. *Iowa Law Review, 92,* 957-1031.

Semmer, N.K., Elfering, A., Jacobshagen, N., Perrot, T., Beehr, T.A., & Boos, N. (2008). The emotional meaning of instrumental social support. *International Journal of Stress Management, 15,* 235–251.

Shannon, C.A., Rospenda, K.M., Richman, J.A., & Minich, L.M. (2009). Race, racial discrimination, and the risk of work-related illness, injury, or assault: Findings from a national survey. *Journal of Occupational Environmental Medicine, 51(4):* 441–448.

Shuman, D.W. (1993). The use of empathy in forensic examinations, *Ethics & Behavior 3,* 289–295.

Shuman, D.W. (2000). When time does not heal: Understanding the importance of avoiding unnecessary delay in the resolution of tort cases. *Psychology, Public Policy, and Law, 6(4):* 880–897.

Shuman, D.W. (2007). How should we address mental and emotional harm? *Judicature, 90,* 248–251.

Shuman, D.W., Greenberg, S.A., Heilbrun, K., & Foote, W.E. (1998). Special perspective: An immodest proposal: Should treating mental health professionals be barred from testifying about their patients? *Behavioral Sciences and the Law, 16*(4): 509–523.

Shupe, E.I., Cortina, L.M., Ramos, A., Fitzgerald, L.F., & Salisbury, J. (2002). The incidence and outcomes of sexual harassment among Hispanic and non-Hispanic white women: A comparison across levels of cultural affiliation. *Psychology of Women Quarterly, 26(4):* 298–308.

Simon, R.I. (1995). Toward the development of guidelines in the psychiatric examination of posttraumatic disorder claimants. In R.I Simon (Ed.), *Posttraumatic stress disorder in litigation* (pp. 31–84). Washington, D.C.: American Psychiatric Press.

Simon, R.I., & Shuman, D.W. (Eds.) (2002). *Retrospective assessment of mental states in litigation: Predicting the past.* Washington, D.C.: American Psychiatric Publishing.

Sims, C.S., Drasgow, F., & Fitzgerald, L.F. (2005). The effects of sexual harassment on turnover in the military: Time-dependent modeling. *Journal of Applied Psychology, 90,* 1141–1152.

Slovenko, R. (2002). *Psychiatry in law/Law in psychiatry.* New York: Brunner-Routledge.

Sowka, M. (Ed.) (1980). National Association of Insurance Commissioners, malpractice claims: Final compilation. Brookfield, WI: National Association of Insurance Commissioners.

Spataro, J., Mullen, P.E., Burgess, P.M., Wells, D.L., & Moss, S.A. (2004). Impact of child sexual abuse on mental health: Prospective study in males and females. *British Journal of Psychiatry, 184,* 416–421.

Stefan, S. (2002). *Hollow promises: Employment discrimination against people with mental disabilities.* Washington, D.C.: American Psychological Association.

Stein, J.A., Golding, J.N., Siegel, J.M., Burnam, M.A., & Sorenson, S.B. (1988). Long-term psychological sequelae of child sexual abuse. In G.E. Wyatt & G.J. Powell (Eds.), *Lasting effects of child sexual abuse* (pp. 135–154). Newbury Park, CA: Sage Publications.

Stiles, W.B. (2009). Logical operations in theory-building case studies. *Pragmatic Case Studies in Psychotherapy, 5,* 9–22.

Stockdale, M.S., & Crosby, F.J. (Eds.) (2004). *The psychology and management of workplace diversity.* Boston: Blackwell.

Street, A.E., Gradus, J.L., Stafford, J., & Kelly, K. (2007). Gender differences in experiences of sexual harassment: Data from a male-dominated environment. *Journal of Consulting and Clinical Psychology, 75*(3): 464–474.

Streseman, K.N. (1995). Headshrinkers, manmunchers, moneygrubbers, nuts and sluts: Reexamining compelled mental examinations in sexual harassment actions under the Civil Rights Act of 1991. *Cornell Law Review, 80,* 1268–1330.

Sullivan, M.K. (Ed.) (2004). *Sexual minorities: Discrimination, challenges and development in America.* Binghamton, NY: Haworth Press.

Sunstein, C., Hastie, R., Payne, J., Schkade, D., & Viscusi, W. (2002). *Punitive damages: How juries decide.* Chicago: University of Chicago Press.

Suter, P.B. (2002). Employment and litigation: Improved by work, assisted by verdict. *Pain, 100,* 249–257.

Sweet, J.J. (1999). *Forensic neuropsychology: Fundamentals and practice.* New York: Taylor & Francis.

Tehrani, N. (2004). Bullying: A source of chronic post traumatic stress? *British Journal of Guidance & Counselling, 32*(3): 357–366.

Tellegen, A., Ben-Porath, Y.S., & Sellbom, M. (2009). Construct validity of the MMPI-2- Restructured Clinical (RC) Scales: Reply to Rouse, Greene, Butcher, Nichols, & Williams. *Journal of Personality Assessment, 91*(3): 211–221.

Tellegen, A., Ben-Porath, Y.S., McNulty, J.L., Arbisi, P.A., Graham, J.R., & Kaemmer, B. (2003). *MMPI-2 Restructured Clinical (RC) Scales:*

Development, validation, and interpretation. Minneapolis: University of Minnesota Press.

Tellegen, A., Ben-Porath, Y.S., Sellbom, M., Arbisi, P.A., McNulty, J.L., & Graham, J.R. (2006). Further evidence on the validity of the MMPI-2 Restructured Clinical (RC) Scales: Addressing questions raised by Rogers et al. and Nichols. *Journal of Personality Assessment, 87,* 148–171.

Terpstra, D.E., & Baker, D.D. (1992). Outcomes of federal court decisions on sexual harassment. *Academy of Management Journal, 35(1):* 181–190.

Tilbury, M.J. (1979). *Civil remedies. Volume 2: Remedies in particular contexts.* Sydney, AU: Butterworths.

Tjaden, P., & Thoennes, N. (2000). *Full report of the prevalence, incidence and consequences of violence against women: Findings from the National Violence Against Women Survey, National Institute of Justice and Centers for Disease Control and Prevention.* Washington, D.C.: National Institute of Justice.

Tombaugh, T. (1997). The Test of Memory Malingering (TOMM): Normative date from cognitively intact and cognitively impaired individuals. *Psychological Assessment, 9(3):* 260–268.

Topa Cantisano, G., Morales Dominguez, J.F., & Depolo, M. (2008). Perceived sexual harassment at work: Meta-analysis and structural model of antecedents and consequences. *The Spanish Journal of Psychology, 11*, 207–218.

Tsushima, W.T., & Tsushima, V.G. (2009). Comparison of MMPI-2 validity scales among compensation-seeking Caucasian and Asian American medical patients. *Assessment, 16*, 159–164.

Tunks, S.P. (1992). The role of litigation in predicting disability outcomes in chronic pain patients. *The Clinical Journal of Pain, 7(4):* 300–304.

Ullman, S.E. (2007). Relationship to perpetrator, disclosure, social reactions, and PTSD symptoms in child sexual abuse survivors. *Journal of Child Sexual Abuse, 16*, 19–36.

Underhill, E. (2007) Sustainable employment and injured labour hire workers: The need for a shift in responsibility? *The Corporate Citizen, 7*(2–3): 19–21.

United States Merit Systems Protection Board [USMSPB] (1995). *Sexual harassment in the federal government: Trends, progress, continuing challenges.* Washington, D.C.: USMSPB, Office of Merit Systems Review and Studies.

Urquiza, A.J., & Capra, M. (1990). The impact of sexual abuse: Initial and long-term effects. In M. Hunter et al. (Eds.), *The sexually abused male: Prevalence, impact, and treatment* (Vol. 1, pp. 105–135). Lexington, MA: Lexington Books/D.C. Heath.

U.S. Equal Employment Opportunity Commission (1992). Compensatory and punitive damages available under §102 of the Civil Rights Act of 1991. *EEOC Notice No. N915.002.* Washington, D.C.: Author.

U.S. Equal Employment Opportunity Commission (1999). Enforcement guidance: Vicarious employer liability for unlawful harassment by supervisors. *EEOC Notice No. 915.002*. Washington, D.C.: Author.

U.S. Equal Employment Opportunity Commission (2007). Sexual harassment charge statistics for EEOC & FEPAs combined: FY 1992 through FY 1996. Retrieved March 11, 2009, from http://www.eeoc.gov/stats/harass-a.html.

U.S. Equal Employment Opportunity Commission (2009a). Sexual harassment charge statistics for EEOC & FEPAs combined: FY 1997 through FY 2008. Retrieved March 11, 2009, from http://www.eeoc.gov/stats/harass.html.

U.S. Equal Employment Opportunity Commission (2009b). EEOC mediation statistics: FY 1999 through FY 2007. Retrieved May 18, 2009, from: http://www.eeoc.gov/mediate/mediation_stats.html.

U.S. Equal Employment Opportunity Commission (2010). Charge statistics: FY 1997 through FY 2009. Retrieved March 11, 2010, from http://www.eeoc.gov/eeoc/statistics/enforcement/charges.cfm.

Vagg, P.R., & Spielberger, C.D. (1998). Occupational stress: Measuring job pressure and organizational support in the workplace. *Journal of Occupational Health Psychology, 3,* 294–305.

Valente, S., & Wight, C. (2007). Military sexual trauma: Violence and sexual abuse. *Military Medicine, 172,* 259–265.

Vasquez, M.J. T., Baker, N.L., & Shullman, S.L. (2003). Assessing employment discrimination and harassment. In A.M. Goldstein (Ed.), *Handbook of psychology, Vol. 11, Forensic psychology* (pp. 259–277), New York: John Wiley & Sons.

Vidmar, N. (1995). *Medical malpractice and the American jury: Confronting the myths about jury incompetence, deep pockets, and outrageous damage awards.* Ann Arbor, MI: University of Michigan Press.

Vore, D. (2005, Oct.). Independent psychological and psychiatric evaluations: Clinical, ethical and practical issues. Paper presented at the American Academy of Forensic Psychology Workshop Series, Vancouver, BC, Canada.

Vrij, A. (2008). Credibility assessments in a legal context. In D. Carson, R. Milne, F. Pakes, K. Shalev, & A. Shawyer (Eds.), *Applying psychology to criminal justice* (pp. 81–96). New York: John Wiley & Sons.

Vrij, A., Mann, S.A., Fisher, R.P., Leal, S., Milne, R., & Bull, R. (2008). Increasing cognitive load to facilitate lie detection: The benefit of recalling an event in reverse order. *Law and Human Behavior, 32,* 253–265.

Wakefield, J.C. (2003). Dysfunction as a factual component of disorder: Reply to Houts, Part 2. *Behavior Research and Therapy, 41,* 969–990.

Wakefield, J.C., & First, M. (2003). Clarifying the distinction between disorder and non-disorder: Confronting the overdiagnosis ("false positives") problem in DSM-V. In K.A. Phillips, M.B. First, & H.A. Pincus (Eds.), *Advancing DSM: Dilemmas in psychiatric diagnosis* (pp. 23–56). Washington, D.C.: American Psychiatric Press.

Waldo, C.R., Berdahl, J.L., & Fitzgerald, L.F. (1998). Are men sexually harassed? If so, by whom? *Law & Human Behavior, 22*, 59–79.

Walfish, S. (2006). Conducting personal injury evaluations. In I.B. Weiner & A.K. Hess (Eds.), *The handbook of forensic psychology* (3rd ed., pp. 124–139). Hoboken, NJ: Wiley.

Walster, E. (1966). Assignment of responsibility for an accident. *Journal of Personality and Social Psychology, 3*(*1*): 73–79.

Wang, P.S., Beck, A.L., Berglund, P., McKenas, D.K., Pronk, N.P., Simon, G.E., & Kessler, R.C. (2004). Effects of major depression on moment-in-time work performance. *American Journal of Psychiatry, 161*, 1885–1891.

Wasti, S.A., Bergman, M.E., Glomb, T.M., & Drasgow, F. (2000). Test of the cross-cultural generalizability of a model of sexual harassment. *Journal of Applied Psychology, 85*, 776–778.

Weiner, I.B. (2007). Rorschach assessment in forensic cases. In A.M. Goldstein (Ed.), *Forensic psychology: Emerging topics and expanding roles* (pp. 127–153). Hoboken, NJ: John Wiley & Sons.

Wiener, R.L., & Winter, R.J. (2007). Totality of circumstances in sexual harassment decisions: A decision-making model. In R.L. Wiener, B.H. Bornstein, R. Schopp, & S. Willborn (Eds.), *Social consciousness in legal decision making: Psychological perspectives* (pp. 171–196). New York: Springer Press.

Weissman, H.N. (1991). Forensic psychological assessment and the effects of protracted litigation on impairment in personal injury litigation. *Forensic Reports, 4*(*4*): 417–429.

Wettstein, R.M. (2005). Quality and quality improvement in forensic mental health evaluations. *Journal of the American Academy of Psychiatry and the Law, 33*,158–175.

White, J., Day, A., & Hackett, L. (2008). *Writing reports for court: A practical guide for psychologists working in forensic contexts.* Brisbane: Australian Academic Press.

Wilczak, A. (2009, May). Gender differences in the occurrence of stalking. Paper presented at the annual meeting of the American Society of Criminology, Atlanta, Georgia.

Williams, C.W., Lees-Haley, P.R., & Djanogly, S.E. (1999). Clinical scrutiny of litigants' self-reports. *Professional Psychology: Research and Practice, 30*, 361–367.

Williams, D.R., & Williams-Morris, R. (2000). Racism and mental health: The African American experience. *Ethnicity and Health, 5*, 243–268.

Williams, J.H., Fitzgerald, L.F., & Drasgow, F. (1999). The effects of organizational practices on sexual harassment and individual outcomes in the military. *Military Psychology, 11*, 303–328.

Williams, K.D. (2007). Ostracism. *Annual Review of Psychology, 58*, 425–452.

Willness, C.R., Steel, P., & Lee, K. (2007). A meta-analysis of the antecedents and consequences of workplace sexual harassment. *Personnel Psychology, 60,* 127–162.

Wilson, J.P., & Moran, T.A. (2004). Forensic/clinical assessment of psychology trauma and PTSD in legal settings. In J.P. Wilson & T.M. Keane (Eds.), *Assessing psychological trauma and PTSD* (pp. 603–636). New York: Guildford Press.

Wingate, P.H., & Thornton III, G.C. (2004). Industrial/organizational psychology and the federal judiciary: Expert witness testimony and the *Daubert* standards. *Law and Human Behavior, 28,* 97–114.

Wissler, R.L., Evans, D.L., Hart, A.J., Morry, M.M., & Saks, M.J. (1997). Explaining "pain and suffering" awards: The role of injury characteristics and fault attributions. *Law and Human Behavior, 21*(2): 181–207.

Wissler, R.L., Hart, A.J., & Saks, M.J. (1999). Decisionmaking about general damages: A comparison of jurors, judges and lawyers. *Michigan Law Review, 98,* 751–826.

Wolfe, J., Sharkansky, E.J., Read, J.P., Dawson, R., Martin, J.A., & Ouimette, P.C. (1998). Sexual harassment and assault as predictors of PTSD symptomatology among U.S. female Persian Gulf War military personnel. *Journal of Interpersonal Violence, 13,* 40–57.

Wood, J.M., Nezworski, M.T., Lilienfeld, S.O., & Garb, H.N. (2003). *What's wrong with the Rorschach? Science confronts the controversial inkblot test.* San Francisco: Jossey-Bass.

Woods, K.C., Buchanan, N.T., & Settles, I.H. (2009). Sexual harassment across the color line: Experiences and outcomes of cross- versus intraracial sexual harassment among black women. *Cultural Diversity and Ethnic Minority Psychology, 15*(*1*): 67–76.

World Health Organisation (2007). *International classification of diseases, injuries and causes of death* (10th Revision, ICD-10-CM). Geneva: Author

Wrench, J. (2007). *Diversity management and discrimination: Immigrants and ethnic minorities in the EU.* Aldershot, UK: Ashgate.

Wright, C.V., & Fitzgerald, L.F. (2007). Angry and afraid: Women's appraisal of sexual harassment during litigation. *Psychology of Women Quarterly, 31,* 73–84.

Wright, C.V., & Fitzgerald, L.F. (2008). Correlates of joining a sexual harassment class action. *Law and Human Behavior.* Retrieved June 9, 2009, from http://www.springerlink.com.ezproxy.csu.edu.au/content/j1608p8674k606k5/fulltext.pdf.

Yip, T., Gee, G.C., & Takeuchi, D.T. (2008). Racial discrimination and psychological distress: The impact of ethnic identity and age among immigrant and United States–born Asian adults. *Developmental Psychology, 44,* 787–800.

Young, G. (2008). Psychological injury and law: An integrative model. *Psychological Injury and Law, 1,* 150–160.

Young, G., Kane, A.W., & Nicholson, K. (2006). *Psychological knowledge in court: PTSD, pain and TBI.* New York: Springer.

Young, G., Kane, A.W., & Nicholson, K. (2007). *Causality of psychological injuries: Presenting evidence in court.* New York: Springer.

Zayfert, C., DeViva, J.C., Becker, C.B., Pike, J.L., Gillock, K.L., Hayes, S.A. (2005). Exposure utilization and completion of cognitive behavioral therapy for PTSD in a "real world" clinical practice. *Journal of Traumatic Stress. 18*(*6*)*:* 637–645.

Zimbroff, J. (2007). Cultural differences in perceptions of and responses to sexual harassment. *Duke Journal of Gender Law & Policy, 14*(*2*)*:* 1311–1341.

Zimmerle, H. (2005). Common sense vs. the EEOC: Co-worker ostracism and shunning as retaliation under Title VII. *Journal of Corporation Law*, *30,* 627–645.

Tests and Specialized Tools

CAPS: Clinician-Administered PTSD Scale (Weathers, Ruscio, & Keane, 1999).

DAPS: Detailed Assessment of Post-traumatic Stress (Briere, 2001)

MCMI-III: Millon Clinical Multiaxial Inventory-III (Millon, 1994)

MMPI-2: Minnesota Multiphasic Personality Inventory-2 (Bagby et al., 2005)

MMPI-2-RF: Minnesota Multiphasic Personality Inventory-2—Restructured Form (Wygant, Sellbom, Ben-Porath, Stafford, Freeman, & Heilbronner, 2007)

OPIE: Oklahoma Premorbid Intelligence Estimate (Krull, Scott, & Scherer, 1995)

PAI: Personality Assessment Inventory (Morey, 1996, 2007)

SEQ: Sexual Experiences Questionnaire (Fitzgerald & Schullman, 1993)

SIRS: Structured Interview of Reported Symptoms (Rogers, 1992)

TOMM: Tombaugh Test of Memory Malingering (Tombaugh, 1997)

TSI: Trauma Symptom Inventory (Briere, 1995)

VIP: Validity Indicator Profile (Frederick, 1997)

WAIS-IV: Wechsler Adult Intelligence Scale-IV (Psychological Corporation, 2008a)

WMS-IV: Wechsler Memory Scale-IV (Psychological Corporation, 2008b)

References for Tests and Specialized Tools

Bagby, R.M., Marshall, M.B., Bacchiochi, J.R. (2005). The validity and clinical utility of the MMPI-2 Malingering Depression scale. *Journal of Personality Assessment, 85(3)*, 304–311.

Briere, J. (1995). *Trauma Symptom Inventory professional manual.* Odessa, FL: Psychological Assessment Resources.

Briere, J. (2001). *Detailed Assessment of Posttraumatic Stress (DAPS).* Odessa, Florida: Psychological Assessment Resources.

Fitzgerald, L.F., & Schullman, S.L. (1993). Sexual harassment: A research analysis and agenda for the 1990s. *Journal of Vocational Behavior, 42,* 97–109.

Frederick, R. (1997). *The Validity Indicator Profile manual.* Minneapolis, MN: National Computer Systems.

Krull, K.R., Scott, J.G., & Scherer, M. (1995). Estimation of premorbid intelligence from combined performance and demographic variables. *The Clinical Neuropsychologist, 9,* 83–42.

Millon, T. (1994). *Millon Clinical Multiaxial Inventory Manual (3rd ed.).* Minneapolis, MN: National Computer Systems.

Morey, L.C. (1996). *An interpretive guide for the Personality Assessment Inventory.* Odessa, FL: Psychological Assessment Resources.

Morey, L.C. (2007). *Personality Assessment Inventory professional manual (2nd ed.).* Lutz, FL: Psychological Assessment Resources.

Psychological Corporation (2008a). *Wechsler Adult Intelligence Scale-IV Technical Manual.* New York: The Psychological Corporation.

Psychological Corporation (2008b). *Wechsler Memory Scale-IV Technical Manual.* New York: The Psychological Corporation.

Rogers, R. (1992). *SIRS, structured interview of reported symptoms: Professional manual.* Odessa, FLA: Psychological Assessment Resources.

Tombaugh, T. (1997). The Test of Memory Malingering (TOMM): Normative data from cognitively intact and cognitively impaired individuals. *Psychological Assessment, 9(3),* 260–268.

Weathers, F.W., Ruscio, A.M., & Keane, T.M. (1999). Psychometric properties of nine scoring rules for the Clinician-Administered Posttraumatic Stress Disorder Scale. *Psychological Assessment, 11(2),* 124–133.

Wygant, D.B., Sellbom, M., Ben-Porath, Y.S., Stafford, K.P., Freeman, D.B., & Heilbronner, R.I. (2007). The relation between symptom validity testing and MMPI-2 scores as a function of forensic evaluation context. *Archives of Clinical Neuropsychology, 22,* 488–499.

Cases and Statutes

Administrative Dispute Resolution Act, 5 U.S.C. §§571–583 (1995)

Age Discrimination in Employment Act, 29 U.S.C. §201 (1967)

Americans with Disabilities Act of 1990, 42 U.S.C.A. §12101 *et seq.* (West 1993)

Americans with Disabilities Amendment Act of 2008, Pub. Law 110-325 (2009)

Antoine-Tubbs v. Local 513, Air Transp. Div., 50 F. Supp. 2d 601 (N.D. Tex. 1998) *aff'd without opinion,* 190 F.3d 537 (5th Cir. 1999).

Baki v. B. F. Diamond Constr. Co., 71 F.R.D. 179 (D. Md. 1976)

Brady v. Wal-Mart Stores Inc., CV 03-3843, U.S. District Court (E.D.N.Y., Central Islip, 2006)

Brown vs. Board of Education, 347 U.S. 483 (1954)

Burlington Industries v. Ellerth, 524 U.S. 742 (1998)

Burlington Northern & Santa Fe Railway Co. v. Sheila White, 548 U.S. 53 (2006)

Civil Rights Acts of 1866, 42 U.S.C. §§1985, 1986 (1866)

Civil Rights Act of 1871, 42 U.S.C. §§1983, 1985, as amended (1986)

Civil Rights Act of 1964, 42 U.S.C. §2000e *et seq.*, as amended (1964)

Civil Rights Act of 1991, Pub. L. No. 102-106, §106 (1991)

Cremin v. Merrill Lynch, Pierce, Fenner, & Smith, Inc., 328 F. Supp.2d 865 (N.D. Ill. 2004)

Crawford v. Metropolitan Government of Nashville and Davidson County, Tennessee, 129 S. Ct. 846 (2009)

Daubert v. Merrell Dow Pharmaceuticals, Inc., 509 U.S. 579 (1993)

EEOC v. Dial Corporation (April 29, 2003), Case No. 99-C-3356 (N.D. Ill)

Equal Pay Act of 1963, Pub. L. No. 88-38, 77 Stat. 56 (codified as amended at 29 U.S.C. § 206[d])

Fair Labor Standards Act, 29 USC Section 201 *et seq.* (1935)
Family Medical Leave Act of 1993, Pub. L. No. 103-3; 29 U.S.C. sec. 2601 (1993)
Franklin v. Consolidated Edison Co. of New York, No. 01-7559 (2d Cir. Apr. 9, 2002)
Glockner v. Department of Veterans Affairs, EEOC Appeal No. 07A30105 (Sep. 23, 2004)
Gonzalez v. Abercrombie & Fitch, Consent Decree, Case No. 03-2817 SI, 04-4730, 04-4731 (US Dist Ct, N.D.Ca, Apr 11 2005)
Halvorsen v. Plato Learning, Inc., No. 05-5325 (6th Cir. Feb. 15, 2006)
Hathaway v. Bennett, 10 N.Y. 108 (1854)
Harris v. Forklift Systems, Inc., 510 U.S. 17 (1993)
Harrison v. Edison Bros. Apparel Stores, Inc., 151 F.3d 176 (4th Cir. 1998)
Hodges v. Keane, 145 F.R.D. 332 (S.D.N.Y. 1993)
Holland v. Barnhart, 01A01372 (October 2, 2003)
Iroquois Nursing Home v. New York State Division of Human Rights, __A.D.3d__(NY A.D.4 Dept. Slip Op. 07320, Oct. 3 2008)
Jenson v. Eveleth Taconite Company, 130 F.3d 1287 (8th Cir.1997)
Kumho Tire Co. v. Carmichael, 526 U.S. 137 (1999)
Labonte v. Hutchins & Wheeler, 678 N.E.2d 853 (Mass. 1997)
Leatherman v. England, WL 1650704 (2001)
Lilly Ledbetter Fair Pay Act of 2009, Pub. L. No. 111-2 (2009)
Meritor Savings Bank FEB v. Vinson, 477 U.S. 57 (1986)
Merriweather v. Family Dollar Stores, 103 F.3d 576 (7th Cir. 1996)
National Labor Relations Act, 1935, 29 U.S.C. §§ 151–169
New York State Dept of Correctional Services v. New York State Division of Human Rights 2008 WL 2682073, 3 (N.Y.A.D. 3 Dept.) (2008)
Oncale v. Sundowner Offshore Services, Inc., 523 U.S 75 (1998)
Patterson v. P.H.P. Healthcare Corp., 90 F.3d 927 (1996)

Perry v. W. S. Darley & Company, 54 F.R.D. 278 (E.D.Wis. 1971)

Pittman v. ANR Freight Systems, Inc., 47 Fed Appx 266 (6th Cir. 2002)

Price Waterhouse v. Hopkins, 490 U.S. 228 (1989)

Rogers v. Equal Employment Opportunity Commission, 454 F.2d 234 (5th Cir. 1971), cert.den., 406 U.S. 957 (1972)

Rupp v. Purolator Courier Corp., 45 F.3d 440 (10th Cir. 1994)

Satchell et al. v. Fedex Express, Consent Decree, Case No. C03-2659 SI, C03-2778 SI (N.D. Cas, Aug. 15 2007)

Schlagenhauf v. Holder, 379 U.S. 104 (1964)

Sheehan v. Daily Racing Form, Inc., 104 F.3d 940 (7th Cir. 1997)

Siljak v. Ravenswood Disposal Serv., No. 02-1026 (7th Cir. Nov. 21, 2002)

The Rehabilitation Act of 1973, Pub. L. No. 93-112 (1973)

Key Terms

Abductive reasoning: Experience-based logic to infer a cause of an observed consequence. Preexisting knowledge is used to develop and evaluate hypotheses to explain incomplete data or the relationship between seemingly independent observations: e.g., to determine that A caused B.

Actuarial test: Psychological testing by means of which a person's personality style or emotional functioning is assessed based on the subject's scores on test items derived through empirical research.

Ad quod damnum: Latin phrase referring to the sum of money proportionate to the harm or injury experienced and sought to compensate non-pecuniary damages such as pain and suffering. Also *ad damnum*.

Adverse treatment: see **Disparate treatment**.

Adverse impact: see **Disparate impact**.

Agnew's General Strain Theory: Theory describing underlying causes of antisocial behavior. It proposes that an individual's failure to achieve positively valued goals, through the absence of positive reinforcement or the presence of negative factors, can cause strain manifested in feelings of anger, frustration, pressure, or alienation. This can lead to the development of antisocial/illegal methods to achieve desired goals (e.g., "acting out"). Increases in the frequency, strength, and duration of strain are theorized to determine the magnitude and overtness of antisocial behavior.

Civil claim: Claim lodged under civil law to enforce a right or request money for damages sustained. Civil claims are made by private parties, while criminal claims are filed by the government. However, civil and criminal claims may overlap at times; for example, in property damage cases, where both a criminal charge and a civil claim for damages may be lodged based on the same conduct. Civil law encompasses business, contracts, estates, domestic relations, accidents, negligence, and all matters related to legal issues, statutes, and lawsuits that are not encompassed by criminal law.

Constructive discharge: Resignation by a worker from employment based on the employer's behavior or the work environment.

If the employee can prove that the employer's behavior and/or working conditions were of such a nature that no "reasonable person" would continue working in those circumstances, the resignation will be considered a wrongful termination for which the employer is liable.

Compelled (mandated) mental examinations: Once a plaintiff makes a claim of psychological injury, the opposing party may seek an independent mental examination of the plaintiff, who is obliged to comply with this request (under Rule 35 of the Federal Rules of Civil Procedure or similar state laws). These examinations focus on the historical and current mental health status of the plaintiff to establish case-related psychological injury.

Compensatory damages: Monetary award to compensate a plaintiff for actual losses and injuries, pecuniary and non-pecuniary, that have been proven. These sums are intended to redress past and future losses to the plaintiff caused by the wrongful conduct of a defendant.

Deposition: Sworn testimony of a witness taken out of court outside the presence of a judge. Part of formal pretrial fact-finding process in a civil case. The witness is placed under oath to tell the truth, and lawyers for each party may ask questions. The questions and answers are recorded and may be used in a later in-court proceeding.

Diminution in value: The loss of value directly resulting from a particular event or series of events. In a legal dispute, the evaluation of this loss forms the basis of proposed compensatory damages and includes the assessment of losses that have already occurred and losses that will occur in future.

Disability: An ongoing physical or mental impairment that substantially limits one's ability to perform one or more major life activities.

Discovery: Formal pretrial litigation procedures during which each party to a lawsuit seeks relevant information and documents from the other side in an attempt to "discover" facts pertinent to the claim. Discovery helps a party find out the other side's version of the facts, and what their witnesses know. Some common discovery devices include depositions, interrogatories, requests for admissions, document production requests, and requests for inspection.

Discrimination: see **Workplace discrimination**.

Disorder: A physical or psychological condition that deviates from "normal" functioning, such as a medical illness or psychological disturbance. The most commonly employed guideline for the diagnosis of psychological disorders is the *Diagnostic and Statistical Manual of Mental Disorders* (American Psychiatric Association, 2000). Within this manual, mental disorders are organized along five categories known as *axes.* The most important are Axis 1 (clinical disorders, including mood, anxiety, thought, and learning disorders) and Axis 2 (personality disorders and intellectual disabilities).

Disparate treatment: intentionally favorable or unfavorable treatment of one or more employees because of their group membership.

Disparate impact: a facially neutral employment action that has a negative outcome on several employees in a protected group.

Duty to mitigate: The legal duty of a plaintiff/victim to minimize the loss resulting from unlawful conduct by taking reasonable and appropriate measures to prevent the increase of damage or exacerbation of an injury.

Eggshell skull: When damage to the plaintiff is more severe than would have been reasonably foreseeable, due to the plaintiff's preexisting vulnerability, the defendant is still held liable for all consequences of unlawful conduct. The term implies that if a person had a skull as delicate as the shell of an egg, and a tortfeasor or assailant who did not know of that condition were to hit that person on the head, causing the skull unexpectedly to break, the responsible party would be held liable for all damages resulting from the wrongful contact, even though they were not foreseeable.

Expert witness: A witness whose specialized knowledge about a topic is helpful in resolving facts in controversy in a legal proceeding.

Evaluating psychologist: Forensic mental health professional trained in psychology who has not previously been involved in an individual's care and conducts an independent assessment of that individual's clinical status, usually where liability is at issue, to determine the cause, extent, and medical or psychological treatment of a work-related or other injury.

Functional impairment: Loss of ability in social, occupational, or personal context that prevents the person from performing in a manner that is considered "normal"; or, if the impairment was acquired, in a manner that was achievable prior to the impairment.

Garden variety damages: Injuries based on the plaintiff's experience of "ordinary" or "normal" levels of psychological distress or suffering following a wrongdoing that do not result in more profound and/or longer-term mental health damage.

General causation of harm: Consequences of wrongful conduct that apply to most individuals.

General damages: See **Non-pecuniary damages**.

Harassment: See **Hostile and abusive workplace environment**.

Hostile and abusive workplace environment: Also known as *discriminatory harassment*. Unwelcome conduct in the workplace that targets one or more employees because of their group membership and substantially interferes with their ability to perform their job duties.

Ideographic: The unique experiences, properties and attributes of the individual that set him or her apart from other individuals. Opposite of nomothetic.

Impairment: Loss of, loss of the use of, or disturbance of a mental, psychological, or physical function.

Malingering: The feigning and/or exaggeration of symptoms of mental or physical illness with the aim to procure external incentives, such as compensation or medication, or to avoid responsibility or evade punishment.

Mental state in controversy: When a plaintiff makes a claim for damages for a psychological injury allegedly caused by the defendant's wrongful conduct, he or she is said to have placed his or her mental state *in issue*. The nature, scope, and cause of the injury may be challenged by the opposing party.

Mobbing: Psychological violence, pressure, bullying, ostracism, harassment, and disturbance in an attempt to force a person out of the workplace through unjustified accusations, humiliation, emotional abuse, and terror.

National Labor Relations Act: U.S. law by which employers are restricted in their ability to fire employees and by which they are prohibited from disadvantaging or discriminating against employees who are members of collective workers' unions.

Nominal damages: An award of monetary compensation that establishes that wrongful conduct has occurred without evidence of harm for which compensatory damages may be awarded. Nominal damages are intended to recognize a plaintiff's legal injury when no actual monetary damages may be discerned. The compensation amount is trivial and is intended as a token. In some courts, nominal damages must be exactly $1.

Nomothetic: Generalisable or shared experiences, properties or attributes of a cohort of individuals, a, class or population and their corresponding personality traits and behaviours. Opposite of ideographic.

Non-pecuniary damages: Also known as **general damages**. Compensation awarded to redress a plaintiff for injuries suffered, such as emotional distress or psychological harm. Non-pecuniary losses such as emotional pain and loss of health are not subject to precise quantification. No exhaustive list of non-pecuniary losses exists, but the losses may include emotional pain; suffering; inconvenience; mental anguish; loss of enjoyment of life; injury to character, credit, and reputation; and loss of health.

Pecuniary damages: Also known as **special damages**. Economic or out-of-pocket expenses or monetary losses incurred in the past or known with certainty to be incurred in the future.

Percipient witness: Witness with knowledge of case facts obtained through direct observation. For example, the witness may have seen or heard the event or have witnessed the plaintiff's injuries.

Proximate cause: Also known as the **legal cause**, this term refers to the primary, independent, and direct cause of injuries. With regard to tort claims, the plaintiff must establish that, without the wrongdoing of the defendant, the injuries or loss would not have been sustained, and that the wrongdoing was the proximate cause of the alleged harm.

Projective test: A form of psychological testing by which a person's personality and emotional functioning are assessed based on their interpretation of and responses to ambiguous stimuli.

The theory is that, due to the ambiguous nature of the stimuli, the person's interpretation of them will reveal underlying and subconscious thoughts, feelings, and attitudes. Projective tests are generally not standardized and lack reliability and validity, and their interpretation is primarily based on subjective or clinical opinion.

Psychological Injury: Also known as **psychiatric injury**. Damage to intellectual or emotional functioning.

Punitive damages: Monetary compensation intended to punish or deter the wrongdoer. These damages may be awarded to the plaintiff in addition to compensatory damages.

Reasonable accommodation: Consideration or adaptations in the workplace that enable a worker to perform his or her job duties notwithstanding that individual's religious practices, or physical or mental impairments.

Retaliation: Also known as **reprisal** or **victimization**. Adverse employment action against a worker because the employee's previous or planned lawful actions contravene the employer's wishes. These actions could include the filing of a complaint against the employer, or refusal to cooperate in illegal activities. A legal claim of retaliation is not limited to discharge from employment but can also be based on other wrongdoings by an employer such as denial of promotion or removal of benefits.

Retaliatory discharge: Dismissal of an employee because the employee's previous or planned lawful actions contravene the employer's wishes.

Reverse discrimination: Claim by the employee that others who belong to a protected class or category received unlawful preferential treatment at work because of their protected status based on their race, gender, disability, etc.

Sexual harassment: Employment actions conditional on acceptance or rejection of unwelcome sexual conduct in the workplace, or creation of an abusive workplace environment based on sexualized behavior or gender hostility.

Special damages: See **Pecuniary damages**.

Specific causation of harm: Consequences of wrongful conduct arising because of factors particular to the individual plaintiff in a specific case.

Tort: From the French word *tort*, meaning "wrongdoing" or "wrongful conduct." In law, it refers to civil wrong: an intentional or accidental (negligent) act causing harm to another person that does not breach a contract. Tort laws outline the criteria for legal responsibility or liability for causing harm or injury to another.

Tort claim: A civil claim for compensation based on damage or injury caused by another person's negligent or intentional conduct comprising a tort, or wrongdoing.

Tortfeasor: A person who has committed a tort/wrongdoing.

Victimization: See **Retaliation**.

Workplace discrimination: Differential and unfair treatment in employment based upon a worker's membership in a protected group (age, disability, ethnicity, gender, national origin, race, religion). This inequality may arise during hiring, promotion, compensation, work content, workload, and termination.

Whistle-blowing: Public-interest reporting of wrongdoing.

Index

About the Authors

Jane Goodman-Delahunty, JD, PhD, is a professor at Charles Sturt University in the School of Psychology and Australian Graduate School of Policing. Her opposition to workplace discrimination stems from her South African origins. She practiced employment relations at the bar in the State of Washington (1983–1992), as an administrative judge for the U.S. Equal Employment Opportunity Commission in Southern California (1992–2001), and as a third-party neutral with Judicial Arbitration and Mediation Services (JAMS) The Resolution Experts (1994–2001). Trained in psychology and law, Goodman-Delahunty is a former president of the American Psychology-Law Society and editor of *Psychology, Public Policy and Law* (2001–2006). She is currently a commissioner with the New South Wales Law Reform Commission, a member of the NSW Administrative Decisions Tribunal, a mediator for the NSW Office of Fair Trading, and president of the Australian and New Zealand Association for Psychiatry, Psychology, and Law.

William (Bill) Foote, PhD, has been in forensic practice in New Mexico for over 30 years. He has served in a number of elected offices, including as president of the New Mexico Psychological Association, and president of the American Board of Forensic Psychology and as a member of the Executive Committee of the American Psychology Law Society. He has also chaired committees in the American Psychological Association, including the Committee on Legal Issues and the Committee on Professional Practice and Standards. He has held faculty appointments at the University of New Mexico in the Department of Psychiatry and the School of Law.